"This book will launch a revolution in how America celebrates."

Teresa Wippel, vice president, Green For Good, GreenForGood.com

"Creating annual holiday traditions, while being respectful of our impact on the world, gives our children a gift that is worthy of being handed down for generations. *Celebrate Green!* is filled with creative eco-friendly ideas and resources you can use to celebrate holidays and make lasting memories with your family."

> **Alan Greene,** MD, FAAP, author *Raising Baby Green* and *From First Kicks to First Steps*, founder, DrGreene.com

"Corey and Lynn make creating eco-savvy celebrations a cinch. Packed with powerful information and practical strategies, *Celebrate Green!* maps out simple and straightforward ways to honor what's good for people, the planet, and communities throughout the year. I love how the authors balance fascinating statistics and the "why" behind going green with some of the most creative and "do-able" ideas I've ever seen. They have proven that making memories and making a difference can blissfully coexist in our holidays and traditions. *Celebrate Green!* is an ideal guidebook to help you live—and celebrate—with intention."

> **Deanna Davis, PhD**, author of *Living With Intention*

"For those of us who sit at parties and worry about all those paper plates and excess gift wrapping, this book is an amazing resource! To have a beautiful celebration, one need not sacrifice anything -- especially the planet."

> **Cambria Gordon**, co-author of *The Down-to-Earth Guide to Global Warming*

"For years I thought there had to be something more to eco-friendly parties than newspaper gift wrapping and brown recycled napkins. Corey and Lynn found it and created a green gold mine full of stylish and creative ideas. Celebrate Green! doesn't just give you a way to celebrate. It gives you a reason to celebrate."

> **Hannah Keeley,** *author of Hannah Keeley's Total Mom Makeover: The Six-Week Plan to Completely Transform Your Home, Health, Family and Life*

"For every occasion, you can find great ideas for green gifts, decoration tips and even recipes for organic and healthy snacks and drinks. Everything is very well organized, simple, and practical. Pick up a copy of this book to be assured you have a fabulous resource guide to celebrate green through the whole year."

Christopher Gavigan, executive director and author of *Healthy Child Healthy World*

"The green movement can feel overwhelming. We all know we need to make some changes, but where to start? Leave it to two moms to find simple solutions to empower the entire family, young and old, starting with making holidays more about green and less about sugar and overconsumption. I am green with envy that I didn't think of that! Brilliant!"

> **Stacey Kannenberg**, author and publisher of *Let's Get Ready For Kindergarten!* and *Let's Get Ready For First Grade!*

"Wow, wow, WOW! The book Corey and Lynn have created is itself a glorious celebration—of imagination, innovation, and most important of all, beauty. With their savvy guidance we discover how to celebrate in loving ways that nourish our souls and enrich our relationships, while also tending to the health of our global future. What a wonderful way for a new generation to learn to celebrate "with small footprints" on our shared mother, planet Earth!"

Marcy Axness, Ph.D., author of *Raising Generation PAX*

"I had no idea there were so many ways to entertain, have fun and give back to the planet all at the same time. Lynn and Corey have so many clever ways to "keep it green" and help the reader do the same with minimal effort involved.

"I thought *Celebrate Green!* was just going to be about green entertaining but it's so much more than that. I loved the recipes, all the tips about basic lifestyle changes anyone can make, mindful traveling, and even ways to recycle that simply never occurred to me.

"It's not only a great read but a great reference book to have on hand all year round. I really can't recommend it enough."

Theresa McKeown, author of *The ABC's of Being Me*

"This book is an essential antidote for those of us who are overwhelmed by the excesses of American holidays, but are not quite sure what to do about it. The authors' wise advice will help anyone realize healthier, environmentally sound holiday celebrations while continuing their own valued family traditions – and quite possibly starting some new ones. Filled with useful and creative recommendations, meticulously researched and up-to-date, *Celebrate Green!* is an invaluable and comprehensive resource not just for the holidays, but for the entire year."

Simeon Hutner, filmmaker

"Because sustainability begins with respecting life, and a huge part of life is celebrating, mother and daughter team Corey Colwell-Lipson and Lynn Colwell's easy-access and idea-filled *Celebrate Green!* offers a refreshing, varied perspective on honoring special occasions in a way that respects all life on our planet, all year long."

Kimberly Danek Pinkson, EcoMom founder

"The word 'celebrate' says it all for this book. So why aren't we being more green? This " no excuses" book has all the answers for knocking down any roadblocks you ever had about recyling and reusing!"

Kathy Peterson, national TV host on Lifetime TV's *The Balancing Act*, celebrity design expert and best selling author of five books including *Kathy Peterson's Great Outdoor Decorating Makeovers on a Budget of $250 or Less!*

"This is more than about green. It's about our lives, our choices, how we behave, who we are, how we show love, how we live, what we identify love with and what we call success. It's about saving our planet, saving our finances, and saving our souls...and having fun doing it. It's about giving our children a completely different world without having to hide them from the truth. Instead, it's opening their eyes to a great new way of thinking. It's so easy, it's brilliant.

"I can't wait to give this to my daughter, friends and family. So much of what we do happens without our even thinking about it. This is an easy, straightforward, not-preachy, informative, intelligent, fact-filled, reference guide...and so much more."

Marylee Martin, writer and actress

Celebrate Green!

Creating Eco-Savvy Holidays, Celebrations & Traditions for the Whole Family

Corey Colwell–Lipson & Lynn Colwell

thegreenyear™
The Green Year®, LLC
Renton, Washington

Celebrate Green! Creating Eco-Savvy Holidays, Celebrations and Traditions for the Whole Family

Copyright 2008 by Lynn Colwell and Corey Colwell-Lipson

Published by The Green Year®, LLC

13003 LK Kathleen Rd. SE

Renton, WA 98059 U.S.A.

Orders@CelebrateGreen.NET; www.CelebrateGreen.NET

Library of Congress Cataloguing in Publication Data

Colwell-Lipson, Corey and Colwell, Lynn.

Celebrate Green!: Creating Eco-Savvy Holidays, Celebrations & Traditions for the Whole Family / by Corey Colwell-Lipson and Lynn Colwell.

1. Holidays – United States. 2. Environmental responsibility. 3. Sustainable living.
4. Gifts.

394.2697   ISBN: 978-0-615-23973-6

The Green Year®, LLC. 2008.

Design: Jeff Duckworth

Cover photos: Holli Dunn

Interior craft photos: I CANDI Studios

We offer a monumental thank you...

First of all to our husbands, Steve (Lynn's) and Ryan (Corey's). We know you cringe every time we bring life to a halt with, "We have an idea!" But once the initial shock is over, you support us as only lifetime partners can, with abiding love, understanding and a willingness to do the math for us.

To Corey's daughters, Zoe and Finn for so generously sharing their mommy with the book creation process. You give us reason to celebrate, no matter the day.

To our families (the list would take up the entire page, but they know who they are), for supporting us through the happy times (getting the contract) and the challenging (our publisher, sadly, going under). Your ideas, contributions and pride in what we're doing keep us going.

To our friends including all of Lynn's Up With People buddies, who, whether green-conscious or not, found the words and the time to share our frustrations and cheer us on—and who promised to buy innumerable books for themselves and to give as gifts. You are gifts to us.

To everyone we contacted to ask for quotes, input and permissions. We could not have written this book without the research and writings of the community of people engaged in doing work that raises our eco-consciousness. This includes scores of "average" people working to untangle the truth and science behind "going green," entrepreneurs who are creating imaginative products from things most people throw away, and those who are implementing the simple changes that can make a real difference. You inspire us.

To those whose lives are tied to the pages of this book including our friend and exceptionally talented photographer, Holli Dunn; our green genius chefs: Mary Purdy, Wenonah Michallet-Ferrier, Joy Stroh, Pam Samper, Jill Westfall, and Debbie Colwell; our talented hand models, Jenny Juang and Kiara Williams; and everyone who saw us through the printing process at Webcom. To the guys at Seattle's A-1 Best Computer, (especially Franklin and David), who saved our lives when Corey's computer crashed several times in the course of preparing this book.

To those who willingly (at least that's what they said), read the manuscript and gave us ideas and input.

And most especially to Miracle Man, Jeff Duckworth, our designer, who took our passion and made it his own. Only because of Jeff's commitment to tight deadlines, his work ethic, flexibility, patience, graciousness, and talent were we able to turn our vision into reality. To say we are bursting-our-buttons proud of this book and overwhelmingly grateful to Jeff for crafting its look and feel, is an understatement.

To every single person who touched our lives before and during this project, whose enthusiasm helped fuel us when ours flagged, we are grateful beyond measure to all of you.

Lynn & Corey

The first step

These days, trying to act in eco-friendly ways can be overwhelming.

Green claims buzz around us like swarms of bees. How do we know, with confusion among even the most well-informed experts, whether what we're doing makes a difference? Some of what has swiftly become gospel to well-meaning "greenies," has not yet been proven. And sometimes, our most well-intentioned actions result in unintended negative consequences.

The plain fact is: We don't know everything about the ultimate impact of acting in what appear to be the most eco-responsible ways.

On the other hand, we do know some things.

A lot of what we know (or think we do), is in this book. (And, we'll admit, even things we're not absolutely, positively convinced of, but that sound reasonable to us, appear on these pages as well, often with a caveat noted.)

Celebrate Green! is not a step-by-step instruction manual. It is not a manifesto of eco-conscious behaviors. It was conceived as a means to bring together ideas that will stimulate you to think and act in ways that may be new to you when you celebrate life's most important moments.

And while the book is filled with ideas we believe can make a difference, they are just ideas. Without people embracing and acting on them, the impact will be nil. But millions of us changing the way we approach and implement holiday activities, cannot help but create a massive effect.

At the same time, we're still learning too and we realize that trying to make dozens of changes at once can lead to frustration and burnout. We suggest you, like us, take it a step at a time.

Choose a few alternatives for your next holiday celebration. You may find that making just one or two adjustments awakens a desire to do more and engages your creative spirit in the pursuit of a better way. The bottom line is, after all the input from experts, do what makes sense to you! When you couple your instincts with some basic knowledge, chances are that instead of feeling like greening up celebrations is a chore and a have-to, you'll discover it can be remarkably fun and gratifying.

Isn't that worth celebrating?

Table of Contents

The Seed

 On Halloween, 2006, I took our young daughters trick-or-treating as I had many times before. As handful after handful of candy filled their buckets, I cringed at the thought of hauling all that junk home. Just then, someone placed a jar of bubbles in my daughter's hand. She and her friends shrieked with joy. A few houses down, stickers from another homeowner received a similar reception. Suddenly it occurred to me that Halloween didn't *have* to be about candy. Kids could be just as excited by treats other than sugary confections. I began to wonder—couldn't Halloween be healthier and still fun? And while we're at it, couldn't Halloween be more earth-friendly too? Wasn't it time?

By all practical measures, the time was, and still is, right for change. On a daily basis we're inundated with stories about lead-laden toys, the childhood obesity epidemic, and shortened life spans of future generations, not to mention environmental concerns about global warming, toxic waterways, and vanishing species of plant and animal life. With so much work to do, I wondered, could celebrating holidays differently really alter our course?

I decided it was worth trying. It made sense to start with Halloween and see what would happen.

I asked moms and dads what they thought about creating a healthier and more earth-friendly Halloween. "Is that even possible?" they asked. "I'm sure that it could be," I replied, always the idealist. In May of 2007 I called my local natural foods store to gauge interest. I asked if they would consider displaying affordable, healthy food and non-food items at Halloween as well making signs that people could hang on windows and doors to show that theirs were healthy Halloween homes. The store's marketing manager responded with an emphatic, "Yes."

A bigger picture soon emerged, one that included treats, but went further. I began to think about costumes, food, party games, and door-prizes and wondered if these might become healthier and more sustainable as well. What could I do to help create this change? What could I do to help provide parents with better alternatives? What could I do to keep the fun and tradition of the holiday intact while creating sustainable solutions?

I quickly realized that I could gather community support for these ideas. After all, change doesn't necessarily take a village, but it's a lot easier and more rewarding when it does.

A few weeks after my conversation with the store, Green Halloween®, an unofficial community movement, was born. My mom came on board and I gathered a dream team of sponsors from around the Seattle area. We involved schools in contests and attended a dozen or more events from the end of September through Halloween night, meeting thousands of children, teenagers, and adults along the way. The icing on the organic cake was that my multi-talented, creative and fun-loving mom hopped on board and became co-"Green Halloween® Lady."

In addition to bringing in sponsorship, we realized early on that this movement had the potential to create wide-spread change by involving a local non-profit whose mission was similar to ours. It was serendipitous and fortuitous that early on I was introduced to Treeswing (Treeswing.org), an organization committed to improving the lives of children through nutrition, exercise, play, and healthy environments. I knew right away that I wanted Treeswing to be our first beneficiary. (In 2008 Green Halloween® would become an official program of Teeswing's.) An important part of Green Halloween®'s mission became to support and partner with organizations that align with our goals.

We launched Green Halloween®'s website, which featured dozens of tips on how to make Halloween healthier and more earth-friendly, from invitations to costumes to recycling leftover pumpkins. At events, we focused on the "treats" aspect of Halloween and brought with us a display of alternatives to conventional candy, including food and non-food items. Expecting that some people would defend Halloween as an intentionally glutinous and delightfully sinful vacation from conscientious eating, parenting, and wise consumer habits, my mom and I steeled ourselves against a potential angry barrage from those who might be less than grateful for our efforts. Indeed, some people, including kids, might wish for us to leave Halloween alone. But by the time October 31st was over, more than 10,000 people had walked past or stopped at our event tables. *Not one single child*, of any age, said they'd rather have traditional candy than the items on our display. Seeing the alternatives in front of them opened their minds to the possibility of change. We were astonished and, truthfully, a little disappointed that we never got to use our speech titled, "Ten reasons Halloween needs a healthy/green facelift."

A week after the inaugural Green Halloween®, I began receiving e-mails from reporters around the country asking to interview me about green Thanksgiving and Christmas ideas. Although our community movement was always meant to expand past Halloween, I was surprised at how quickly the ideas caught on. By January of 2008, my mom and I had formed The Green Year®, a company focusing on healthy and earth-friendly holidays and celebrations. Green Halloween® and The Green Year® seek to make changing for the better fun. Our goal is to create holiday traditions we can all be proud of.

No one knows what the future holds, but I'm hopeful that the green movement is the right path. In the coming years, The Green Year® will continue its efforts to build bridges between consumer demand and merchandisers' and retailers' efforts to make holiday products healthier and more earth-friendly. We expect that as time passes, more and more holiday products will be produced with health and sustainability in mind. Encouraging people to think green about holidays will be unnecessary because eco-wise holiday traditions will be woven into the fabric of every celebration. In the meantime, I hope you find this book to be an entertaining and useful guide that will help you take the first steps toward celebrating green.

Cheers! – Corey

When Corey approached me to talk about introducing green into celebrations, I enthusiastically jumped on board. Not only did the concept make sense to me, but more importantly, in terms of starting a movement, her timing was perfect. Al Gore's film, *An Inconvenient Truth,* had galvanized the nation, and people were beginning to understand how a complex concept like global warming might affect not only generations to come and far away places, but them and those they love—today. Organic products have found their way onto the shelves of major retailers that only a few years ago scoffed at the possibility. Granted, the reason is more economic than philosophical, but the point is, change has arrived. Green is good.

Actually, come to think of it, I grew up in a greener time, a simpler time, when no one I knew stored bags of candy at home, so getting some at Halloween was a *real* treat; when cleaning up after a party meant washing dishes, utensils, and table linens—by hand; when no one could tell you'd been celebrating the night before from the line of plastic bags snaking down the driveway; when leftovers were wrapped in paper, not plastic, and lemonade was made from scratch only in the summertime because grocery stores in winter stocked three kinds of apples, but nary a lemon and the only way you could get those yellow beauties was to live in Florida or California or visit there and return with a dozen stashed in your suitcase. We certainly never topped off a Thanksgiving dinner with grapes from South Africa or pears from Chile.

As I recall, holidays and celebrations were more about people and less about things. My mother was an interior designer, but her Christmas party tables were simply and elegantly set with linen cloths, matching napkins, white china, a line of poinsettias, and a few tapered candles. The need to impress via excess had not yet reared its ugly head as cultural norm. Keeping up with the Joneses was an expression I remember hearing, but it had more to do with general upward mobility than toddler birthday parties designed by Martha and catered by Wolfgang Puck. Gross consumerism was on its way, but had not yet taken hold. I recollect having to wait to take in the magical holiday store windows in New York City until after Thanksgiving. These days, it's not unusual to see employees stringing lights or tinsel and tossing "snow" around Santa's photo studio in a department store before Halloween!

I'm not saying we need to celebrate as they did in the Stone Age, but as Corey began describing her vision for Green Halloween®, I realized the hypocrisy of "going green" every day of the year *except* for celebrations and holidays. Frankly, I no longer, in good conscience, can act as though excess, unhealthy and un-earth-friendly activities don't matter if I engage in them only a dozen times a year. They do matter for one reason. I'm not the only person living on Earth. Multiply what I do in the name of ease, thrift, fun, or simple ignorance by billions. Both the problem and the solution become apparent.

When I started down this road, I had no idea of the number of alternatives available to people interested in living their eco-values every day of the year. I quickly learned that environmentally friendly options are not a pipe dream, but in most instances, realistic choices. So why not green up my celebrations? All the excuses I use to avoid doing what I should evaporate in the face of the facts.

Our goal in writing this book was to open minds to potential and possibilities. We are not the green police. We want everyone to continue to enjoy every single celebration, but not to walk through them mindlessly as if the choices we make, as easy as they are, are unimportant.

There's a lot in this book. You might feel overwhelmed as you read about the ways in which every aspect of every celebration can be boiled down to its least harmful essence. You might even think there's too much information or that you don't want to take away from your celebrations by focusing on their downside potential. But I believe that change comes when we understand the consequences of our actions. Once we know the pros and cons, we can make informed decisions rather than sleepwalk through what has become routine or even traditional. Just because we've always done something a particular way doesn't make it right, especially in view of our developing knowledge of its impact.

Take a tip from me. Don't worry about digesting or even reading all the information in this book. Just open to the pages on the event you're going to celebrate. Choose a few ideas to start and get going. Doing something, after all, is way better than doing nothing.

Lynn

Green Holidays 101

In 2007, Green Halloween® took Seattle by storm. Its purpose was to create healthier and more earth-friendly holiday traditions, starting with Halloween. Its success was overwhelming, and soon people from all over the country were asking, "When is Green Halloween® coming to *my* city?" With the environmental movement gaining momentum (even big box stores had jumped on the bandwagon), it was a little surprising that holidays had been virtually ignored. The connection might seem obvious now that you're holding this book in your hands, but until recently, "eco-wise" and "celebrate" rarely shared a sentence.

Indeed, celebrating is often synonymous with *un-earth-friendly* acts including excessive energy consumption and waste generation. From Thanksgiving through the December holidays, for example, landfills see an increase of 25% more litter, which not only takes up room, but furthers global warming through off-gassing. Birthday parties, weddings and office parties likewise contribute to these problems with their emphasis on excess rather than earth-friendliness. Individuals who do their best to be green during the rest of the year may toss it all out the window on holidays or special occasions because they're in a rush, think it's easier, or aren't aware that alternatives exist. But here's the good news: You *can* enjoy the year's holidays and celebrations *and* be good to the planet. And here's the better news: earth-friendly holidays are easy, affordable, fun, and of course, rewarding. *Celebrate Green!* will show you how.

Chances are, in your everyday life, you're already making a difference. You may recycle, use your own shopping bags (at least *some* of the time), and turn lights off when you leave a room. These are all great places to start. Holidays and celebrations are no different than any other day of the year in that choices motivated by reducing, reusing, and recycling (the 3Rs) are likely to be the most eco-wise. So from planning a party to buying gifts to writing thank you notes, green celebrations should always begin with the 3Rs.

HERE'S THE GOOD NEWS: YOU CAN ENJOY THE YEAR'S HOLIDAYS AND CELEBRATIONS AND BE GOOD TO THE PLANET.

Jubilee Farm, in Carnation, Washington, used to be certified organic. Now they're not. No, pesticide contraband wasn't discovered in their barn. The farm's owner, "Farmer Erick," decided to un-certify his farm. This might seem like a strange thing for a man passionate about sustainability to do, especially in light of the fact that organic food sales increased by 20.9% in 2006. But Farmer Erick decided to go certification-free when he came to the conclusion that he could grow food sustainably without having to pay the "virtue tax" associated with certification.

After polling his CSA (community supported agriculture) customers, who all agreed that the tax was not worth it (when they knew firsthand that their veggies were just as organic as they would be if they were certified), Farmer Erick ended his certified organic status, went into his fields, and continued growing food using the same organic and biodynamic methods he'd used all along.

Farmer Erick says that if he were ever to wholesale, he'd seek status again because otherwise retail customers wouldn't know his foods were grown organically. This story reminds us that it's good to get to know the farmers you buy your food from on site, through CSAs, or at your local farmer's markets. If their products are not certified organic, ask them about their practices, and if they claim to be organic, ask them about this too. While it's true that some farmers (or the people who sell their food) may make false claims, it may also be true that a Farmer Erick near you is using sustainable methods but just isn't taking any credit for it. Our tip when it comes to local organic food is a three letter word: A-S-K.

The 3 Rs

Greening your holidays and celebrations is easy to do when you remember that every product has a lifespan. (Wedding dresses and New Year's champagne don't just appear via Fairy Godmother.) Holiday/special occasion items (and the parts/ingredients used to make and package them) were at one point grown, manufactured, and/or created. Growing, manufacturing, and creation processes impact the planet in large and small ways depending on energy usage, chemicals employed, and waste management practices. After products are made, they are packaged, transported, and stored until they are purchased, transported, and finally used. At some point, the products or their parts may be disposed of, which requires the use of more energy and precious resources. The 3Rs enable you to make green choices during any and all steps along the way while planning, enjoying, and wrapping up your celebrations.

Reduce

...buying less may be the best option of all. Less pollution. Less Waste. Less time working to pay for the stuff. Sometimes, less really is more. – StoryofStuff.com

Hands down, the most earth-friendly of the 3Rs is reducing. Reducing cuts down on resources needed to produce products and trims waste generated by production, transportation, use, and elimination of the product. Reducing is a gift to our wallets, our waist lines, our waterways, and our world. But of all the 3Rs, reducing may be the hardest to do, especially during holidays and celebrations.

As Americans, we've come to believe that stuff equals love and acceptance. So it follows that we believe more stuff equals more love and acceptance. Birthdays, Valentine's Day, Mother's Day, and more give us the opportunity to show our friends and family just how much we love them by showering them with stuff—often beyond our budgets and certainly beyond need or even reason. Having all the latest clothes, cars, and gadgets makes us feel more accepted. Because these beliefs are so ingrained, reducing may feel like an unwelcome challenge, yet *reducing is the single most important choice* because it helps our planet the most. So, whether you try reducing first or last, we challenge you to a holiday/celebration reduction diet. How much stuff can you *not* buy and still show others you care, have a great time, and create wonderful memories? You may be surprised.

Reducing does not mean going without, although we don't think the Earth would complain if this were the case. In fact, great green strides can be accomplished through the items we *do* buy, by choosing products that are more earth-friendly (more on that later). But reduction itself can be achieved in many ways. You can reduce the overall amount of things you buy, such as decorations, party-favors, or party garb; or, you can reduce the amount of stuff that is used to create or package products, giving preference to items that minimize impact on the Earth such as wrapping gifts in other gifts (eliminating/reducing the need for wrapping paper), by making party food from scratch, or by buying food sold in bulk or that is not pre-packaged. You can reduce through limiting the number of petroleum-based products you buy and can reduce your eco-footprint by consolidating shopping trips, using alternative transportation, and shopping locally. You can reduce the amount of energy you consume during the holidays by lowering the thermostat during a party, making use of the body-heat generated by your guests. See? It's not so hard. The key here is buying and using less. Simple.

All things being even, trimming your eco-wasteline during holidays might be the most challenging, but it also reaps the greatest rewards, not just for our planet and our bank-accounts, but for us as well. Children and adolescents benefit from learning moderation and simplicity, especially when modeled by adults around them. In a study published in 2007, researchers found that materialism and low self-esteem are reciprocal in nature (they are both caused and affected by the other). The study also discovered that as materialism decreases, self-esteem increases. Clearly, efforts to curb consumerism are worthwhile.

Americans make up five percent of the world's population, yet use 30% of the world's resources. The way we celebrate does nothing to enhance our reputation as a nation that cares about the fate of the Earth and its people.

But of course, there is hope. And as we've said, it's not all that difficult. Here are three easy ways to reduce excess holiday consumerism:

WOMEN GOING GREEN:

According to the U.S. Census Bureau, women control 80% of household spending, do 60% of the online shopping, and buy 81% of all products and services. Women also spend five *trillion* dollars per year, and this amount continues to grow. What if each and every woman began to think sustainably and (when reducing and reusing was not an option) spent a percentage of her dollar "votes" on people or earth-friendly products and services? The website BigGreenPurse.com and the One in a Million campaign are working to find out. Their plan is to encourage one million women to shift $1,000 of their household budgets to eco-friendly products and services. Think $1,000 is a lot of dough? Think that'd be too hard to do? Break it down into months or weeks and you'll see that the number is small when you consider that most food, household, and personal care products, clothing, and services are available in green alternatives. If you're still unsure, grab a friend, your mom, or daughter and pledge to give conscientious consumerism a try. Green is your color, girlfriend!

1. **Apply the 25% rule.** When shopping for everything from décor to hors d'oeuvres, aim to buy 25% less than you normally would. Chances are, you'll discover that you and your guests don't miss that 25%. In fact, no one may notice at all. If 25% is easy, why not challenge yourself to progressively higher reductions until you find a number that works for you? Imagine how many resources would be saved, how much energy preserved, and how much waste reduced if everyone trimmed their buying habits by just 25%.

2. **Focus on quality rather than quantity.** If you are in the market for birthday gifts, for example, seek items that are going to last and be used and/or cherished for a long time. Just say no to disposable gifts and items that may break or will need to be replaced soon, such as electronic items that quickly become obsolete. For children, toys that are made of natural materials such as wood are usually sturdy, safe, and often so lovely that they'll become heirlooms.

3. **Buy local.** Buying locally generally reduces resources used and waste caused by transporting goods over long distances. Each ingredient in an average Thanksgiving dinner, for example, travels about 1,500 miles to arrive on your plate. A 2007 study determined that one Christmas dinner for eight people in the United Kingdom generates an equivalent to 44 pounds of carbon dioxide emissions. Feeding the country is equal to driving a car around the globe 6,000 times. Jet-setting food unnecessarily creates tons of carbon dioxide emissions when you consider the fact that meals can come from closer to home. So look for all your special occasion goods at local stores or farmer's markets and ask for locally grown or made products. For more on eating locally, visit 100MileDiet.com.

Reuse

Reusing is great for the planet because it means that resources for new products are being preserved and new waste is not being generated. Like reducing, reusing saves money and gives us the opportunity to exercise our creativity and resourcefulness. Reusing is similar to recycling, but in general, reusing involves repurposing items at least once, and optimally an infinite number of times. Green celebrations almost always include some form of reusing before, during, and after special occasions. Whether costumes, tableware, or gift wrap are on your list, before buying new, consider ways in which previously used items can serve new purposes. The following chapters offer dozens of ways you can reuse during your holidays and celebrations, but here are a few general tips:

1. **Plastic or paper? Say "No thanks" to both.** The Average American uses between 300 and 700 bags per year. If every American tied the bags they use in one year into a line, it could wrap itself around our planet 760 times! And instead of breaking down, as plastic bags degrade, they contaminate water and soil and endanger wildlife. Even "biodegradable" plastic bags may not actually break down in the landfill. But paper bags made of virgin wood are no better. A study out of Germany found that manufacturing paper bags uses 1.49 times the amount of energy and causes greater emissions of sulfur dioxide, nitrous oxide, carbon monoxide, and methane than creating plastic bags. In addition, paper bags create significantly more volume of waste. According to this same study, if plastic bags were banned worldwide, 17 million acres of trees would be needed to meet the demand of shoppers. Reusable shopping bags are the key. Remember to use yours not just while shopping for holiday food but also for clothing, gifts, and everything else you buy.

2. **Beg, borrow, or steal.** Okay, scratch begging and stealing, but borrowing can be a great way to reuse and repurpose items such as tableware, special occasion clothing, and even Christmas trees. If friends and family members don't have the items you're seeking, look for rental shops and consignment stores instead of buying new. Craigslist, Freecycle, eBay and other Internet sites offer reusable items at low or no cost, while garage and thrift-sale shopping often reveal treasures perfect for holidays and other celebrations.

3. **Reusing creates tradition.** Reusing the same decorations, tableware, and activities year after year is a great way to establish or carry on traditions that bring joy and meaning to your family's life. Instead of trying to outdo yourself with new decorations each year, holidays and special occasions can be made more meaningful by reusing the same décor (or at least some of the main items) year after year.

4. **Exercise caution when acquiring previously used products that may be unsafe.** Many recalled toys, for example, end up in garage sales and on eBay and thrift stores, while antique store tableware may contain lead. Use websites like

So, it's a typical Monday night, Cedar's been settling down, so I'm blogging away. I thought Cedar had totally settled when I heard a scream of complete insanity coming from the bathroom. "MOM! Hurry…." And when I can't make it there in 3 seconds flat, "MOM! NOW!"

On the way to the bathroom I'm thinking, *Did Cedar fall, crack his head, break the toilet?* He usually calls me mama —mom when there's trouble. Uh, oh. No good thoughts are in my head, that's for sure.

I run into the bathroom and Cedar is standing smack in the middle of the room; just standing there, frozen, with no pants or undies to be seen either, I might add. I rush over to my half-naked child and start checking for blood and bruises and asking him if he's ok.

Cedar says he's fine, and I say, "Well, what are you screaming for? I thought you were hurt!

Now, this child, who I'm trying really hard to be mad at for scaring me to death, holds up an empty toilet paper roll and says calmly (and I quote), "Can I recycle this?"

Me: "What the? That's why you were screaming?"
The boy: "Yeah."
Me: "WHY?"
The boy: "Because I've always really wanted a pirate telescope, and now I can recycle this tube into one."

Sigh. What are you gonna say to that?

Contributed by Jennifer Chait, TreeHuggingFamily.com blog

HealthyToys.org and products such as home lead test kits to ensure that your efforts to save the Earth don't harm you or your loved ones.

Recycle

Recycling is another good way to bring a little green into your family's celebrations. Recycling diverts unnecessary waste from landfills and breathes new life into objects that may have seen better days. But while recycling is certainly high on the list of things people should do all year long, keep in mind that recycling itself uses resources. Recycling your paper, plastic, and glass goods after a party, for example, is better than sending them to a landfill, but those products must be picked up, transported, recycled into something else (possibly with new packaging), and transported again. So of the 3Rs, recycling should be done only if reducing and reusing are not possible.

 Another thing to keep in mind is that just because an item has the recycle symbol on it, or says it's made of eco-friendly or recyclable packaging, does not mean that you will be able to recycle it. That's because many recycling stations accept only certain types of recyclables. Case in point: I live in King County, Washington, just outside of Seattle. When my hard plastic food processor bowl recently broke (as I was preparing Christmas Eve dinner), I cringed at the thought of it ending up in a landfill. Our local government seems to place a priority on environmental issues and yet, after placing a few calls, I discovered that the bowl, made out of a #7 plastic, is in fact recyclable… but not in my area. The waste management person I spoke with said the only solution was to *speak with my local and state politicians about creating additional means of recycling* in my area. For now, only soft plastic bottles and containers as well as paper items, some types of electronics, and yard and food scraps may be recycled. Everything else, recyclable or not, goes into the landfill if it cannot later be reused or repurposed. (In some cases, such as with electronics, you may be able to return products for recycling to the company that manufactured the item. Before throwing a geographically non-recyclable recyclable in the trash, check with the company that manufactured it to see if they'll accept it for recycling.)

But the term "recycling" also includes giving priority to products that are made from recycled, rather than new, raw materials. Although energy and resources may still be consumed in recycling products such as paper, plastics, and glass, buying recycled means saving virgin resources, some of which are non-renewable. So next time you're in the market for new goods for your next holiday or celebration, look for recycled products.

Gifts made from recycled materials are getting easier and easier to find. For the next Mother's Day, how about a vase created from recycled glass, a handbag sewn from recycled or reused candy wrappers, or a cozy fleece scarf knit from recycled bottles? Recycled content paper goods such as wrapping paper, invitations, and thank you notes can easily be found online and in some forward-thinking stores. (Look for products with a recycled content that is 100% post-consumer waste.)

Composting is another form of recycling. In addition to buying products that are made using recycled and recyclable materials, if you're unable to reuse the products later, try to select items that can be recycled through composting. Your family's Christmas tree, for example, can be composted rather than trashed, and WorldCentric.org sells compostable cups and plates that are not too colorful but still oh so green.

The 3 Gs

While the 3Rs is a household term, we hope the 3Gs will soon attain the same status. We believe that any discussion of earth-friendly holidays and celebrations should include a consideration of the following concepts: good for people, good for the planet, and good for the community. Just like the 3Rs, the 3Gs are meant to inform decisions and behaviors and to provide a simple way to remember our sage, earth-friendly suggestions. Also, as with the 3Rs, you don't have to do all of them at once. Starting with just one will make a difference.

The 3Gs can be applied to all of our holiday and celebration choices. To demonstrate their use, let's say you are shopping for Halloween goodies to give to neighborhood trick-or-treaters. In this scenario, you find yourself conflicted about the idea of buying a ten-pound bag of conventional candy, and so you consult GreenHalloween.org for a list of healthier and more earth-friendly items. After scanning the list, you decide that you'd still like to give away candy and notice that Green Halloween® suggests several alternatives to conventional sweets. One company sells lollipops made from organic ingredients and packaged in corn-based, biodegradable wrappers. You're wondering how this candy fits with the 3Gs. Let's explore.

Good for People

Is this option good for people (including children and adults)? Well, it's true that these lollipops are still candy, but organically grown ingredients are not grown using pesticides, so these would be a healthier choice than conventional options. In addition, the lollipops contain no artificial ingredients, flavors, or coloring, no preservatives, no lead, no high fructose corn syrup, and no hydrogenated oils.

If you were considering handing out non-food items to your neighborhood's little ghosts and goblins, treasures such as polished rocks, play dough, stickers, and recycled content toys may be considered "healthy" as well, as long as they're free of lead and other toxins, even if they are not meant to be ingested. Products that are healthy for people should pose no long- or short-term threats.

Great. So the lollipops fit under "good for people." But wait.

Meeting the "good for people" criteria also means good for the people who come into play long before a product reaches your hands (or mouth). The people who grow, make, or manufacture items are often left out of the earth-friendly equation, and yet what's good for the planet is often good for them as well. Organic farmers and workers, for example, are protected from the exposure to cancer-causing chemicals that conventional farmers are exposed to, so buying organic foods or foods with organic ingredients supports this type of people-friendly farming. The lollipops you'd like to hand out on Halloween contain organic ingredients, and so they would fall under the good for people category. Of course, chemicals are not the only risk to people who make products. Unsafe working conditions, unfair wages, and child labor are just some of the un-people-friendly practices that, unfortunately, do take place. Choosing products that are made in the United States or that are Certified Fair Trade help ensure that people are not being harmed to make the holiday items you and your family will enjoy.

BUYING ONLINE?

Search out companies that give a portion of their proceeds to non-profits you'd like to support. And check out GoodSearch.com, a philanthropic search engine that donates a hefty 50% of advertising revenue to your charity of choice.

Good for the Planet

Is this option good for the planet? Products made with organically produced ingredients are always better for the Earth than products made from conventionally grown ingredients that have been sprayed. Pesticides (including insecticides, herbicides and fungicides) used in conventional farming leach into soil and groundwater. Furthermore, organic farming conserves energy and prevents soil erosion. The lollipops you've chosen not only are organic, they are packaged using a corn-based material, and so may be considered doubly good for the Earth. Petroleum-free packaging is generally preferable to plastic packaging made from fossil fuels because (1) oil is not a sustainable resource; (2) plastic packaging can contaminate products, especially food products with toxic chemical residue; and (3) some plastics are non-recyclable (or are simply not recycled) and end up in landfills where they continue to leach into groundwater and don't bio- or photo-degrade for hundreds of years or more. Food-based packaging utilizes renewable resources and is compostable and biodegradable. Lastly, you discover that the lollipops are made in America, but not in a town nearby. Ideally, products are local, but when this is not an option, using American-made products may be more earth-friendly than using products from abroad due to the extensive waste produced by shipping products from out of the country.

Good for the Community

The third "G" is good for the community. We believe that being good to one's community (local, national and/or global) is an essential feature of being green. Once again, what is good for the Earth is usually good for people and for our communities. Choices in this category include those that actively give back. For example, if the company that sells the organic lollipops contributes a percentage of its revenue to a non-profit organization, the lollipops would fall under the good for community category. Other ways companies can give back to their communities are to contribute large numbers of products to families in underprivileged neighborhoods, encourage their employees to volunteer in the community on company time, or sponsor community-based events and movements such as Green Halloween®.

Although bioplastics may seem like an ideal way to green up our American obsession with bags and packaging, bioplastics have their opponents. This scrutiny is based on some serious concerns about food-based plastics, from the massive amounts of energy (and fossil fuels) it takes to produce some of them to the fear that many bioplastic products may not biodegrade as expected. Other potential negative effects include the impact of bioplastics on deforestation, world food prices, water supply, genetic engineering, and soil erosion, not to mention the fact that mixing bioplastics with conventional plastics can cause serious damage to existing recycling operations. With these (and other) concerns, what's a shopper to do? For issues that are not black and white (as many aren't), we suggest that you ask questions, use your judgment in a given situation, and choose the best option available. Also, stay abreast of the latest eco-developments with bioplastics and the issues surrounding them and, whenever possible, make your voice heard through letters, e-mails, or votes.

We developed The Green Year label to highlight holiday and special occasion products that are people- and/or Earth-friendly and to benefit Treeswing, a non-profit leader in promoting children's health. For information on becoming a featured vendor and using our label on your product(s), go to our website, CelebrateGreen. NET.

Eco-Savvy Seals

While many green guidelines eschew excessive acquisition of goods, at some point nearly everybody shops. But shopping does not mean your R's and G's should be put aside. Your eco-savviness can remain alive and well when the products you choose are also eco-savvy.

Whether you're purchasing decorations or after party clean-up supplies, look for products that sport one or more of the following logos, seals, or stamps. These marks indicate that the products you've selected fall under one or more of the 3R and 3G categories, helping make eco-smart decisions easier. (Note: This is not a comprehensive list.)

1% For The Planet	Forest Stewardship	Quality Assurance
CCOF Trade Association	Council	International
Certified	Green-e	Rainforest Alliance
Co-op America	GreenGuard	Recycled Content
Dolphin Safe	Green Seal	Salmon Safe
EcoLogo	The Green Year®	SmartWood Certified
Energy Star	Leaping Bunny	Trees for the Future
Fair Trade Certified	Luxury Eco Stamp	USDA Organic
Fair Trade Federation	Marine Stewardship	
Food Alliance Certified	Processed Chlorine Free	

FOR A THOROUGH LIST AND DISCUSSION OF MEANINGFUL AND MEANINGLESS ECO-LABELS AND TERMS, WE SUGGEST *IT'S EASY BEING GREEN: A HANDBOOK FOR EARTH-FRIENDLY LIVING* BY CRISSY TRASK.

Celebrate Green FAQ's

Even when going green for holidays and celebrations feels like the right thing to do, you may have questions that need addressing before you take your first eco-friendly step. The most common questions we hear are:

The holidays are expensive enough. Won't going green break the bank?

A common perception is that earth-friendliness costs an arm and a leg. It's true that some earth-friendly products cost more, but when you apply the 3Rs, you almost always end up saving money. If, instead of decorating your living room at Christmas as though you're vying to win an America's Most Beautiful Home contest, try reducing the amount of décor you purchase and focusing on *people* over things. You will save money even if you purchase more costly earth-friendly products because you're buying less.

But the higher price of some earth-friendly products also may be deceiving, since most will save energy, time, and/or money in the long term (not to mention the fact that they may help save the planet). LED Christmas lights, for example, may run up to double the cost of traditional Christmas lights, but use up to 90% less energy and last 25 times longer. LED lights are cooler and therefore safer, decreasing the possibility of burns and fires, and are virtually unbreakable, reducing replacement costs.

Like LED lights, organic food and clothing may cost more up front, but they don't cost us the planet and may save money over time. When we watch what we put in and on our bodies and lead healthier lives, our future healthcare costs are expected to be lower.

Having said all this, not all earth-friendly products cost more when compared to their conventional counterparts. A trip down the aisle of your local health food store or co-op will reveal good-for-you and good-for-the-earth products in a spectrum of prices, some lower than name brand items. Coupons, rebates, in-store and Internet specials, and combining purchases, buying in bulk (such as by the case), or splitting shipping with friends also can save a bundle. But don't expect to compare the purchase price of eco-wise products and items found at your dollar-discount store. Those products usually are made in other countries by people who are not paid a living wage, which is how manufacturers can afford to charge so little. Don't bite. Cheap, un-earth-friendly goods cost us all in the end and are almost never worth the price.

All in all, being a green consumer means thinking short- and long-term, weighing the costs and benefits, and making choices that are right for us and our families.

How to save some green while going green:
1. **Plan ahead.** Almost everything goes on sale at some time or another. If you know you are going to purchase earth-friendly party decorations, find the ones you want, then buy when they are at their lowest price. Gifts will most likely offer the biggest savings if you avoid purchasing while in emergency mode.

1. **Get everyone involved.** Trying to make changes to long-held traditions without the support of others in your household can be tough. But when you make it a family challenge to replace, renew, and really think about what you want to do, it can not only be good for the planet, but can create a unique bonding experience.

2. **Make it fun.** If people believe that making changes is going to be enjoyable as well as worthy, they'll be more likely to pitch in.

3. **Plan ahead.** This is probably the biggest challenge to making changes around holidays and celebrations. Last-minute buying generally means choosing things that are not good because their availability may be limited. We'd suggest sitting down once a year with the family calendar. Think about how far in advance of each holiday you need to plan and shop, then mark time on the calendar to do that.

2. **Do online searches for "organic coupons," "green coupons," or "eco-coupons."** Some organic companies offer e-coupons if you sign up for their e-newsletters. Check out your favorites.

3. **Support Community Supported Agriculture (CSA).** CSA's allow the public to buy directly from farmers. Typically, with a CSA, you'll pay a monthly fee and receive a box full of fresh, seasonal produce delivered to your door or a drop-off site. OrganicConsumers.org and LocalHarvest.org have state-by-state guides to help you find a nearby CSA.

4. **Buy organic foods in season and freeze for use later on.** If you pick organic strawberries or blueberries in summer and freeze the fruit on cookie sheets, you can make organic blueberry pies at Thanksgiving.

5. **Join a buying club or co-op.** Stores like Costco are now selling organic foods, and co-ops allow you to share the expense with others. Co-ops can be brick and mortar or arranged with groups of friends or neighbors.

6. **Buy in bulk.** Our local co-op gives us 10% off when we order products by the case. (This co-op also gives members 10% off once a month, so if we buy a case on that day, we end up saving 20% over purchasing the product individually.) Buying in bulk is generally cheaper because you're not paying for packaging.

None of the stores near me sells earth-friendly products. Do I have to live in a big city to turn my celebrations green?

Issues of access are a concern for many people who would like to go green for holidays, celebrations, and in their everyday lives, but don't think the stores near them have the products they're looking for. Fear not; eco-savviness is not geographically determined. While cities like San Francisco, Seattle, and Los Angeles are likely to offer more earth-friendly retail stores per capita than smaller ones, many big-name stores and "clubs" now sell earth-friendly or earth-friendlier products, including enough food, clothes, and gift items to turn any celebration green.

But even if you live in a two-mule town, you have access to the same earth-friendly goodies that eco-wise Tinsel Town residents use by shopping on the Internet. A quick online search will reveal products for every holiday, celebration, or occasion that are perfectly wonderful and eco-friendly. Even sites like Amazon.com sell green products (and by joining Amazon's "Subscribe and Save" program you can get free shipping as well as additional savings). When shopping on the Internet, remember to plan ahead. This will save time and even money while reducing the likelihood of last-minute impulse buying of expensive, overly packaged, un-earth-friendly products at your local stores.

Regardless of where you shop, remember that going green requires not a single cent. Reducing and reusing, especially, can be done for free and are worth mountains of gold to the Earth. We can't shop our way out of global warming, but we can create sustainability by changing our everyday habits. To make the biggest impact, no matter where you live, celebrate green by being conscientious about what you buy and don't buy, do and don't do, not just for special occasions but in your everyday life as well.

I'm so confused by all the green terms and logos. How do I know that the companies I'm buying products from can be trusted?

Don't be fooled by greenwashing.

According to TerraChoice Environmental Marketing (TerraChoice.com), greenwashing is defined as "the act of misleading consumers regarding the environmental practices of a company or the environmental benefits of a product or service." Their research points out the "six sins of greenwashing": (1) a hidden trade-off; (2) no proof of green claims; (3) vagueness; (4) irrelevant green claims; (5) lying or exaggeration of claims; and (6) promoting the lesser of two evils (such as organic cigarettes or bottled water from a company that claims to use less plastic in the product line).

Eco-savvy shoppers should not be fazed by misleading marketing. Attempts to befuddle you into buying products is a scheme now being practiced by some companies that are losing profits to authentically green products. Instead of changing their own products or sources, they may slap meaningless terms (or even a meaningless seal) on their bottles or boxes and cross their fingers that you'll take the bait. Some companies may stretch the truth, say that their product is free of a toxin that was outlawed decades ago, or try to confuse you by making up terms. Don't buy it.

REMEMBER THAT THERE IS NO SUCH THING AS A ZERO ENVIRONMENTAL IMPACT PRODUCT, ONLY PRODUCTS WHOSE FOOTPRINTS ARE REDUCED WHEN COMPARED TO OTHER SIMILAR PRODUCTS. THE ONLY TRULY GREEN, 100% SUSTAINABLE CHOICE IS ABSTINENCE (SOUND VAGUELY FAMILIAR?). SO IF GREENWASHING TERMS ARE LEAVING YOU UNCERTAIN AS TO A PRODUCT'S REAL IMPACT ON YOU OR THE PLANET, YOU MAY WANT TO CONSIDER GOING WITHOUT OR HOLDING OFF ON YOUR PURCHASE UNTIL YOU CAN BECOME MORE INFORMED.

NATURAL VS. ORGANIC: BE A SMART SHOPPER

A product labeled 100% organic is entirely organic.

A product labeled 100% natural has little meaning.

It's easy for consumers to confuse the terms "organic" and "natural." The United States government's definition of "organic" must be followed in products carrying this label, while there is no government definition of "natural." So a company can pretty much call a product 100% natural regardless of its contents. By the way, by law, fish, salt, and water cannot be labeled "organic."

To confuse things, you might see a Certified Naturally Grown label. Goods carrying this label have been grown to USDA organic standards. But many small scale, direct-market farmers may choose this certification over the USDA's for reasons including cost.

Although Certified Naturally Grown is not a third party certification, we think it's worth a look. Read about it online and decide for yourself.

While the following terms are not red flags (and some may be used appropriately by trusted sources), they also mean very little because none of the terms is certified by the government or any third-party agency. Look instead for products that sport the previously mentioned seals, and if you have any doubt as to whether a product is what it says it is, a quick online search should reveal its manufacturer's true colors.

Popular "greenwashing" terms include:

Biodegradable	Natural
Cruelty free	Non-toxic
Free range	Recycled/Recyclable
Green	

For more information on this topic, check out GreenwashingIndex.com and Re-Modern.com for a fairly comprehensive glossary of green and greenwashing terms.

Just reading through all this seems overwhelming. I don't have the time or energy to do all this, especially during the holidays or when I'm preparing for special occasions.

We know it may seem like a lot to absorb, especially if some of this is new to you, but keeping in mind the following points may awaken (or revitalize) your "can do" attitude:

1. **Doing something is better than doing nothing, and you don't have to take every step we mention to make a sizeable impact.** Perhaps you can start by choosing the one or two suggestions which seem most doable for you and your family. You can always increase your efforts on the next holiday.

2. **Get your whole family involved.** Have a family meeting to discuss how everyone can contribute to the greening of your next holiday. Do it way in advance of the occasion. Choose from our list of ideas.

3. **Flavor our suggestions with your family's own values and traditions.** Putting your own stamp on green celebrations will make the process more fun. You may find that celebrating green becomes a tradition your family will cherish and pass on for generations to come.

Why can't we just celebrate like we used to and leave saving the planet for the rest of the year?

Your sentiments are certainly understandable. Holidays and special occasions should be times of joy, and making these changes may seem like a damper, or, at the very least, a lot of work. But like everything else, it's all how you look at it. If going green feels like a drag, it might very well turn out to be. When making green choices is framed as a gift to yourself and to future generations, you could actually enjoy the ride. Try keeping in mind that making earth-friendly adjustments is simply important to do, like brushing your teeth, and you might find it easier to accept them as part of the cost and opportunity of living during these pivotal times.

The reason it's important to green up our celebrations is that holidays and special days are plentiful. If special occasions were all bundled together and commemorated in one big, global shindig, that one big day might set us back some, but we could use the rest of the year to make up for it. But holidays and special days don't happen on one day only in one place; they occur throughout the year in homes, schools, and places of work across the globe. With 6.6 billion (and growing) people on our planet, that's a lot of celebrating for a lot of different reasons, be they personal, familial, national, cultural, or religious.

Think of it this way: Imagine that everyone on the planet has two jars. One jar is labeled with a plus sign, the other with a minus sign. Now envision that every single one of our daily choices can be concretized as tiny pebbles, which are then placed in one of the jars. Did you make or buy a handmade gift for your niece for her birthday instead of choosing another Barbie? One pebble is added to the plus jar. Did you leave your Christmas lights on overnight? One little pebble is dropped into the minus jar. It is true that these choices in and of themselves will not save or destroy the planet, but what happens over time, year after year? The jars will start to fill as the number of pebbles grows until you can see very clearly how your good and not-so-great choices have added up. This is called the cumulative effect, and its consequences affect all of us because (don't forget) 6.6 billion other people also have jars of their own.

Of course, not all decisions are black and white, good or bad. Many are in between or a little of both. So while it's true that the Earth has some ability to regenerate and recover,

Last Easter, a candy company unveiled its "eco-egg." The candy is not organic. The chocolate is not Fair Trade. The product was declared "eco" because individual pieces were sold unboxed, reducing waste. While we applaud efforts to lessen packaging, we believe that attaching the phrase "eco" to an otherwise unchanged conventional product is at the very least a stretch, and at worst an example of greenwashing.

it needs more time than we are giving it. We can't hide from the fact that the path we've collectively chosen is moving us towards depletion, and meaningful change is therefore important *every day*. So start small, start where you can, and watch your plus jar fill faster while your minus jar's growth slows. And as you get into the swing of things, as green choices evolve into habits, celebrating green is sure to become an enjoyable and rewarding part of your family's traditions.

In a Nutshell

Eco-savvy celebrations always include aspects of reducing, reusing, and recycling as well as choices that are good for people, the planet and/or the community. But how many of the 3Rs or 3Gs you choose or in what way you apply them is completely up to you. Earth-conscious celebrating is not a one-size-fits-all destination; *it is a process*. So regardless of where you fall on the proverbial Green 'O Meter, as long as you're taking some steps, however tiny, you're making a difference.

AS LONG AS YOU'RE TAKING SOME STEPS, HOWEVER TINY, YOU'RE MAKING A DIFFERENCE.

Spring

The first time I saw a daffodil poking its beak through the soggy ground outside our home in Seattle, I nearly gasped. It was so exciting! Springtime was here!

It wasn't until I moved to the Northwest that I really understood what all the fuss was about. In southern Arizona and southern California, where I'd spent my youth and early adulthood, I only experienced two seasons—summer and almost-summer. In Tucson, it was either hot or scorching or sweltering with rain, and in Los Angeles, it was either hot or barely cool with rain, but really what's the difference? Basically, I lived in summertime all year 'round. Even the surroundings were static. The cacti always seemed oblivious to the month (they bloom, but if you sneeze, you miss it), and flowers in California were in a perpetual state of exuberance. No change, no death and rebirth, no ebb and flow. Our family could have celebrated Christmas in bathing suits and no one would have thought a thing of it.

But now that I get what springtime is all about, I'm all about spring. It's a beautiful, inspiring, and energizing season highlighted by holidays that seem tailor-made for green. In this chapter, we'll take a look at creating an eco-savvy Easter, Earth Day, and Mother's Day. And if St. Patty's Day, Passover, Arbor Day, or Cinco de Mayo are your thing, not to worry; we'll give you a few green pointers there as well.

Easter

I have a friend who *swears* that when we were little girls, she saw the Easter Bunny, live and in color, at my house. Even today, as a successful, bright, and sane mother of two, she gets chills when she recalls the memory of the mythical creature hopping past my bedroom window one night during a sleepover in 1979. Since I've never met anyone else who has seen the Easter Bunny, and since no one on my block owned a bunny costume (Star Wars costumes had been trumping sales of fairytale creatures for some time), I have no other choice but to believe that what she saw was true. So in case you've been wondering all your life what the Easter Bunny looks like, here it is: He's seven feet tall (one foot of which is ears), thin (minus the pot belly), and white as snow. He was also sporting a "scary" looking expression which, at the time, my friend thought might have been a sign of wickedness, but now believes was an expression of being overwhelmed and underappreciated. Any mother could decipher that.

But Easter is about more than commercialized, albeit real-as-they-get, bunnies. In fact, Easter, as it is generally celebrated today, combines Christian, Jewish, pagan, and ancient traditions focusing on rebirth and renewal, both of which have been symbolized throughout the history of humankind through the humble egg.

Eggs have been (and still are) involved in the teachings, artwork, and lore of nearly all cultures and religions worldwide. To both ancient and contemporary people, eggs represent springtime, fertility, birth, or resurrection, while the yolk often symbolizes the sun (sunny-side up, anyone?). When it comes to eggs, ancient Egyptians, Greeks, Romans, Hindus, Buddhists, Jews, and Christians can all agree: eggs are a powerful reminder of life and promise. A multitude of mythical and religious figures, including Jesus, have been depicted in everything from hieroglyphs to artwork, emerging from eggs or eggshells.

Coloring eggs, a well known Easter tradition, also spans geography, time, and belief. While coloring eggs in pastel shades is generally thought to be an imitation of the colors of eggs found in nature, lore suggests that colored eggs hold deeper meanings and even power. Ukrainian myth says that the Madonna brought eggs to Pontius Pilate when she asked him to spare the life of Christ. But when Pilate's guards denied her request to see

Pilate, she cried tears which fell on the eggs she carried, turning them into a rainbow of colors. During the Jewish celebration of Lag B'Omer, held in the springtime, colored eggs symbolize God's promise to Noah to never again destroy the world by flood. In Southern Asia, the Chinese and some tribal groups have used the cracks in boiled painted eggs to prophesy the future.

Suffice it to say that eggs are, have been, and always will be a key part of springtime celebrations. With this in mind, the question for you is, which eggs are most eco-friendly, humane, and healthy?

There is nothing like fresh-laid eggs from happy chickens, and if you're celebrating an eco-Easter, this is a great place to start. Our friend Petra has five pet chickens that provide her family with eggs so beautiful they don't need any dyeing. Inside their blue and pink shells shine deep yellow yolks that, when cooked, boast an intense flavor not found in store-bought eggs. If you don't have a hen-owning friend like Petra, try to locate a nearby farmer with free-range chickens who sells eggs via delivery, farmer's market, co-op, or pick-up. Or check out LocalHarvest.org to locate local eggs not only from chickens but also geese, ducks, and more.

Our pointers for green eggs (sans ham) include:
- Think sustainable, eco-friendly, and cruelty-free
- Choose eggs sold in earth-friendly compostable or recycled/recyclable cardboard packaging over plastic or Styrofoam. Or bring your own basket or container to your local farm or farmer's market.
- Select certified organic, certified humane, vegetarian-fed, and cage-free (though unscrupulous famers may stretch the term 'cage-free' by providing chickens with only limited amount of time and space outdoors).

Eggstreme Dyeing

Every year my friend Nikki and I host an Easter party for our kids and friends. The first year, we asked everyone to bring eggs and something to color them. A few guests contributed dye pellets. Others brought foods such as beets and onions, which we'd heard also work in egg dyeing. While the store-bought dye pellets did the job, the food-dyed eggs took the cake, turning ordinary white and brown eggs into the sweetest shades of pink, blue, and yellow. From then on, our eggs went au natural.

Dyeing eggs with food is not only the most eco-friendly option; it's an easy, educational family activity. Using food to dye food is cool because you never know what you're going to get. Experiment with more or fewer ingredients, more or less time in the pot, and with white, brown, and speckled eggs from different types of birds for a variety that is sure to win child, parent, and Easter Bunny approval. (If you're short on time but can plan ahead, 100% organic egg dye also can be ordered online.)

How to Dye Eggs Naturally

What you'll need:

- A variety of eggs, washed and dried
- Foods for dyeing (see below)
- Cardboard egg crate, wire rack, or shoe box lid with silver dollar sized holes (for drying eggs)
- 4 cups of water
  - 2 tbsp of white vinegar
  - Pots for cooking
  - Strainer (for cold dyeing method)
  - Beeswax crayons or rubber bands
- Tongs or slotted spoon

Dyeing Methods

Hot method. Combine uncooked eggs and ingredients for a single color in a large pot. Bring to a boil, then simmer for at least ½ hour (for deeper colors, simmer longer). Remove with tongs, pat dry, and place in a crate or on a rack or box lid. Once dry, rub with vegetable oil for a shine or leave with a matte finish.

Cold method. (Safer for younger children.) Boil eggs. Avoid overcooking so shells remain intact. Next, mix dye ingredients, boil, and simmer as above. Remove dye from heat, cool and strain, reserving dye in bowl. Carefully place hard-boiled eggs in dye and leave in for at least ½ hour (or longer for deeper color). Remove with tongs, pat dry, and place in a crate or on a rack or box lid. Once dry, rub with vegetable oil for a shine or leave with a matte finish.

You can create a variety of colors with a few ingredients by dyeing some eggs with the hot method, some with the cold, and varying the amount of time eggs are exposed to the dye.

Eggstra Decorating Tips

If you'd like your eggs to sport patterns, shapes, or words, use a beeswax crayon to draw the design *before* the egg is dyed. Older kids can paint on melted beeswax with a thin brush.

If using the hot dyeing method, be very careful when decorating fragile uncooked eggs, or use pre-hard boiled eggs. Beeswax will melt off during the hot dye process if eggs are left in too long, but will remain using the cold method. If you want the wax area to disappear after cold dyeing, dip the egg in warm water just until the wax melts, or place in a 200-degree oven for a few minutes.

Want stripes? Wrap the egg with rubber bands. Or, for a tie-dye look, rub shells with vinegar and enfold in onion skins, secured with kitchen twine or rubber bands. Next, hard boil without dye (or do the same with an already hardboiled egg and just leave onion skin on overnight). Adding a tablespoon of oil to the dye will create a marbled effect.

Create another look by holding a small leaf or blade of grass against the egg with a piece of pantyhose tied tightly around it. Then dye. When the dye is set and the hose is removed, an imprint of the object should appear.

Basket and Eggcessories

Frequently made of plastic, Easter baskets are often assembled by people making unfair wages. These baskets most likely end up in a landfill following the holiday. In our house, we reuse the same Easter baskets year after year. Most of the time, they are kept in my closet where I secret items I don't want my children to get hold of, like my collection of lost teeth. (If my kids ever discover this cache, the Easter Bunny and the Tooth Fairy will be cruelly unmasked in one fell swoop.) A less risky option would be to find baskets

Try the following natural dyes for a variety of tones. Begin by using approximately four cups of fruits and veggies, two tablespoons of white vinegar, and one tablespoon of spice for every four cups of water. Adding more of the natural dye ingredient (in addition to a proportionately higher amount of vinegar) or soaking for longer (try overnight!) will create darker colors. Canned, fresh, and frozen fruits and veggies work, but fresh foods seem to result in the darkest hues. As always, choosing organic and local foods is preferable. Be sure to eat, use, or compost any leftovers. Note that chemicals (such as chlorine) and minerals in your water may affect the dye's intensity.

◉ **Pink/red**: Beets, cranberries/cranberry juice, pomegranate juice, red grape juice, red onion skins, rhubarb stalks (chopped), raspberries, some types of tea

◉ **Orange**: Yellow onion skins (from about 12 onions), paprika, chili powder

◉ **Yellow**: Lemon peels, orange peels, carrots (shredded), cumin (ground), turmeric (ground)

◉ **Green**: Spinach, some types of tea, golden delicious apple skins (may be a green/yellow)

◉ **Blue**: Blueberries/blueberry juice, purple grape juice, red cabbage, blackberries

◉ **Purple**: Violet blossoms + 2 tsp lemon juice, hibiscus tea

◉ **Brown**: Strong black coffee, tea, dill seeds, black walnut shells

at garage sales and thrift shops, then reuse them after Easter for gifts instead of using wrapping paper. If your child is not going on an egg hunt, the Easter Bunny could also deliver his goodies in a cloth bag, hat box, or other container that can be enjoyed or used later. You can also make a lovely basket in any size from scraps of fabric.

Eggological Grass

About two weeks before Easter, my daughter's kindergarten class planted wheat grass in straw Easter baskets lined with repurposed aluminum pans. Just in time for Easter, the baskets were filled with lush, bright green grass that perfectly cradled her pastel, naturally dyed eggs. (After Easter we juiced and drank the nutrient-dense grass.) Other alternatives to petroleum-based plastic Easter grass include raffia, strips of organic nori (shimmery green seaweed available in paper-like sheets), shredded recycled paper, or strips of green (or multi-colored) fabric. You also can use a grass-colored silk scarf or cotton play cloths, available online.

Un-Eggscusable-Plastic Eggs

It's a given that plastic eggs are not eco-friendly, but if you'd like to hide treats and treasures inside, what other options do you have?

- Discover plastic eggs at yard sales or thrift shops and reuse them every year.
- Don't use plastic eggs; hide the treasures themselves (in addition to naturally colored, hard-boiled eggs).
- Use paper/cardboard eggs that come in two pieces and can be filled just like plastic ones.

Candy Eggsamination

Easter is the second biggest holiday for candy sales after Halloween, and sales are growing every year. Popular Easter candies include chocolate eggs (a tradition that started in Europe in the early 1800s) and Marshmallow Peeps (several hundred million of which are consumed each year).

Easter candy, like rest-of-the-year candy, can be cursed with all the ills you know so well (after reading this book), such as artificial colors, preservatives, and unhealthy fats, just to name a few. Specifically, Easter candy may contain unpronounceable (and unmentionable) ingredients (some of which are petroleum based) like hexametaphosphate, magnesium stearate, polysorbate 60, and sorbitan mono-stearate, as well as a rainbow of synthetic dyes (Red 40, Yellow 5, Blue 2, and Yellow 6) that may trigger hyperactivity and attention difficulties in susceptible children in the short term and possibly cancer in the long term.

But your little honey bunnies don't have to fear—candy is still a child and eco-friendly option when it is made from real (not synthetic) and organically grown ingredients and eaten in moderation. But where does the Easter Bunny find such eco-savvy treats? Global Exchange's online store not only sells organic, Fair Trade chocolate eggs, they also offer tantalizing gift baskets for kids and adults, as well as a Fair Trade Easter Action Gift Pack that includes streamers. Other online and local retailers sell organic and vegan jelly beans. Plan ahead to order online, or look for (or ask for) organic and Fair Trade candy at your local health foods store.

Tips:
- Feed your child a healthy and filling meal or snack before heading out to hunt for eggs filled with candy (even organic candy).
- Buy an egg mold and make your own chocolate eggs using organic, Fair Trade, shade grown baking chocolate from your health food store (for more on chocolate, see the section on Valentine's Day).
- Remember to give priority to products with less packaging and packaging that is recycled and/or recyclable, compostable, or made from renewable resources.
- Passionate about peeps? Buy organic, real-food marshmallows at your local health food store, or search the Internet for recipes on how to make your own. Even vegetarians can enjoy homemade marshmallows by substituting kuzu (plant based) or agar-agar (sea vegetable) for gelatin (animal based).
- Instead of candy, hide (or fill eggs with) fruit leather, homemade GORP with carob chips and dried fruit, or Annie's organic Bunny Grahams (Annies.com).
- If you are going to give out candy, ensure that it is organic and made from real foods (instead of artificial ingredients).

Eggological Gifts (Instead of Candy)

Of course, one healthy option is to forgo candy all together and stick to useful, amusing and/or healthy non-consumables. Below are some great alternatives kids of all ages will enjoy. (Some will fit in eggs, some won't, but they'll all be a hit with youngsters). For more ideas visit CelebrateGreen.NET.

- Kits such as:
  - Ingredients and decorations for making homemade muffins or cookies
  - Gardening tools and seeds (How about seeds for easy-to-grow "Eco Easter," also known as Evergreen Japanese Iris?). Other ideas are herb gardens or potted plants.
  - Wool felting kits (for making eggs and bunnies)
- Free-trade musical instruments (including wooden egg shakers)
- Play silks made from silk or cotton in a rainbow of colors
- Saplings
- Wooden baby farm animals (ideally from certified sustainable wood)
- "Bunny Money"—good for points towards an outing, activity, or special book, toy, or clothing item
- Organic cotton, wool, or soy stuffed bunnies, chicks, or baby farm animals (buy or sew/knit your own), or organic cotton lamb puppet
- Vintage papier-mâché eggs
- Beeswax crayons or modeling clay (in an array of springtime colors)
- Egg-shaped, artisan sculpted 100% beeswax candles from BigDipperWaxWorks.com

Eggcellent Animals

Even though a fuzzy bunny or fluffy chick might seem like a sweet Easter gift, buying a child an animal is not recommended unless your family thoughtfully addresses all the issues around doing so. Animal welfare agencies around the country are inundated by thousands of animals-as-Easter-gifts when their adoptive families no longer want to care for them. We tend to forget that bunnies and chicks grow into adult animals who may not be quite so cute and who require loving care for the rest of their lives.

But there *is* someone you can buy bunnies and chicks for: a person in need. Through Heifer Project International (Heifer.org), you can make contributions of rabbits, chickens, sheep, and other animals to help people around the world become self-sufficient. (HPI uses strict animal welfare guidelines and also focuses on environmentally sound agricultural techniques, gender equity, HIV/AIDS education, microenterprise, urban agriculture, and youth-focused programs.) If HPI doesn't appeal to you, some local farms may also allow you to visit their animals year round. And of course, you can always make or buy organic cotton or wool stuffed bunnies and chicks (check out the adorable stuffed huggables made with SOYSILK brand fiber at Shopatron.com), or give your child books with drawings or photos of baby animals.

And if you really, really want to incorporate a new family member for Easter, make sure your home and family are suited for the kind of animal you'd like to welcome, then consider adopting an orphaned pet. If you wait until after Easter to select your new companion, animal shelters are likely to have a large number of abandoned Easter pets just waiting for a second chance. On Easter you can give your child a card or hand-made gift certificate that says, "On X date, we'll be picking out your new bunny/bird/cat/dog/etc." Include a book in your child's Easter basket about caring for that type of animal, as well as products and toys the animal will need. Between Easter and adoption day, prepare for the pet by making/buying its bedding, securing outside fences or gates, and ridding your home and yard of objects that might be hazardous to your pet. By the time adoption day arrives, your child's Easter gift will be welcomed home to a safe and prepared environment.

Eggcellent Food

All the egg boiling and blowing you'll be doing may create an eggcess of eggs; but don't waste food by tossing it out (unless it's gone bad, and even then, it should be composted). Add chopped boiled eggs to pasta or green salads or make our yummy egg salad for an easy, quick lunch or dinner. If you empty eggs for decorating, you'll end up with a bounty of raw egg, so plan accordingly and serve herb omelets or vegetable quiche, warm or cold, at your brunch.

But eggs aren't the only food worthy of Easter. Carrots offer a nod to the dear 'ol Easter Bunny and are a healthy addition to all aspects of the Easter meal. My kids love fresh carrot juice and carrot cake muffins. Whenever possible, use local and organic carrots, of course.

FRUITY DECOR

How about sprucing up the meal with organic edible fresh flowers to top salads, eggs, or coconut sorbet? Or make a "flower basket" from fruit that is so pretty it can also serve as a centerpiece. Here's how:

1. Use flower-shaped mini cookie cutters and melon scoopers on a variety of fresh, colorful, organic fruit. Leave grapes and berries whole.

2. Thread fruit onto bamboo skewers and push the opposite end of the skewers into a hallowed-out melon placed upside-down in a basket lined with a dish.

3. Add sprigs of mint or wheatgrass.

4. Take a picture before everyone consumes your beautiful, fruitful work of art.

Eco-Egg Salad
● ● ● ● ● ● ●
Choose local and organic ingredients whenever possible

An easy, light, filling lunch for after the grueling hunt.

INGREDIENTS
Local, humane, organic eggs (hard boiled and peeled)
Organic mayo (store bought or homemade)
Locally bought or garden grown onion, celery, and herbs such as parsley, dill, and chives
Salt and pepper

Directions
Serve on a bed of local/garden greens or on homemade bread or crackers.

Safety tip: Don't eat eggs that have been unrefrigerated for more than two hours. At our Easter party, we dye using the hot method, then hide the eggs, have the hunt, and bring everyone back inside for the egg-peeling and egg-salad-making celebration—all under two hours from boiling time.

Deggcor

It's easy and affordable to include eco-friendly Easter décor in your holiday tradition by using natural materials that reflect the colors, textures, and symbolism of springtime. Here are some ideas for decorating your home or event for the Easter holiday:

● Nothing says springtime like fresh flowers, whether they come from a florist, your garden, or a meadow nearby. If you're buying flowers, look for those that have been organically grown, and if you're growing them yourself, whenever possible, use organic seeds and compost/fertilizer. Choose reused vases or those made of recycled glass or repurposed mason, milk, or juice bottles. If desired, spruce up with natural or colored raffia.

● Who says Christmas is the only holiday where we're allowed to make use of ornaments and a tree? Make an Easter tree out of a potted tree, birch branch, or blooming forsythia. Decorate with painted eggs hung from ribbon, eggs decoupaged with photos, or diminutive handmade bunny and bird ornaments. An Easter tree can be as large or as small as your imagination and space allow.

CARROT GINGER SOUP
● ● ● ● ● ● ● ● ● ● ● ● ●
Choose local and organic ingredients whenever possible

SERVES 4 TO 6
INGREDIENTS

3 cups of carrots, peeled and rough cut
1 medium onion, rough cut
1 clove garlic, smashed
½ cup white wine
1 tbsp ginger, peeled and chopped
1 cup orange juice
2 cups vegetable broth
2 tbsp uncooked brown rice
1 tbsp peanut butter or Tahini

DIRECTIONS

Put onions and wine in a soup pot. Steam with a lid on till onions are soft. Add all other ingredients except peanut butter. Cook till carrots are soft. Puree mixture in food processor or blender. Add peanut butter if serving hot. Good with a dollop of sour cream.

Contributed by Joy Stroh, Salud! chef, Whole Foods Market, Bellevue, WA

◉ Use blown and painted or decoupaged eggs in a bowl as a centerpiece. Place them alone, atop live wheatgrass, on a mirror, or on one of the other plastic-grass substitutes previously mentioned.

◉ Attach strings to decorated eggs and hang from doorways or walkways, chandeliers, door-fronts, or curtain rods.

Eggtivities

Beyond eggs, baskets, and gifts, it's the family activities that make Easter a memorable and enjoyable holiday tradition.

In my youth, Easter Sunday meant waking up very early in order to attend a sunrise service at our church in Tucson, Arizona. The service was held outside, with the congregation facing the Catalina Mountains, and as the sun rose, the sky would turn from gray to bright hues of pink and purple, swirled together with streaks of clear blue.

After church we headed to my cousins' house where my aunt had prepared a gourmet spread which we kids would hardly notice because we had more important things in mind: tackle tag, or actually, tackle the oldest and tallest cousin, Wade. Only after we'd grass-stained every inch of our Easter fashions would we gather excitedly for the big hunt. Our Easter Bunny usually left a mixture of hard-boiled and plastic eggs filled with jelly beans, and he always found the best hiding places, like in cactus holes, under the dog's dish, in a dry birdbath, or in a rock garden. After we'd discovered every last egg, we'd chow down on Aunt Debbie's always delectable lunch, then play music and sing together.

Our Easter celebrations often included games and activities all nine cousins and six aunts and uncles could enjoy together. One year, we made Easter bonnets out of newspaper and odd bits of this and that. Another time we fashioned baskets out of papier-mâché. One year when I was too old for Easter egg hunts, my mom and I created one for my dad. Instead of candy, we hid reused plastic eggs filled with strips of paper that said things like, "You are the most eggceptional dad in the world!" or "Happy Easter, your eggcellence!" We had fun from start to finish on that one, and it was hysterical to watch my father hunting for eggs on his hands and knees like an overgrown kid.

If, like us, you believe that being green means emphasizing people over objects, consider Easter activities that decrease attention on things (i.e., candy and gifts), while increasing joy, togetherness, and great memories. A few more ideas:

- Blown and decorated Easter eggs. Wash eggs with warm, soapy water and pat dry. Stick a pin through the top of the egg and make a larger hole in the bottom. Using a small syringe or your own wind-power, empty the shell (reserve egg for later). Decorate using water-based paints, colorful bits of paper (or tree-free paper), magazine images, or photos. You can also glue on spices, rice, or other small bits of dry food or natural materials.

- Fill blown and decorated eggs with recycled paper and tin foil confetti for a smashing (but messy!) party favor.

- Make a shell mosaic. After blowing and dyeing eggs, crush the shells and use to decorate other eggs or items to be used as gifts or décor.

- Make Easter baskets or an Easter piñata by papier-machéing a balloon and decorating with recycled and/or natural materials.

- Enjoy a reverse egg hunt. Give each child a number of eggs and set the timer. Adults close their eyes while kids hide the eggs, then parents have to find them.

- Try the old-fashioned bunny hop. Turn on the music and teach everyone the "Bunny hop," or make up your own steps and have fun!
- Go hunting in the dark. Get up before dawn or wait until nighttime to hunt for your eggs in the dark. Use flashlights (crank operated or rechargeable battery-powered, of course) or low lighting to aid in the search.
- Put on an Easter-themed puppet show with bunny, chick, and lamb sock-puppets. Kids can make up their own show, as well as make the puppets if they like.

Be a Good Egg

If springtime reminds us of renewal, then what better time of year to renew your family's vision of a sustainable future and to take steps to rejuvenate our planet or communities? Inspired by the season, people across the globe are finding ways to make the world a better place this time of year. In an effort to combat deforestation, for example, Kenyan Nobel Peace Prize Laureate Wangari Maathai said that people across the globe should plant trees at Easter to symbolize revival for our planet and its inhabitants. Churches are paying attention to the impact of their traditions and are making conscientious decisions about the resources they use, such as palm leaves (used for Palm Sunday). According to the *New York Times*, increasing numbers of churches are now purchasing ethically and sustainably sourced palm leaves while religious leaders ask, "Is God Green?" and direct worshipers to biblical references mandating humans to be stewards of the planet. And did you know that generations long gone found ways to do good during Easter? The old tradition of using hot cross buns as Easter treats began when European monks made and served them to the poor.

What "good egg" traditions can you and your family create?

No Budget Earth Day Celebration

Free or Low-Cost Gifts to Celebrate Our Planet

Even if you've never "celebrated" Earth Day before, you're reading this book, so maybe you'd like to join in the fun and start a new family tradition.

Whether you want to devote five minutes or the entire day on April 22 to celebrating our planet, we've got ideas for you and none costs a penny. If you don't have the supplies on hand to do these activities, skip them. The idea is that the only price attached is in time and attention. (How long you spend is, of course, up to you. Our list is merely a guide.)

Ten-Minute (or Less) Ideas:

- Turn your thermostat down two degrees and keep it there. In the summertime, set the AC two degrees higher.
- Send Happy Earth Day e-cards to a half dozen friends.
- E-mail your state or national representatives about a green initiative.
- If you're in the supermarket, track down the manager and encourage him or her to source local products.
- Make signs to put on the mirror over faucets to remind family members to turn off water when they are brushing their teeth. (You can save an average of nine gallons every time you do this.)
- Cancel subscriptions to newspapers or magazines you don't really want.
- Go online to CatalogChoice.org to free your mailbox from junk mail.
- Call several people and arrange to carpool for an upcoming event such as a child's sporting activity or a club meeting.
- Go online and join a group like Sierra Club, World Wildlife Fund, Kids for Saving the Earth, the Wilderness Society or Co-op America.
- Make a family pledge to walk everywhere today.
- Talk to the principal at your children's school about instituting environmental education in the curriculum.
- Check to see that your tires are correctly inflated.
- Sign the "Healthy Yard Pledge" at Audubon.org.

- Go to sites like Care2.com, TheHungerSite.com, Ripple.org, or FreeRice.com. Click on the links to make donations (some at no charge to you) to environmental or humanitarian causes.
- Join an earth-aware campaign at RootsAndShoots.org.

Half-hour Ideas:

- List some un-earth-friendly habits in which you engage and make a written agreement with other members of your family or group to change at least one of them.
- Check to see if you really need all the lights you're currently using. If some are not necessary, but you want to keep a bulb in the fixture for the sake of appearances, partially unscrew the bulb so it won't turn on. Be careful not to unscrew too far; you don't want the bulbs falling out!
- String a laundry line and dry clothes naturally.
- Clean your refrigerator's condenser coil.
- Calculate your carbon footprint at ProjectHouse.vpweb.com.
- Dig outside. If you live in an apartment, see if you can find someone with a garden who will allow you to plant or weed. Just get your hands into the dirt. Feel the ground that feeds and supports us all.
- Tune up your heating system. If you don't know how, this is a great day to learn about it by going online or visiting the library.
- Skip washing dishes by hand today. Instead, load the dishwasher fully and set to air dry. Using a dishwasher with large loads saves significant water and energy as compared to hand-washing dishes. And while you're at it, scrape off food, but don't prewash, especially if you have a newer dishwasher. Cleaning one or two plates by hand if they're not totally clean beats letting the water run while you're rinsing an entire load's worth.

One-Hour Ideas:

- Walk around your neighborhood and pick up trash.
- Install low-flow shower heads and faucet aerators in every bathroom in the house.
- Make up an Earth Day song with family and/or friends.
- Take a family bike ride.
- Get out a calendar and plan one earth-friendly activity each month for the next year.

- Read with your kids. Pick a book of interest to your budding environmentalist from the list at PlanetPals.com or from your local librarian.

- Put on an eco-fashion show. Collect items from around your home and garden and gussy up your duds. Be creative! Glue pebbles on your shoes. Make a shirt out of newspaper pages. You get the idea. Be silly. Have fun. Make the driveway your runway and strut your green garb for friends and neighbors.

- Gather the family to discuss what each member can do to improve his or her earth-friendly behaviors. Turn it into a competition if you like. Each family member, depending on age, can choose from a list of eco-friendly behaviors that he or she will adopt during the next year. Write each member's pledge down. Keep track, and the following year regroup to see how well you've done. Create an award for the winner. A little cash incentive might not be a bad idea either. One family puts pennies in a jar every night and at the end of the year uses that for a prize that goes to the most eco-conscious family member.

- Head to the library and play some eco-friendly games. If they don't have any, ask if they would consider purchasing one like *Let's Save Our Earth*, a non-competitive learning game that teaches kids and adults alike about simple things each of us can do to help the planet. Or bring your own and supplement the game by searching for books to take home that explore the game's topic in more detail.

- If you happen to be washing clothes today, do it in cold water. By using cold, you'll eliminate the majority of environmental impacts since 90% of the energy involved in washing clothes by machine goes to heating the water, not to running the machine. Unless clothes are heavily stained, cold water can get them clean enough.

- Walk through your house and unplug any item with an LED light that could be a drain on electricity. A variety of appliances, such as microwaves, toasters, laptops, and washing machines with doors left open, can draw power so anything electrical with an accessible plug should be unplugged when not in use. If the plug is hidden, install a "smart strip" or use a remote control outlet system.

Half-Day to Whole-Day Ideas:

- Take a hike and play games like Nature Alphabet where you look for things along the way that begin with each letter of the alphabet.
- Visit an organic farm.
- Build a compost bin out of recycled materials.
- Read up on worm composting and go in search of some of the little wigglers.
- Choose a topic of interest to your family related to the Earth, recycling, buying less, or whatever interests you. Shoot a video or create a book about the topic from your point of view. This can be a lot of fun. A video could be as simple as asking the same question of everyone in the family and recording their answers. Or you might take it outside. Maybe there's an area in your neighborhood where people dump trash, or a weedy lot that could be a community garden. Once you've finished your project, you might want to share it with other people, in school or even local officials, who might help solve the problem. Shot a video? Why not enter it in the International Family Film Festival (IFFilmFest.org), or if you live in the Northwest, the Youth Film Festival of the Northwest at NWFilm.org.
- Build some bird houses out of recycled materials. Plastic bottles, milk cartons, wooden boxes—all can be converted into birdhouses. Check the Internet for instructions.
- Make a solar oven.
- Choose some art projects to do as a family. Download a list of endangered species and create your own hand-drawn calendar featuring one species each month. Or, take crayons and paper, go for a walk, and find a pretty place to sit and draw your natural surroundings and wildlife.
- Attend or volunteer at an Earth Day event. Find one at EarthDay.net, EPA.gov/EarthDay, or the Nature Conservancy.
- Help launch a community garden.
- Don't buy *anything* today.

Mother's Day

We're surely not the first people to think of this, but the Earth *really is* like a mother.

Of course, the obvious similarity is that without the Earth, we would not have life, but going deeper we find the Earth exhibiting many mom-like qualities. The Earth provides us with everything we need to grow into fine human beings and then leaves us to decide what we'll do with our lives. She presents us the resources to heal and to flourish and appreciates some loving care, at least once in a while. Like an understanding mom, the Earth patiently tolerates a certain amount of naughtiness from her 'children' who may take for granted all the work she does to maintain a safe and nurturing home. The Earth's children scurry about and clamor for possession of her precious resources like puppies for milk. But if we push our Earth-mother too far, when disregard and disrespect cross the line, the Earth reminds us of her power, and indeed seems to get a little, or even a lot, angry. After too much neglect, it is she who may need the healing.

Mother's Day is the perfect opportunity to thank moms for all that they do—to tell them that their often unappreciated, tireless efforts have not gone unnoticed (at least not on one day a year). But saying "thank you" to your mom doesn't have to be at the expense of Mother Earth. Mother's Day is the perfect opportunity to remember that simple gestures of love, respect, and appreciation are all that *any* mother could ever desire.

Cards

At least half of all moms in an iParenting.com survey ranked a card as the top item they wanted for Mother's Day. No wonder. A card may be nothing more than a folded sheet of paper, but when heartfelt sentiments echo words of admiration, gratitude, recognition, and love, the simple result is transformed into a meaningful gift that may be more cherished than any store-bought present ever could be.

Mother's Day cards may be handmade or purchased, but it is important to remember the history of materials used in any card you choose. Reusing paper such as previously used card fronts, photographs, magazine pages, and bits of colorful paper reduces environmental costs associated

MOTHER'S DAY SHOULD BE RENAMED GUILT BUYING DAY.
—RIDER THOMPSON, FOUNDER, SUSTAINABLE IS GOOD

with new card production and, as a bonus, saves money. Mint tins, small jewelry boxes, and other found objects can create one-of-a-kind cards that are gifts in and of themselves.

If you don't have the time or inclination to make a card from scratch, you can still give your mom the card she really wants (and go easy on the planet) by supporting companies that use tree-free sources to create cards. According to Tree-Free.com, replacing every greeting card sold in the United States with tree-free options would save:

- 650 million pounds of wood or 2.25 million trees that supply enough oxygen for 1.2 million people every year.
- 1 million BTUs of energy—enough to power an average household for 3.8 million days.

MAKE IT FOR MOM!

SWEET POTATO & CHIVE PANCAKES

Choose local and organic ingredients whenever possible

SERVES 4

These savory cakes not only use seasonal and healthy ingredients, but they will delight your taste buds and may become your next comfort food!.

INGREDIENTS

3/4 pound sweet potatoes
1 cup whole wheat flour
3 1/2 tsp baking powder
1 tsp salt
1/2 cup corn meal
1/4 cup chopped fresh chives
2 eggs, beaten
1 cup milk/soymilk/rice milk
1/4 cup butter, melted (You can also use olive oil)
1/4 cup your favorite local cheese, shredded

DIRECTIONS

Place sweet potatoes in a medium saucepan of boiling water and cook until tender but firm, about 15 minutes. Remove skins and chop into chunks. Place in blender or food processor and blend until smooth. *Add flour, baking powder, salt, corn meal, chives, and milk. Blend until you have a smooth batter. Add cheese and either gently stir batter or blend on very low. Lightly grease a pan with butter or olive oil and turn on medium-high heat. Drop batter mixture onto pan using a medium-sized ladle and cook until golden brown, turning once with a spatula when the surface begins to bubble.

* If you don't have a blender/food processor, you can also mash the sweet potatoes by hand and then add the other ingredients into the bowl and blend with a whisk or large fork.

Prep Time: 25 minutes
Makes 10 medium-sized pancakes

Contributed by Mary Purdy, certified nutritionist and registered dietitian. Seattle, WA, www. NourishingBalance.com

● 196 million pounds of greenhouse gas emissions, the equivalent of the exhaust from driving a compact car for 256 million miles.

● 916 million gallons of water, which would provide enough water to take 53 million eight-minute showers.

● 105 million pounds of solid waste, the equivalent of 3.6 million 32-gallon garbage cans of waste.

In some cases, tree-free options trump even 100% post-consumer waste recycled and sustainably harvested cards because, aside from the obvious benefit that they save trees, tree-free cards are free of chemicals (such as chlorine) and use less energy to produce. Sustainable tree-free greeting cards originate from sources including kenaf, sugar cane, bamboo, denim, garlic, hemp, mango, banana, rice, coffee, and believe it or not, animal dung! Of course, e-cards are always the most ecological. ThreeLeafCards.com has beautiful, video e-cards for Mother's Day and all year 'round.

Gifts

If there is such a thing as a national conscience, it comes into play every Mother's Day. Not give your mother a gift? That's downright un-American, not to mention more guilt-inducing than driving around in a Hummer while espousing green living.

As we've said in other sections of this book, the best strategy when it comes to buying any item is to think about whether or not it's necessary.

Advertisers have us convinced that mothers equate the amount of money spent on Mother's Day with the amount of love their children have for them. We flock like lemmings to purchase the latest and greatest when what most mothers really want, according to the iParenting.com survey, *is to be recognized*; whether with a card or gift seems to matter little.

Many moms feel misunderstood, overworked, and unappreciated. So the best gift for most moms is one that shows you understand, that lightens her load, and that demonstrates your appreciation for what she does.

Turning Mother's Day gifts green might start with a frank conversation with mom on the topic. And of course, we have lots of suggestions for items you can make instead of buy, experiences you can try together, or things you can do for her that will show your love in the profound way that a purchased gift simply can't match.

That said, according to eMarketer, small business owners in the United States believe Mother's Day brings in more revenue than other big holidays such as Valentine's Day, Easter, Father's Day, and Halloween. A 2008 poll conducted by BIGresearch and published by the National Retail Federation (NRF) reported that in 2007, 90.8% of the American population was expected to buy something for Mother's Day, spending an estimated $15.8 billion on gifts including spa, facials and massage ($1.1 billion), jewelry ($2.7 billion), flowers ($3 billion), or a Mother's Day outing ($2.9 billion). Overall, consumers were expected to spend an average of $138 for the holiday.

Any way you slice it, it seems, moms are being showered with stuff.

Although green consumerism is on the rise, it is unclear how many sons and daughters plan to use their $138 in an eco-savvy way. If what NRF President and CEO Tracy Mullin says is true, "For mom, it's the thought that counts," then wouldn't it stand to reason that thinking about you birth mother *and* your Earth mother would earn you bonus points?

So what's a green kid of any age to do? If you're ready and the time feels right, have that discussion about the meaning of Mother's Day gifts. If you want to make a gift or recycle something you already own into a truly heartfelt and spectacular gift, go for it. But if you're not ready to forsake buying just yet, at the very least take a look at all the earth-friendlier and ethically sourced items that are available. These, and more choices, are available simply by doing an online search.

Eco-Diva
Jewelry (see below for more information)
- Recycled record jewelry: LauraBeamer.com
- Fair trade jewelry made by artisans around the globe: WorldofGood.com
- 100% recycled cork cuff bracelet: VitaminDesignShop.com

I love to collect quotes and I think a lot of moms enjoy that as well. When I was in Europe years ago, I took a photo of a sign that said, "Please ask for a quote." At the time, I had no idea why I snapped that shot. But eventually, I decide to make a gift for a friend with quotes she loved and I found the picture, cut it up and glued it to the front of my book. The cover is fashioned from a piece of corrugated cardboard cut into an unusual shape just for the fun of it. The inside pages are paper lunch bags cut in half and turned on their sides. The journal's owner can put memorabilia inside the bags if she likes.

Shoes/Purses/Shopping Bags

- Handmade shoes: Mohop.com
- Shopping bags that fold into a small ball and can be sent back to the company when their life is over: ChicoBag.com
- Buy or make a purse from candy wrappers or other trash

Clothing

- Ahimsa Peace silk stole: FindGift.com (Ahimsa Peace Silk is made from the cocoons of wild and semi-wild silk moths of India. Unlike with conventional silk, in production, the pupae are not stifled or killed.)
- Natural raffia hat: HelenKaminski.com
- Organic cotton clothing: UnderTheCanopy.com

dECOr-Savvy Mom

- Bamboo vases, boxes, bowls and other decorative items
- Fair trade telephone wire baskets from Africa: BridgeForAfrica.org
- Fair trade Nicaraguan mother and child vase: MoonDropClothiers.com

Gourmet Cook Mom (or Food and Wine Connoisseur)

- Chocolate of the month club—Endangered Species: ChocolateBar.com
- Eco friendly dinnerware and teapots: TerraKeramik.com
- Solar cookbook (and oven you or the kids can make)

Deserves Some Pampering Mom

- Clean the house with an eco-maid service
- Lotions, soaps, shampoos from SaveYourWorld.com (sale of one product=purchase of one acre of rainforest), or Lulu Life Virgin Sudanese skin care products made by rural women in Sudan from Swahili-Imports.com
- Organic cotton, bamboo, or hemp robe

Media Mom

- For the magazine-lover — a subscription to *Organic Spa* (printed with earth-friendly dyes and eco-conscious paper manufacturing) or *Natural Home* (printed on paper that is made with 100% de-inked, post-consumer fiber and is processed chlorine free)
- Subscription to the Sundance Channel. On Tuesday evenings, they air special programming called "The Green." They report on sustainable businesses, recycling, green fashion, and organic farming, among other things. All this is followed by a film related to the environment.
- How can you not get her an MP3 player and point her in the direction of green podcasts?

Gardener Mom

- Hemp garden gloves: Gaiam.com
- EcoForms pots (for plants) made from renewable grain husks, inside or out, durable and lightweight: TheGreenGardenStore.com
- *Weed 'Em and Reap: A Weed Eater Reader,* by Roger Welsch.

Crafty/Artistic Mom

- Hand-dyed yarn
- Hemp sketch book or journal, watercolor, sketch, or drawing paper: EcoArtWorks.com
- Stockmar "natural" watercolor paints: AToyGarden.com

Works Outside the Home, or Mompreneur

- 100% recycled material Laptop Green Sleeve: Act2GreenSmart.com
- A local Ladies Who Launch seminar or "incubator": LadiesWhoLaunch.com
- Motherboard business card case: Eco-Artware.com

Mom on the Go

- Dissolving paper shampoo or soap: X-TremeGeek.com
- Hemp waist pack: Hempmania.com
- Eco-travel guide book, or *Code Green* (lists 100 eco-wise travel ideas) from Lonely Planet books

Gifts for Every Mom

- Tickets to an upcoming flower show, art show or classes, or a computer trade show, for that matter. Pick her favorite activity and there's bound to be an event she'd love to attend.
- Honor Mother Earth and your mom by planting a tree or rose bush. Make a sign that designates when it was planted and for whom.
- For moms who are far away, organic gift baskets: EcoExpress.com

Meaningful Mother's Day Activities

(None of these ideas costs any money.)

- Ask your mom to discuss her growing up years. Moms rarely have time, and who asks them to talk about themselves? You'll gain as much as she does from listening to (and maybe making a video) of her funny or heartfelt memories.
- Call a mom who isn't your own, but who has played an important role in your life. This might be a relative or a friend. Let her know how much she means to you. You also could e-mail a celebrity mom who has inspired you in some way.

- Make your mom "Queen for the Day." Present her with a crown at breakfast and do whatever she wishes throughout the day.
- Make up words about your mom to a familiar melody and sing it in front of other family members and friends. Get everyone to join in on the chorus.
- Create a tradition you will carry out every year on Mother's Day. For instance, make a simple candle holder and light a candle while listing all the things you appreciate about your mom.
- Look through family scrapbooks together.

More on Gifts of Jewelry

My Grandmother had five granddaughters and a husband with foresight. Over the course of several years, in the last decade or so of their lives, my granddad gave my grandmother five rings to someday leave for the girls; a gift from him to her and from them to us. Prior to my grandma's death, she called each granddaughter to her home and asked which ring she would like to have.

The rings were yellow gold bands topped with a variety of gemstones or small diamonds. Some were solitaires, while others held clusters of stones shaped like a flower or heart. They were all lovely, but my eyes were drawn to two rings placed to the side of the box. These rings were not large or shiny. My grandma noticed my gaze. "Those are just some old rings. You really wouldn't want them, would you? These over here are worth much more."

I asked my grandma where the simple ones came from.

"Oh, this one is the engagement ring your granddad gave to me before he could afford much more…. Don't you want this one over here with a bigger stone?"

"And what about this one?" I asked.

"This one belonged to my aunt, your great-great aunt. But it is so old the band is paper thin. How about this one, instead? See how much more substantial it is?"

My grandma didn't seem to understand why I'd choose a plain, worn out ring over something newer and more impressive, but she was so "tickled" that I was interested in their histories that she gave me both rings and called it a day.

By buying gifts from or making a contribution in your mom's name to one or more of these organizations, you can help women around the world and in your own neighborhood as well as give your mother something she'll love:

1. WomenForWomen.org
2. GrandmotherProject.org
3. ChangingThePresent.org/women/gifts
4. Shop.TheBreastCancerSite.com
5. MadeBySurvivors.com
6. GlobalFundForWomen.org

ROCK OUT—JUST GO FOR ETHICALLY SOURCED ECO-BLING.
—IDEALBITE.COM

Jewelry can be a beautiful gift, but it's important to remember that each piece and each component within the piece has its own history.

If you're planning on giving your wife, mom, or grandma jewelry this Mother's Day, you're not alone. The National Retail Federation says that about 32% of Americans buy jewelry gifts on Mother's day, spending over two billion dollars during the month of May. Because jewelry is such a popular component of the Mother's Day tradition, we'd love to point you to eco-perfect options. But while researching jewelry for this book, we came to only one diamond-clear conclusion: jewelry is a murky subject. Here's the scoop on the two most popular Mother's Day jewelry items: diamonds and gold.

"DIAMONDS ARE FOREVER" IT IS OFTEN SAID. BUT LIVES ARE NOT. WE MUST SPARE PEOPLE THE ORDEAL OF WAR, MUTILATIONS AND DEATH FOR THE SAKE OF CONFLICT DIAMONDS.
—MARTIN CHUNGONG AYAFOR, CHAIRMAN OF THE SIERRA LEONE PANEL OF EXPERTS

Diamonds

 While working out with a Pilates DVD one day, I was on my tummy following the "strap pulls" move when the instructor said to rest my forehead on the backs of my hands, shaped together into a diamond. "Everyone *loves* diamonds," she gushed, intimating that simply thinking about the gem might somehow make me feel wealthy and chic while sweating through the next set of butt-firming exercises.

It's certainly true that a lot of people love diamonds. And it's also true that a lot of people love to *give* diamonds (or jewelry with diamonds in it) to the women they love, especially on Mother's Day. And why wouldn't they? Since at least 500 BC people have prized these jewels for their beauty, durability and usefulness. Whether jewelry features diamonds or is accented by them, the stones are considered the crème de la crème of jewels and have been equated throughout history and in many societies with love, strength, and longevity. What more could you want for your mom? But unless you've been living under a diamond-encrusted rock for the last few years, you'll know that diamonds may not be the best choice for conscientious consumers.

Of the millions of carats of diamonds mined each year, a small percentage are considered conflict diamonds (also known as blood diamonds, dirty diamonds, and war diamonds). Conflict diamonds originate from war-torn countries and are used to fund violent crime, war, and terrorism. The mining, trade, and sale of these diamonds are also likely to include the exploitation of people (including children) as well as environmental degradation. Although efforts have been made to ban the trade and sale of conflict diamonds (such as through the Kimberly Certification Process), they still make their way onto the market, albeit in comparatively small numbers, and are estimated to account for a minimum of $23 million dollars worth of sales each year.

Even with a certificate claiming that a diamond is conflict-free, the reality is that it might not be. According to Amnesty International's website (AmnestyUSA.org), "Despite its pledge to support the Kimberley Process and Clean Diamond Trade Act, the Diamond Industry [sic] has fallen short of implementing the necessary policies for self-regulation. The retail sector in particular fails to provide sufficient assurance to consumers that the diamonds they sell are conflict-free."

Add this to the facts that an estimated 20% of the world diamonds are "controversial diamonds" (not originating from war zones but still may be smuggled or mined by abusive labor practices) and that each and every carat requires about 250 tons of earth-moving.

So what's an aware and caring son, daughter, or husband to do? Be part of the solution by ensuring that stones you buy for Mother's Day and other holidays are conflict-free. The Conflict-Free Diamond Council (ConflictFreeDiamonds.org) was established in 2004 to end "the trade of conflict diamonds by creating consumer demand for Certified Conflict-Free Diamonds." The website features in-depth information on conflict diamonds and where to buy conflict-free ones. Amnesty International and Global Witness also have published *The Diamond Buyer's Guide*, which suggests asking the following questions of the jeweler no matter where you buy your diamond:

- How can I be sure that none of your jewelry contains conflict diamonds?
- Do you know where the diamonds you sell come from?
- Can I see a copy of your company's policy on conflict diamonds?
- Can you show me a written guarantee from your diamond suppliers stating that your diamonds are conflict-free?

Here are some alternatives to conventionally mined diamonds:
- High glimmer, low guilt cultivated diamonds. High quality cultivated or created diamonds are virtually indistinguishable from mined diamonds, and yet avoid the environmental and human toll associated with some conventionally mined diamonds while being

less expensive and, according to some accounts, more durable. Instead of waiting billions of years for the Earth to combine unimaginable pressure with 2000° to 3000°F temperatures, cultivated diamond experts use artificial methods to imitate the Earth's process to create a human-friendly, low-impact, sustainable "women's best friend." ApolloDiamond.com, Gemesis.com, and Chatham.com make high quality, created diamonds and gemstones employing various innovative techniques. "Combining modern technology and engineering with old-world artisan skill," Charles & Colvard's lab-cultured Moissanite diamonds (made through a patented process) cost less, and according to the company, have more fire, brilliance, and luster than their mined counterparts.

⦿ It is true that diamonds are durable and timeless, giving truth to the phrase, "a diamond is forever." So instead of buying new, look for used. Pre-owned, vintage, or antique diamonds can look as brilliant as the day they were first cut, and their age adds charm and history, especially if the diamond belonged to someone in the family. According to Michelle Kozin, the author of *Organic Wedding*, diamonds from before the 1880's predate conflict-era stones as well as industrialized mining techniques and are therefore more people and earth-friendly choices.

⦿ Go on a diamond hunt. The Crater of Diamonds State Park in Arkansas is the world's only diamond mine that allows the public to dig for their own gems. To date, 70,000 diamonds have been unearthed. Although you'll pay a fee to dig, any diamonds, semi-precious stones, or minerals you find are yours to keep. (In 1924 a 40.23 carat diamond, the "Uncle Sam," was discovered there!)

> GOLD MINING IS ONE OF THE DIRTIEST INDUSTRIES IN THE WORLD. IT CONTAMINATES DRINKING WATER, DESTROYS TRADITIONAL LIVELIHOODS, AND DISPLACES INDIGENOUS COMMUNITIES.—OXFAM AND EARTHWORKS' NODIRTYGOLD.COM

Gold

We're sorry (really, truly) to be the ones to break it to you, but gold is controversial too. Although Mother's Day is the second biggest gold-giving holiday after Christmas, "good as gold" may no longer be an accurate descriptive term. The problem, once again, is the human, social, and environmental impact of mining gold, 80% of which goes into making jewelry. And it isn't just the fact that making a single gold ring can generate tons of toxic waste while using high amounts of energy and water. Experts say that conventional gold mining practices exploit and endanger

1 Seeking used, vintage, and antique jewelry is an ideal eco-option.

2 Mined metals and stones are not the only materials suitable for jewelry. TouchWoodRings.com makes and sells exquisite custom rings from an array of beautiful and durable woods that are mostly found or discarded. Knowing that precious metals and stones may come with a higher price than just the financial one, rings such as these are a great eco-option that don't require aesthetic sacrifice.

3 No gold on hand? How about making Mother's Day jewelry gifts from easy-to-find, reused, natural, or low-impact materials? All you need is something to punch a hole in the object and a bit of wire or some jump rings (found at any craft store). Have fun searching for everyday objects that might be meaningful or just plain fun when turned into a charm for your mom to wear on a chain or ribbon. Lynn made the necklace charms on page 45 and 50 with the found objects including hardware, a slide mount and a "diamond" from a child's pretend crown.

4 No matter what material jewelry is made from, before buying it, ask to make sure that all of the components are sustainably and ethically sourced.

humans (human rights violations, health and safety risks, risks to women and families) and have devastating effects on the environment (air, water, land, and other resources) and surrounding communities (economic, public health, and cultural tolls). The No Dirty Gold Campaign, sponsored by Oxfam and Earthworks, seeks to make gold shine again by asking jewelry retailers to accept and implement the campaign's Golden Rules criteria of social and environmental responsibility. Jewelry retailers such as Tiffany's and Co., Ben Bridge, and even Wal-Mart have joined No Dirty Gold, making reduced-guilt gold choices in a spectrum of prices available to American consumers.

Along with the No Dirty Gold project, Greg Valerio, a jeweler and poverty/human rights activist, is leading the fight against dirty gold. Valerio hopes to drastically increase the worldwide sale of ethically sourced gold, which, according to a 2008 Reuters story, is now less than one percent of the $56 billion gold jewelry business. His company, one of the world's first retailers of ethically sourced gold and platinum jewelry, is working with the United Kingdom's Fairtrade Foundation to include gold as a product that can be Fair Trade Certified. While certification has not yet been attained (as of this printing), Valerio is hopeful that gold will soon have the same inclusion and oversight that is available to certified Fair Trade products such as tea, coffee, and chocolate. He sources "green gold" or "oro verde" from a mining cooperative in South America, which, according to Valerio's Cred Foundation, seeks "to protect people and the planet, and to develop products for Ethical/Fair Trade markets to provide a fair deal for local workers." More information about green gold can be found at GreenGold-OroVerde.org (click on "English") and on Valerio's website CredJewelry.com.

GreenKarat.com is another great source for information on this issue. They advocate and sell recycled/post-consumer gold (as well as cultured diamonds): "ethically responsible jewelry." According to GreenKarat, there is enough gold "above ground" (i.e., in bank vaults) to supply demand for the next 50 years, and yet 2,500 tons of gold is mined each year. GreenKarat also offers a cool program called Green Assay, whereby customers can track the ecological footprint of each component of jewelry purchased from their company. In addition, they've created the myKarat program which "allows customers to send in unused and broken jewelry for store credit, or to be reused (it can be so meaningful to use grandma's gold in a keepsake piece), or donate the value of the jewelry to an environmental organization of their choice." Matt White, president of GreenKarat, says that the myKarat program "provides several ways an individual can make a difference."

Other online and brick-and mortar jewelers use recycled gold too, so be sure to ask for it. Buying recycled gold might seem like a small step, but in the words of GreenKarat, "Long-term progress is realized when consumers internalize new values and infuse them into custom… Buying recycled gold is one of the most ecologically and socially responsible choices a consumer can make."

You can also make use of recycled gold by custom-creating your Mother's Day gift. How about surprising your wife or mom with a "new" and unique piece of recycled gold jewelry custom-made for her by working with a local jewelry artisan? Underused or consignment-shop gold can be melted by a smith and remade into something eco-fabulous that any woman would cherish.

Most precious metals and precious and semi-precious stones have been mined and therefore negatively impact the environment in some way. In fact, Larry Innes, director of the Canadian Boreal Initiative, wrote, "The fact is that today, no one can sell a diamond, gold, or any gem and say it was mined responsibly." So no matter where the jewelry comes from, you'll want to be cautious of companies that label their products as green or ethically sourced without clarifying for you where the materials came from and how they got there. Get to know your jeweler before buying gifts for Mother's Day and other special occasions. Ask questions, and as Green Assay's site says, "evaluate your purchase through the lens of your own values." The extra time and effort put into finding a reliable source will be an additional gift to your mom. In her heart of hearts, would any mom want to wear jewelry knowing that its beauty was a result of suffering or conflict?

Additional resources for beautiful and eco-considerate jewelry:
- TobyPomeroy.com (using 100% reclaimed gold and silver)
- VerdeRocks.com (vintage and ethically sourced materials)
- KirstenMuenster.com (ethically sourced, found, and recycled)

For more information on the environmental issues related to jewelry, check out:
- GemEcology.org
- MiningWatch.ca
- MadisonDialogue.org
- CommunityMining.org
- EthicalMetalSmiths.org

Arbor Day:

The Holiday that was Born Green

On a spring day in 1998, I stopped by a nursery to pick up some seeds. Before I could get through the gate, a woman stopped me to cheerily announce, "It's Arbor Day. I'm giving away free trees. Would you like one?" She'd uttered two magic words in one sentence—free and tree. Of course I wanted one!

She showed me the choices, explaining the pros and cons of each. I settled on a tamarack because while it looks like what we know-just-enough-to-be-dangerous gardeners think of as an evergreen, its needles turn a glorious gold in fall before they drop. She handed me a 10-inch stick, slender as a pencil lead, a few scraggly roots peeking through the plastic bag.

To be honest, I was not optimistic. What a pathetic excuse for a tree! Trees are supposed to block the sky, not lie in your hand like an uncooked strand of whole wheat spaghetti. A 300-foot tall sequoia or a 3,000-year-old baobab. Now *those* are trees! It seemed unlikely that in my lifetime, what now easily slipped into my purse would ever surpass our puppy in height.

But evidently, even in this negative frame of mind, I held a grain of hope that the stick might grow because when I returned home, I sought out the perfect spot for it. I wanted to be able to see it from the kitchen window as it would, hypothetically, lend a much needed bright fall highlight to our pine-packed landscape. After soaking the twig, I dug a hole and plopped it in. I vowed to keep my eye on it and would, as it turned out, constantly caution my husband not to hack the poor thing to pieces with the weed whacker.

"Don't forget to watch out for the tree," I'd mention to him as he walked out the door ready to spend eight minutes trimming our postage stamp lawn.

"Where is it again?" he'd ask.

"Right there," I'd answer, pointing.

"Where?" he'd ask, scrunching up his eyes.

I'd throw on a jacket and walk purposefully in the direction of the literal stick-in-the-mud. But week after week, to my embarrassment, I'd amble in circles, trying to spy the tree among dozens of similar branches that had fallen and stuck in the ground. It usually only took a few minutes. But still.

Anyway, the following spring, once the snow melted, much to my shock, I realized the stick had sprung a bunch of branches and seemed to have shot up at least a foot like some hormone-heavy teenager. It actually looked like a real tree!

Within another year or two, it stretched taller than I, which, while not obscuring the sky, still gave me a feeling of immense relief and, I'll admit it, joy.

By the time we sold the house in 2005, the tree topped our roof line.

The moral of the story is this: If you happen to be at a nursery on Arbor Day (officially the last Friday in April, but celebrated on different dates in different states according to their best tree planting times—look online at ArborDay.org for your state date), and someone attempts to thrust a pitiable twig into your hand, take it.

Bring it home, and plant it according to directions. Keep away deer and weed whacking maniacs. Water if needed.

Wait a year or two and witness a miracle.

For only $10, you can join the Arbor Day Foundation at ArborDay.org and receive *ten free* trees selected from those that will flourish in your location. They will arrive looking just like mine did, but follow the directions and not only will you enjoy them as they grow, but of course, you'll be doing something great for the environment.

An enjoyable Arbor Day activity is to borrow a plant identification book from the library, then go on a walk with your family and try to identify as many trees, flowers, or other gifts of nature as you can. Keep an ongoing list, maybe in a small notebook. Whenever you travel as a family, plan a hunt and add to the book.

Cinco de Mayo (Verde)

Like most places in the world, Mexico faces a host of environmental issues. What better way to celebrate Cinco de Mayo than to learn about some of these challenges, and even better, if you can afford to do so, contribute either financially or through volunteer opportunities.

Some examples:

PulmoAmigos.org

Amigos para la Conservación de Cabo Pulmo, A.C. (Friends for the Conservation of Cabo Pulmo—ACCP) is a community organization founded in 2002 by fishermen, dive guides, residents, and housewives in the local community to promote conservation of the natural resources of the Cabo Pulmo National Park. The park, located on the east cape of Baja California, includes the only hard coral reef in the Sea of Cortez and is one of just three living reefs in North America. Unfortunately, the reef is threatened by decolorization, unregulated fishing, snorkeling, and scuba diving, and increased sediment discharges as a result of tourist developments and unrestricted vehicular traffic along the beaches, which also threatens sea turtles.

TheRainForestSite.com

Click on the icon and a contribution will be sent on your behalf at no charge to you.

EcoLifeFoundation.typepad.com/monarchs

The forests of Mexico are home to monarch butterflies which travel thousands of miles each year to overwinter there. In recent decades, however, the forests have begun to disappear at the hands of those seeking wood. You can help by funding the planting of tree seedlings in the butterflies' overwintering area in Michoacán, Mexico, through the work of The Michoacán Reforestation Fund, winner of the 2002 Smithsonian Magazine/USTOA Conservation Award.

EcologyFund.com

Mexico is one of the most bio-diverse countries on earth. The Ecology Fund is working with Mexican organizations to safeguard some of the country's most endangered species by protecting what is left of their habitat.

VEGETABLE ENCHILADAS, GUATEMALAN STYLE

Choose local and organic ingredients whenever possible

SERVES ABOUT 4

INGREDIENTS:

8 corn tortillas
peanut oil or other oil for sautéing
3 tbsp grated grana padano or other nice parmesan

FILLING:

1 cup prepared mashed potatoes
1/2 to 3/4 cup shredded jalapeño jack cheese or sub
   Monterrey jack style soy cheese
3/4 cup frozen corn kernels
1/2 green pepper, diced
2 banana peppers (mildly spicy), diced
small stick/or half stick celery, diced
1 cup carrots, shredded
1/4 cup onion, diced
1/2 to 3/4 tsp dried oregano
salt (1/2 tsp)
fresh ground pepper (a few turns)

FOR THE SAUCE:

large can pureed tomatoes
1/2 onion, chopped
2 cloves garlic smashed, whole
1 tsp salt
1 1/2 tsp cumin powder
1/2 tsp chili powder
dash cayenne powder
1 whole dried chipotle pepper, poke to release flavor
1 cup water

DIRECTIONS:

Preheat oven to 375 degrees

Combine all ingredients for the sauce in a med sauce pan, except the water. Simmer while you prepare the rest of the dish, stirring frequently.

In a very hot, dry (cast iron) skillet, roast the corn kernels until slightly blackened to give a smoky flavor. Remove to a bowl. Add the onion, celery, and peppers. Sautee until browned. Remove to a bowl. Rinse the pan with a small amount of water and add to the sauce. The browned bits will add flavor to the sauce. Combine mashed potatoes, roasted vegetables, cheese, and raw carrots together. Season with oregano, salt, and pepper. Set aside.

Puree the sauce in a blender, adding the water. Depending on how spicy you want the sauce, you may remove the chipotle prior to pureeing. Taste the sauce and season with salt if needed.

Heat about 1-2 tbsp oil in the cast iron skillet. Dip each tortilla in the hot oil to soften; stack on a plate. Roll the filling inside the tortillas, approximately 2 - 3 tbsp in each to distribute evenly. Put a small amount of sauce in the bottom of a small baking dish, then line with the filled, rolled tortillas. Cover with the rest of the sauce and cover with tin foil. Bake in a 375-degree oven for 35 minutes.

Remove foil and top casserole with grated Parmesan cheese just before removing from oven. Serve with sliced avocado, shredded lettuce, and red cabbage. Sour cream or yogurt optional (good for quenching the heat).—

Contributed by Wenonah Michallet-Ferrier

Most piñatas you purchase are made from papier maché. Layers of newspapers are laid over a shape or frame, then glued down with eco-friendly flour paste one piece at a time. This type of piñata can be a lot of fun for a group to construct, but frustrating for small children.

Our easy-to-make version wouldn't cut it for older children, but the little ones can get in on the action by both making the piñata and breaking it.

1. Decorate the outside of a paper grocery bag with non-toxic paints, found decorations, and recycled paper. Staple some pieces of yarn or strips of paper hanging off the bottom of the bag.

2. Fill the bag with a combination of balled-up newspaper or magazine pages and healthy or non-food treats. Check out the Halloween section of this book for ideas.

3. Lay a long piece of string about one inch in from the top edge of the bag.

4. Fold the top of the bag over the string and staple the bag closed.

5. Using the string, hang the piñata from a tree branch or clothes line and let the kids take turns trying to hit it. With young children, you don't need to cover their eyes, but moving the piñata up and down as they attempt to whack it adds to the laughter. Of course, keep everyone back and away from the child who is swinging the bat.

OrganicConsumers.org/Chiapas

The OCA seeks to demonstrate that indigenous cooperatives and community groups can obtain Fair Trade and organic certification for their coffee, cacao, and other crops so as to guarantee a living wage to producers. They are working in Chiapas, Mexico, where human health as well as biodiversity is being threatened by genetically engineered corn. You can join OCA at no cost and support their efforts to promote a safe, healthy, sustainable, and socially responsible global food system.

Quartos.org

Three month internships for ages 21-35 working with children educating them about the environment. Must be fluent in Spanish, flexible, and enjoy working in other cultures.

If you'd like to support a more earth-friendly Mexico by purchasing Fair Trade, sustainable, or organic products, here are a few suggestions:

- Hand-woven organic Mexican fabrics
- Oaxaca Loom Exports, environmentally responsible custom designed fabrics and textiles made from organic green cotton and ecological naturally colored cotton from OaxacanStuff.com
- Mexican folk art Fair Trade Nativity, from TenThousandVillages.com
- Recycled glass margarita glasses from MagellanTraders.com

A few interesting eco-issues in Mexico:

- Land area under organic management and total value of organic production in Mexico is expanding at a rate of 45% a year—twice the rate of expansion in the United States. Coffee is by far the country's most important organic crop. Herbs, mangoes, oranges, field beans, apples, papaya, avocado, soy, bananas, cacao, African palm, vanilla, and pineapple make up the rest of the organic roster. The United States, Germany, Holland, Japan, England, and Switzerland are the biggest buyers of Mexico's organic produce.
- Mexico was the first country in Latin America to open a plant to recycle old plastic bottles into new ones. When the plant was opened in 1995, it was the biggest of its kind in the

world, which is a good thing since Mexican citizens consume more sugary drinks than any other nation on Earth and has one of the lowest recycling rates in the world.

- Mexico recycles only about six percent of its solid waste, compared to 10% in Colombia and approximately 15% in Peru. Fewer than 20% of residents of Mexico City separate recyclables from trash, yet the city's only landfill is on the brink of closure. Political wrangling and lack of awareness are cited as reasons why more is not being done, although some progress is being made.

- Sugar production from cane can use large quantities of water. At the San Francisco Ameca plant in the State of Jalisco, Mexico, after action was taken to recycle water and minimize waste, water consumption was reduced 93% and pollution entering the water was cut by 20%. This is significant because during the annual harvest season, the plant processes 4,800 tons of sugarcane.

Green Grub for St. Patrick's Day

 Even though I never set foot in Ireland, I grew up believing a few immutable truths about St. Patrick's Day. I know I'm not alone when I say I associated the day with the following:

1. Wearing of the green
2. Corned beef and cabbage
3. The four-leaf clover, also known as a shamrock

Well, there I was innocently researching organic corned beef so I could write something for this section when I ran across Frances Shilliday's website. He shot down my preconceived notions one by one:

1. If you want to associate any color with St. Patrick, blue, the color of the original Irish flag, would be the more natural choice.
2. Corned beef was not eaten in Ireland except by a royalty now and then. When Irish immigrants landed on New York's lower East Side, they looked for a cheaper alternative to bacon and most likely learned about corned beef from their Jewish neighbors (according to the History Channel).

I JUST WANT TO PUT SOMETHING STRAIGHT ABOUT WHAT SHOULD BE ON YOUR PLATE,

IF IT'S CORNED BEEF YOU'RE MAKIN'

YOU'RE SADLY MISTAKEN, THAT ISN'T WHAT IRISHMEN ATE.

FRANCES SHILLIDAY, 2004

IT'S EASY BEING GREEN ON ST. PAT'S DAY

1. Wear an organic T-shirt with a green greeting.
2. Heft an organic beer.
3. Plant something green.

3. The authentic Irish shamrock has three leaves, not four. And even then, the plant that pops up labeled as shamrock in U.S. flower shops and groceries every March is not the one St. Patrick was reported to have used to illustrate the doctrine of the Holy Trinity. That probably was wood Sorrel, a plant best propagated by root cuttings and therefore less likely to be exploited as a holiday symbol than its prolifically seeding cousin, the "three leafed clover" of I-hate-weeds-in-my-lawn fame.

While these discoveries might have been devastating, seeing as they completely destroyed my childhood fantasies, I actually felt quite grateful to Mr. Shilliday since I couldn't seem to find any sources for either organic corned beef or organic shamrock cuttings.

That being said, I suggest we "green up" our St. Paddy's Day celebration for the sake of the planet, if not as a tribute to St. Patrick. We can start by thinking about what we eat.

While we may be wrong in thinking of corned beef as an Irish basic, we wouldn't be far off by starting our St. Patrick's Day with a true staple of the Emerald Isle, a heaping bowl of oatmeal (make mine organic) awash in water, organic milk, or buttermilk.

And although we have been disabused of the notion that green is the color of the day, we're not ready to give up on that one. So just for the fun of it, why not think about how to get a bit 'o green into every single dish on March 17th? Because if you leave out the corned beef (which is about 30% fat anyway) and concentrate on green, St. Patrick's Day could be one of the easiest and healthiest holidays we have.

To green up what you eat in a fun way, do not add artificial food coloring to potatoes (which we used to do when I was a kid). Little did we know then that traditional food coloring may contain heavy metals, such as lead and mercury, as well as myriad chemicals, according to the FDA. Instead, here's a concept: use real food to add color.

Whether it's slicing an avocado in scrambled eggs, mixing a 100% green salad (kale, arugula, pea pods, and beans, for example), turning potatoes screaming green with pureed cooked spinach or a more muted sage using organic green salsa, chopped cilantro, or other herbs, or making lime sorbet topped with crushed pistachios, let your imagination and taste buds run wild.

Passover

The Sustainable Seder Plate

Passover (Pesach) is the Jewish tradition's "eat seasonal" poster child. It is a time to notice and celebrate the coming of spring. The special plate that holds items for the Seder (Passover's traditional meal) abounds with seasonal symbols: the roasted lamb bone celebrates lambs born in spring; karpas symbolizes the first green sprouts peaking out of the thawed ground; and a roasted egg recalls fertility and rebirth.

Passover offers a perfect opportunity to combine the wisdom of a traditional Jewish holiday with our contemporary desire to live healthily and sustainably in our world. Even if you don't normally think about sustainability, we encourage you to try it out this Pesach.

And if you're not Jewish? Not to worry, these ideas can be applied to all celebrations.

Every Charoset tells a story. Charoset's mixture of apples and nuts is already healthy and delicious and, when made with local (organic where possible) apples, sustainable. Charoset also offers you the chance to explore other cultures within the Jewish Diaspora. Google the word "Charoset" to find recipes from Russia, Spain, Holland, Yemen, Turkey, Surinam… or ask your guests to bring their own favorite charoset recipe and have a taste-test.

Fairly traded pecans. EqualExchange.com offers a line of fairly-traded pecans grown by an agricultural co-operative in Southwest Georgia. What better way to infuse your Charoset with the taste of justice? They also make a great pre-dinner nibble for hungry Seder guests.

Sprout your own Karpas (greens). If you can't find locally grown greens to dip for karpas, sprout your own! Although many sprouts come from corn, soybeans, and other "chametz" (foods that are traditionally not consumed during Passover), in just two to three days you can have fresh, delicious quinoa sprouts that you "grew" yourself from SproutPeople.com.

Horseradish doesn't grow in a bottle. Buy and grate fresh horseradish root for your Seder plate. When it comes time for the Hillel sandwich, hold up an ungrated root so your guests know where that bitter stuff comes from. Make sure to have some of the beet-dyed, jarred horseradish on hand, just in case your Aunt Bess looks forward to it every year.

Free-range betza (egg). Buy organic, free-range eggs, and be willing to pay slightly more for them. They taste better, come from more humanely treated chickens, and support farmers who are making it possible for you to eat good food.

Roast a beet. If you're going vegetarian for your seder (see below), substitute a roasted beet for the roasted lamb shank.

Adapted from *The Jew & The Carrot*: Hazon's blog on Jews, food, and contemporary life (JCarrot.org).

Summer

We're going to preface this section by saying that *we know* the summer equinox is not until after Father's Day and well after Memorial Day. But the fact is that more than any other season, summer is a state of mind. Regardless of the month in which Memorial Day actually takes place, by the end of May or beginning of June (depending on where you live), the first vaguely warm day has everyone out in short sleeves looking much happier than they had been the day before. Time to haul out barbecues, bathing suits, and sunscreen, and with them comes the almost genetically predetermined propensity to want to celebrate.

Whether it's because the sun is out, school is out, or you'd rather be out, by the time Father's Day rolls around, celebrations and gatherings are morphing into laid back affairs focusing on friends, family, and the great outdoors. What could be more perfect for the eco-friendly?

Following are our tips for ways to celebrate green during the summer-is-a-state-of-mind holidays such as Memorial Day, Father's Day, and the 4th of July, starting with the quintessential summer celebration, the barbecue.

Green Grillin'

Traditionally, Memorial Day launches the beginning of barbecue season, with July 4th and Labor Day rounding out the top three grilling holidays of the year. Grilling is a national pastime, enjoyed by about 60 million Americans on each of the aforementioned holidays alone. Since grilling often is the central feature of summer get-togethers, as the kitchen is for indoor parties the rest of the year, it may come as no surprise that three out of four homes in the United States own at least one barbecue grill.

But as fun as a backyard barbecuing might be, grilling has its drawbacks for people and for the Earth. So before you fire up, consider the type of grill, the materials to be burned, the type of food to be cooked and what you'll use to clean your grill when the party's over.

The Grill

Nationwide, the estimated 60 million barbecues held on the Fourth of July alone consume enough energy—in the form of charcoal, lighter fluid, gas, and electricity—to power 20,000 households for a year. That one day of fun, food, and celebration, says Tristram West, a research scientist with the U.S. Department of Energy, burns the equivalent of 2,300 acres of forest and releases 225,000 metric tons of carbon dioxide. —SierraClub.org

With so many grills to choose from and with the potential for human and planetary impact so great, the first question when it comes to grilling is, which category of grill should you choose? Each type—wood, coal, propane or electric—comes with its own environmental price tag. Solar grills, clearly the most eco-savvy choice, have yet to generate the kind of enthusiasm that will make a difference.

Wood and Charcoal Grills

Wood and charcoal burning grills are the second most common types. People who use them say they enjoy the flavor this kind of grilling provides. But good taste comes at a price. Burning wood and charcoal contributes to unhealthy air quality and smog, which has both short- and long-term health and environmental impacts.

Using wood as a heat source can lead to deforestation. If you have a wood burning grill, choose slower-burning and faster-growing hardwood species like mesquite and hickory.

In America, charcoal follows wood as the most common heat source for grills but is even harsher on the planet than wood. Charcoal releases more greenhouse gasses, carbon monoxide, soot, and particulate matter than wood, creates more ground-level ozone (especially when coupled with lighter fluid), and can lead to increased deforestation. Traditional briquettes (made from a number of natural and synthetic products meant to improve binding and combustibility) contain substances such as borax, coal dust, and sodium nitrate so lump charcoal (which contains no additives or binders) is a healthier option.

Avoid using lighter fluids as they release VOC's (volatile organic compounds) and may contaminate food with petrochemical residue. Try a chimney starter (purchased or made) for a more eco-wise option.

Gas Grills

Sixty-one percent of American grills use propane. Both natural gas and propane are cleaner burning and more energy efficient than wood or coal grills. Still, keep in mind that gas is a non-renewable resource and using it comes at a cost to the environment.

Electric Grills

Only seven percent of Americans utilize electricity as a heating source for their grills. Electric grills emit 99% less carbon monoxide and 91% less carbon dioxide than charcoal grills and 21% less carbon dioxide than propane grills. While electric grills certainly have a leg up over other grill types, the electricity they consume still leads to emissions.

Hybrid Grills

Hybrid grills offer the ability to use gas and or charcoal or wood for flavor and have the same pros and cons as grills in both of these categories.

#1 Green Grilling Source: The Sun

 I grew up in Tucson, Arizona, where summertime temperatures often topped a suffocating 105 degrees. One cool summertime trick every young Tucsonan learns is how to cook an egg on the sidewalk. But you don't need heat to use a solar grill, only sunlight.

According to one online retailer of solar grills, burning the briquettes produced annually by just one manufacturer causes 13 billion pounds of pollution. It will come as no surprise then that solar energy wins our bid for the cleanest and most economical type of grill available.

Solar grills take more time to cook food, don't work without direct sun, and don't come with all the accessories and accouterments of high end grills, but they can be used for everything from meat to veggies without the added financial and environmental costs of electricity or heating sources such as wood, charcoal, or gas. And because solar grills do not smoke or burn food, your meal is healthier too. They also tend to be lightweight and portable, which means you only need one for all of your summertime celebration needs, and because the grill utilizes the sun rather than fire, a solar grill can be used anywhere open fire is banned, such as on balconies or in dry woods. Simple solar stoves can be made for free (you can easily find directions on the Internet) but some cost as much as $250 (about half the price of the average gas grill).

Note to All Grillers

If, like us, you live in an area where even in summer sun can't be counted on, you may want to have a traditional grill on hand for cloudy-day barbecues. Regardless of which kind you buy, look for quality construction and materials that will last. Even if the initial cost is higher, you'll reduce strain on the environment by using one sturdy grill rather than purchasing lower quality or disposable ones that collapse after one season. Stainless steel and porcelain enameled cast iron grills are more efficient and will last longer than those made of chrome-plated aluminum. Also, over time, chrome plating can wear off, exposing your food to toxins.

MEMORIAL DAY

Whether or not you know a military man or woman who lost his or her life while in the service of our country, Memorial Day provides an opportunity to do something thoughtful for, or in the memory of a service person or their family. Planting trees, dedicating park benches, or stepping stones or contributing money towards permanent memorials or sculptures are gifts that will be enjoyed and appreciated by countless others for many lifetimes to come.

In addition, don't let the fear of grilling not being eco-friendly deter you from celebrating your summer holidays with a barbecue. You do have to eat, and using your indoor stove will also consume energy. Instead, think about the 25% rule we discussed in Chapter 1 and see if you can reduce the amount of time the grill is used or if the amount of food you grill can be trimmed. Favor fresh, uncooked (raw), seasonal veggies and salads with grilled fare serving on the side.

Warning: To prevent carbon monoxide poisoning (dizziness, nausea, and even death) never use a wood, charcoal, or gas grill to heat a home, and always use in well ventilated areas.

The Food

It's true. Grilled food tastes *good*. But wisely grilled food tastes good too, and cooking in an environmentally sustainable way feels even better, so here are a few grilling tips to please not only your taste-buds but also the planet.

- Use local, organic foods whenever possible. Farmers markets are the perfect source for seasonal ingredients. Go to LocalHarvest.org to locate farmers markets near you or to 100MileDiet.org for food sources within one hundred miles of your home.
- Choose a veggie burger over meat. Veggie burgers use one hundred times less water and ten times less energy to produce than animal-based burgers. In addition, a University of Chicago study (2005) found that going vegetarian reduced greenhouse gas emissions more than using a hybrid vehicle. Veggie burgers can be purchased or made easily at home using a variety of legumes.
- If purchasing soy or corn based veggie burgers, look for products that say non-genetically modified (non-GMO).
- The average American will eat 67 pounds of beef and 59.2 pounds of chicken per year, much of it grilled. If you are going to consume either, it's important that what you put on your grill is not only tasty but healthy too. When grilling meat and poultry, choose certified USDA organic. While the demand for free-range, organic, humanely raised animals is on the rise, concentrated animal feeding operations (CAFOs) provide Americans with the bulk of their animal food products. CAFOs contribute significantly to pollution and other health threats such as higher bacteria levels, so

CAN'T AFFORD A HYBRID CAR? HOW ABOUT A HYBRID GRILL?

The Tulsi-Hybrid solar cooker efficiently cooks meat, veggies, and even pies and breads at temperatures up to 400 degrees. Operates on solar power when the sun is shining, and when it's not, on as little as 200 watts/110v AC of electric power, or about 13¢ worth. For more information see SunBDCorp.com.

Grilled fruit makes a delightful summertime treat that kids and adults enjoy as appetizers, side-dishes, or dessert. Buy local, organic fruit whenever possible.

1. Use an array of fresh (not over-ripe) fruits including berries, peaches, apple, pear, mango, melon, kiwi, banana, pineapple, seedless grapes, etc.

2. Wash, peel (if needed), and chop fruits into one-inch cubes, or leave whole if the fruit is small.

3. Pile fruit onto a stick from your tree (soaked), bamboo (soaked), or stainless steel skewers. Kids will love to help with this. Brush with lemon juice to preserve the color.

4. Although grilled fruit (especially locally grown and seasonal) is sweet and sensational on its own, for a twist, you can try a pre-grill sprinkling of sugar and cinnamon or a dusting of olive oil, white grape juice, honey, or liqueur.

5. Place on a further edge of a warm (not hot) grill for 6-8 minutes for most fruit (harder fruits such as apples may need up to 15), turning a few times.

6. Remove from grill and enjoy alone or with organic yogurt or ice-cream.

look for the organic label or check out EatWellGuide.org for farmers near you who are committed to healthy and sustainable practices.

◉ Choose hormone-free meat and fish (the FDA does not allow pigs and poultry to be given hormones), and poultry and fish that were raised without the use of antibiotics.

◉ Look for the "Certified Humane Raised and Handled" label to ensure that animals were raised with access to pasture. Go to EatWellGuide.org for reputable farms in your area.

◉ Choose meats from grass fed animals. "Mad cow disease" (Bovine spongiform encephalopathy) is caused by cows eating by-products of other cows. Note that grass-fed meat is leaner and must be cooked accordingly.

◉ Don't be fooled by low priced meats. Cheap, factory farmed burgers, hot dogs, and sausages come from animals that may have been inhumanely raised and fed on diets of soy (which may have been genetically modified and grown at the expense of rain forests). Inexpensive sausages and hotdogs may contain more connective tissue, fat, and artificial ingredients than meat.

◉ Choose low-mercury, wild (not farmed) fish, and carry a *Seafood Watch Pocket Guide* (available from MBayAq.org by the Monterey Bay Aquarium) in your wallet to help make the right seafood choices for you and for the environment, or go to TheGreenGuide.com for updated information on the healthiest and most sustainable seafood options.

◉ Do not buy (or grill) unsustainably sourced shrimp. Shrimp farming is thought to be responsible for 32% of the destruction of southeast Asia's "rainforests of the sea," known as mangroves. Wild caught shrimp from Oregon is a safe, sustainable choice for grilling and a lighter alternative to hamburgers.

◉ Choose organic, all-natural and/or homemade marinades (try Consorzio's Baja lime or mango cilantro at Consorzio.com) and sides such as pickles, ketchup, mustard, and mayo (not to mention the local and organic burger toppers such as lettuce, tomatoes, and cheese.)

◉ Choose food products that have limited or, preferably, no food packaging, and avoid products packaged in single servings. Give preference to products sold in bulk.

◉ Know how many guests to expect and buy accordingly so you don't waste food and packaging. If you have leftovers, send your guests home with repurposed glass jars filled with the remaining grub.

- According to the National Cancer Institute, the carcinogenic substances that occur when grilling at high temperatures may increase the risk of colon, pancreatic, and breast cancers. Reduce your exposure to these substances by using lean cuts, trimming excess fat before placing meat on the grill, marinating well and avoiding overcooking or charring food.
- Add flavor to meats and veggies with fresh herbs, or try flavorful skewers from SeasonedSkewers.com.

DELECTABLE!

Spicy Lentil Burgers

● ● ● ● ● ● ● ● ● ●

Choose local and organic ingredients whenever possible

This makes a tasty alternative to your typical burger and provides both protein and fiber. The added herbs and spices aid in digestion, provide some healthy antioxidants, and allow for an extra burst of flavor

INGREDIENTS
3 cups water
2 cups lentils *
½ large onion, chopped
3 tablespoons olive oil
2 cloves garlic, minced
1/2 cup fresh cilantro or parsley, finely chopped
2 tablespoons tamari soy sauce
1 tbsp lemon juice
1 tbsp umeboshi plum vinegar or brown rice vinegar
1 tbsp cumin
¼ tsp cayenne pepper

*2 15-oz cans of lentils can be used in a pinch too

DIRECTIONS:
Boil water and add lentils, reduce heat and simmer uncovered for 30-40 minutes or until lentils become slightly soft. Meanwhile, sauté onion in 1 tablespoon olive oil for 5 minutes. Add garlic and sauté an additional 5 minutes. Place in bowl and add cilantro, tamari, lemon juice, vinegar, and spices. When lentils are done, place in a mixing bowl and allow to cool in the freezer for 10 minutes. Remove from freezer and mix well with other ingredients, forming into good sized patties. If patties are extra moist, use a little whole wheat flour as a binder.
Place on a grill and allow for 6 minutes of cooking on each side.
If you are not grilling, heat remaining 2 tablespoons of olive oil in a frying pan and fry up the patties, turning periodically, allowing for approximately 6 minutes on each side.

Contributed by Mary Purdy, certified nutritionist and registered dietitian. Seattle, WA, www. NourishingBalance.com

Clean-Up

When your barbecue is over, avoid cleaning your grill with chemicals. Instead, try SoyClean's safer soy based Grill Cleaner or Orange Plus (made with orange oil). Better yet, go bottle-free by scraping food from the grill with a Martin Grill Gadget (GrillGadget.com) and a little old fashioned elbow grease.

Barbecue Party Activities

Summer celebrations and parties may not need planned activities when they're outdoor at the beach, park, or other local. But if you're looking for some fun, cooperative games for your summertime party, here are a few ideas:

- **Camouflage.** Hide objects around the yard. Give everyone a (recycled) piece of paper and ask your guests to find the objects and write them down—but don't tell anyone else where they are. Set a timer. Whoever finds the most wins.
- **Identify a tree.** Lead someone who is blindfolded to a tree. The person is allowed to feel, smell, and listen. Move person away from the tree. Spin him around, then have him try to identify which tree he was led to.
- **Greenie.** All wander around with eyes closed except the Greenie who has eyes open but cannot move. When people bump into each other they must say "Greenie". Only the Greenie is silent. On meeting the Greenie they join hands or work along to the end of the Greenie line and take a free hand and open eyes. The area in which you're playing should be relatively small.
- **Pass the veggies.** Sit in a circle. First pass a hard shell squash around the circle with your feet. Next stand, tuck a round squash under your neck, then pass it to the next person without using your hands.
- **Unusual musical chairs.** Instead of people being out when the chair is removed, they have to sit on someone who is still in a chair. Eventually everyone is sitting on one person!
- **Calling all animals.** Everyone choose a partner. With the partner, choose an animal and the sound the animal makes. Each person decides whether the animal name or sound will be hers. Everyone puts on a blindfold. At the word go, everyone starts shouting out their animal or sound. The object is to find your partner by listening for

the correct word or sound. Since more than one group could use the same animal and sound, this game might not be as easy as it seems.

Something bugging your summer party?

Let's face it; few things spoil a summertime celebration more than a cloud of uninvited, multi-legged guests. Instead of giving DEET as a door prize or relying on petroleum-based citronella candles that may or may not do the trick, check below for people and earth-friendly options to keep the bugs at bay:

● Try sprays (to repel), or traps (to attract), that are chemical-free and make use of essential oils (or even bug pheromones!) to do the job with less risk to your family and the planet.

● Do-it-yourself fruit fly traps can be made by pouring a small amount of apple cider vinegar in a jar and placing a cone, with a small hole at the tip, made of rolled paper into the jar so that the tip of the funnel rests just above the vinegar. Fruit flies will be attracted to the vinegar but will get stuck in the jar. Clean and repeat every other day until flies are gone.

● Bats are wonderfully efficient at ridding their environments of mosquitoes, saving money, and eliminating the need for toxic lotions and sprays. If you don't have bats in your area, Gaiam.com sells bat houses you can install high in a nearby tree to entice some near. You'll need to plan ahead though, as it can take a year or more for bats to locate the new home you've planned for them.

● Check your yard, roof, and surrounding area (including saucers under planters) for standing water where mosquitoes lay their eggs and remove water or its ability to pool.

● Before buying bug spray or lotion, check with CosmeticDatabase.com to ensure that the product you're using is safe. The essential oils of lemon eucalyptus and geranium are natural bug repellants. Just add a few drops to water and spray. (Check with your pediatrician before using any repellant, natural or not, on children under age three.)

Father's Day

When I was two, I gave what proved to be my most memorable Father's Day gift. It was a T-shirt on which I'd drawn a Mr. Potatoheadish-looking picture of my dad and the words, "I love Daddy" in permanent crayon. I think I remember fearing that he might not appreciate my budding artistry, but didn't have to worry as it became clear the minute he opened the gift that he *loved* it. I might have been a bit deluded, but he wore the T-shirt all the time (okay, on weekends, when he was mowing the lawn and no one was home but us and the dog), until you could see through the fabric. By the time I left for college, I assumed the shirt had been recycled into a kitchen rag. But years later, after giving birth to a daughter of my own, my mom presented me with a gift featuring my faded Father's Day T-shirt drawing. She'd cut out the picture, sewn it onto a pillow, and preserved it for me. I suppose my dad might have been happy to be relieved, after so many years, of the duty of wearing that shirt (and the need to convince his daughter that the shirt was the greatest he'd ever laid his eyes on). On the flip side, I was sure happy to see it again.

This t-shirt might be an illustration of reusing and recycling to the uber-degree, but it's also an example of how Father's Day giving and receiving can create gifts that last a lifetime—like it or not.

In fact, according to ShopLocal, over 50% of polled dads are never fond of their Father's Day gifts. Perhaps this is because 64% of those polled felt fathers were difficult to shop for, or maybe because nearly 40% of the respondents left their Father's Day shopping until the last minute. Although I'm guessing no official research will confirm my hunch, given my proclivity for green, I'm hoping that a big reason for paternal dissatisfaction might be this: Dads long for more earth-friendly gifts.

Altogether, sons and daughters spend $8.6 billion on Father's Day purchases (as opposed to the $11.4 billion spent on mothers). The average Father's Day gift costs about $90. That's a lot of money spent on a lot of presents that may or may not be enjoyed and that may or may not end up in landfills. Although he might not state his gift preferences as clearly as mom, chances are what dad really hopes for is a gesture of love and appreciation.

This year, instead of adding to the waste, look for ways to honor your dad that keep him and our other Mother (Earth) happy by adding a green twist. Whether your dad pooh-poohs global warming, or whether he's deep green to the core, he's sure to appreciate the effort you make to celebrate him in an earth-friendly way.

Gifts

Father's Day, like many holidays, tends to be gift-focused. But as we've discussed in other chapters, gifts don't have to be things, don't have to cost money, and don't have to cost the Earth. Since you know your dad better than we do, ask yourself what he might like. Would your pop enjoy some one-on-one time with you and/or your kids? Would he appreciate a thoughtful poem, a funny, home-made video card, or a limerick about one of his humorous quirks? Would he like to go on a hike, canoeing, or fishing, or would he enjoy a museum, car show, or concert? Would he be pleased with a home-cooked meal, someone to clean out the gutters or organize his cluttered office? Before spending a cent, think about giving your dad the gifts of your time, energy, and enthusiasm—the gift of you.

If you'd like to offer your dad something concrete (not that you're not concrete), consider purchasing an item crafted by a local artisan or, even better, by you. My dad clearly appreciated his handmade "I love Daddy" shirt, and children of all ages can make similar gifts by using non-toxic fabric paints on T-shirts or caps (look for organic cotton or hemp) with messages such as, "Best Dad, Hands Down" (with handprints), "#1 Dad," or other messages you invent or find on the Internet. You can also print photos on T-shirts from your computer.

If handmade is not your thing and you'd like to purchase a gift for your dad, before heading for the store (online or off), be sure to remind yourself about applying the 3Rs and 3Gs to potential purchases.

Here are some ideas for Father's Day gifts that meet one or more of our green criteria, beginning with the top selling Father's Day gifts of all time.

Clothing and Accessories

Apparently dad needs a little help with his fashion sense. Two of the top three Father's Day gifts are neckties and shirts, although ties win the icon award for this special day. So to green up your Dad's wardrobe starting on Father's Day, instead of the standard tie, how about choosing a luxurious hemp (Ecolution.com) or non-silk vegan tie (JaanJ.com)? Organically grown cotton, hemp, or other eco-wise fabric shirts (as well as shorts, pants, outerwear, and hats) can be found for all occasions online and in retail stores such as Whole Foods Market and REI.

Or how about offering dad the ability to tread lightly on the Earth with a new pair of eco-friendly shoes by Simple, Earth Shoes, Ecolution, or Timberland? Making these shoes consumes fewer natural resources. They are also made from recycled or sustainable materials, require less energy to make, and/or produce markedly fewer greenhouse gas emissions during manufacturing. Eco-wise shoes also come in styles ranging from flip-flops to office-worthy, so there's a choice for every dad.

Hemp is the green material of choice for bags such as briefcases and backpacks because it is grown pesticide-free, is naturally anti-microbial and is 1.5 times more durable than cotton. Ecolution.com, ArtisanGear.com, HempBasics.com, and Rawganigue.com all sell bags and packs that dad can use for office, travel, or every-day use. (Browse these sites for other great gifts for dad including Frisbees , wallets, toiletry kits, belts, socks, and even guitar straps.)

The third top selling Father's Day gift is the humble razor, two billion of which end up in landfills every year. Recycline's Preserve Razor Triple has a recyclable handle made from 100% recycled plastic. To cut down on waste, only the blade section needs to be replaced.

A rechargeable electric razor may last for years and also saves on waste, even though it may not be made of ideal materials. Another eco-savvy choice is the old-style flat model. It might take some getting used to, but straight razors never have to be replaced, and as a bonus, using them makes any dad look undeniably cool. But our top green pick for razors is one run off solar power—perfect for home, car, or camping – and gentle on the Earth to boot.

But what to give Dad if you'd like to think outside the box? Here are some unique, eco-friendly ideas sure to please even the pickiest of papas. (For more ideas or additional places to find these items, do an online search for the item and "green," "eco," "recycled," or "sustainable," or visit our site, CelebrateGreen.NET.)

The Car Guy
- Gift certificates to your local car wash (which reduces groundwater contamination and saves water and energy over do-it-yourself washings).
- Key ring made from recycled traffic signs (Eco-Artware.com).
- LED tire pressure gauge to ensure you're not using more gas than necessary (Gifts.com).

The Good Sport
- Recycled bottle-cap fishing lures (BottleCapLure.com).
- Golf at a golf course certified for environmental stewardship after taking Audubon International's Green Golfer Pledge (GolfAndEnvironment.org). Include a set of non-toxic, biodegradable, water-soluble Eco Golf Balls (EcoGolfBalls.com).
- Canoe paddles made from sustainable wood (EchoPaddles.com).

The Green Thumb
- A Veriflora-certified Japanese Maple Bonsai or Miniature Tuscan Olive Tree for home or office from OrganicBouquet.com.
- Gardening calendar printed on 100% post-consumer waste recycled paper.
- People powered or electric lawn mower (push mower may double as a gym membership).

The Nature Lover or Outdoorsman

- A TerraPax Field Bag (TerraPax.com) made of undyed hemp, flax, and vegetable/bark tanned leather. The closure is made from naturally shed antlers.
- Klean Kanteen is made of lightweight stainless steel and will keep your dad hydrated (plastic bottle-free) without leaching chemicals into him or the Earth. SIGG bottles come in large and small sizes, as well as flask and thermos-styles.
- Hand cranked emergency lantern, flashlight, or radio (Amazon.com).

The Techie

- Business card holders, money clips, desk clocks, and luggage tags made from reused circuit boards (Eco-Artware.com).
- Solar backpack or messenger bags from voltaicsystems.com. All handheld electronics are made from recycled PET such as soda bottles. UV and water resistant.
- Water-powered clock (Gifts.com).

The Bookworm

- Books such as:
  - Inspiring—*Leaving Microsoft to Change the World: An Entrepreneur's Odyssey to Educate the World's Children* by John Wood
  - Lighthearted—*Wake up and Smell the Planet: The Non-Pompous, Non-Preachy Grist Guide to Greening Your Day* by Grist Magazine
  - Educational—*In Defense of Food: An Eater's Manifesto or The Omnivore's Dilemma: A Natural History of Four Meals* by Michael Pollan
  - Practical—*Beat High Gas Prices Now!: The Fastest, Easiest Ways to Save $20-$50 Every Month on Gasoline* by Diane MacEachern

The History Buff

- Cuff links made from buffalo nickels, Indian head pennies, and Mercury dimes (Eco-Artware.com).
- Old maps. Try to find the place where your dad was born.
- Vintage photographs that might have special meaning for your dad (i.e., the town outside the United States from which his family stems, or a distant relative of whom your dad is proud).

COREY AND LYNN'S TOP FIVE GREEN GUY GIFTS

1. Two person organic hemp hammock (EcoPatio.com)
2. BrewOrganic.com brewing supplies
3. Portable hybrid solar power charger (Solio.com)
4. SierraClub.com membership
5. Stainless steel coffee mug

The Traveler
- Join your dad on a mission to better the world through GreenVolunteers.com.
- Hemp trifold wallet (Rawganique.com).
- Environmentally and people friendly luggage tags (Footprint-es.com).

The Chef or Food and Drink Connoisseur
- Sustainable, formaldehyde-free bamboo kitchen tools (BambuHome.com).
- Knife sharpening. Instead of buying new knives, make the old ones like new with professional sharpening in your area or through HolleyKnives.com.
- Recycled glass martini glasses made in California (GreenFeet.com).

The Coffee or Tea Addict
- A basket filled with organic, Fair Trade, shade grown coffee, a stainless steel travel mug, and a coffee sock (an alternative to disposable coffee filters).
- Organic tea and infuser mug (ShopStashTea.com),
- A gift card to Tully's or other organic café.

The Film Buff
- A subscription to socially conscious films, delivered right to Dad's door (EarthCinemaCircle.com or IronWeedFilms.com).
- A library card. Libraries offer free videos and DVDs including many classic films.

The Do-it-Yourselfer
- Flexible, solar-powered LED lamp.
- Solar patio lights.
- Energy saving device such as Powerguard. Saves money and reduces emissions by up to 30% (SoGoGreen.com).

Mr. Mom
- Recycled truck inner tube tire diaper bag for Daddy (GreatGreenBaby.com) or gender neutral and PVC-free diaper bags (Fleurville.com).
- Cloth or recycled plastic shopping bags.

The Pampered Papa (Dads deserve some pampering too!)
- Gift certificate for a massage at a local eco-spa.
- Organic and all-natural skincare products such as shaving gel, soap, face wash, and lotion. Before buying, check with Environmental Working Group's CosmeticDatabase.com to be sure the products you're buying for Dad are safe.

ECO-ELECTRONICS

If you're thinking about buying dad an electronic gadget this Father's Day, remember to consider the gift's impact on the environment.

- Give preference to products powered by the sun, gravity, human power or, at the very least, rechargeable batteries. Solio.com sells a recharger that works for almost any portable electronic device.

- Look for tech products that are made with sustainability in mind, are energy efficient, and are made with reduced hazardous materials (check out MyGreenElectronics.org or GreenElectronics.com.) For example, LCD HDTVs will last longer and use less energy than non-LCD televisions.

- Be aware of planned or perceived obsolescence. Think twice before buying electronics, even for your techie Dad, if you think they are of poor quality, won't last long, will need to be replaced soon, or will need multiple additional components in order operate or fully enjoy.

- Offer to recycle Dad's old electronics or to find someone who is willing to take them off his hands. Place an ad on Freecycle.com, but if this is a no-go, look on MyGreenElectronics.org for electronic recycling centers near you. Even if you didn't buy the Father's Day gift at Staples, this retailer is the first to accept all electronics for recycling as part of their Eco Easy program.

- Organic cotton, hemp, or bamboo sheets, towels, and/or robe (Rawganique.com or VivaTerra.com).

The Guy Who Has Everything

For the dad who has everything, you might consider making a donation in your dad's name to a charity or organization that reflects his history, career path, or passions. A search on the Internet will reveal hundreds of worthy causes that include everything from tree planting and conservation (Tree-People.org) to micro-loans for entrepreneurs in developing countries (Kiva.org) to carbon neutral credits that offset everything from travel to weddings (TerraPass.com). After you make the contribution in your dad's name, most organizations will send him a note and information about their mission.

Dad Was Right

No matter how you choose to celebrate dad, we're sure he'll appreciate hearing from you that he was, in fact, right all along. Right about *what*, you ask? About turning the lights off, cleaning your plate, and wearing sweaters instead of turning the heat up (or on), for starters. Although it may have taken a few decades for you to see the light (and never mind the fact that Dad was trying to save a buck and not the planet), be sure to let Dad know that you heard him loud and clear and that you're grateful for his efforts. And regardless of whether or not you and your dad agree on politics, religion, or your spouse, this year, be sure to toast to one more of his timeless, sage tips: *always* respect your Mother (Earth). Now that's wisdom worth celebrating.

Handmade Father's Day Gift Ideas

Daughters and sons of all ages (and with a spectrum of artistic talents) can make unique Earth-considerate Father's Day gifts their Dads will cherish. Although an Internet search will reveal hundreds of activities, here are a few to get your creative juices flowing:

- **Recycled book clock.** Find an old book that your dad enjoyed or one that reflects a hobby or interest. At a craft store, pick up the face and clockworks (be sure to choose one with the correct stem length). You can glue on a hangar or place the clock on a small stand depending on the size of the book. Clocks, of course, can be made from other items including records, photographs glued to a stiff backing, or even tools. You can draw or paint a clock face on almost anything.

- **Barbecue apron and utensils.** Make an apron (free patterns are on the Internet) or purchase an organic or hemp one. Use non-toxic paints to stamp or draw barbecue-related items or a saying such as, "My dad (insert name) Barbecues Better than Your Dad." If your dad already has barbecue tools, you can fancy them up by sanding the wood handles, then painting them. You could make a barbecue tool hangar by taking a piece of wood, screwing in some hooks, adding hooks at the top, and hanging it from the wall above the barbecue. One more idea for the griller: a grill cover made from old denim shirts. or better yet, an old raincoat!

- **Game center.** Recycle or repurpose a small night stand with a drawer. Paint the entire piece or sand and stain it a new color. Paint a checkerboard pattern on top, then the words "Dad's fun and games" on the drawer.

- **Manly wind chime.** If those words don't seem to go together, they will when you use some fishing line to craft a wind chime out of old nuts, bolts, metal screwdrivers. and other such tools and hardware.

- **Initials on a shirt.** If you know how to embroider, you can use a shirt he already has or purchase an organic denim or dress shirt and embroider his initials or an icon for a favorite hobby (a fish, bicycle, or golf club) on the pocket.

- **Gardening tools.** For a gardener, wood burn his name on his gardening tools and while you're at it, clean and sharpen any he owns that need it.

Lean, green grillin' machine!

NUMBER ONE DAD

4th of July:

Red, White, and Green

The 4th of July—parades, fireworks, bon fires, corn, and watermelon. Summer has arrived. And with it, a host of activities ripe for a green makeover, or at least a touch up.

Why not celebrate Independence Day in a new way? Make this the day you declare your independence from things that harm people, the Earth, and the community? Below are lots of ways to get started.

Fireworks

 Hate to break it to you, but for most people, the highlight of July 4th is not so green. You guessed it; we're talking about fireworks. We grappled and argued about when to hit you with this information: at the beginning or the end of this chapter. I was in favor of hiding it in the middle. But Corey's sensible approach won out and here it is front and center.

If you prefer to hide your head in the red, white, and blue sand (my propensity), skip this section and head right for the food.

Many Americans believe it just wouldn't be the 4th of July without the boom, blast, and beauty of fireworks. After all, the very first Independence Day in 1777, the year after the Declaration of Independence was signed, was marked by a "grand exhibition of fireworks" in communities up and down the Eastern seaboard.

Reading the following from the *Virginia Gazette*, Williamsburg, Virginia, from July 18, 1777, it is understandable why we feel compelled to continue the custom.

"The ...exhibition...concluded with thirteen rockets on the commons, and the city was beautifully illuminated. Every thing was conducted with the greatest order and decorum, and the face of joy and gladness was universal. Thus may the 4th of July, that glorious and ever memorable day, be celebrated through America, by the sons of freedom, from age to age till time shall be no more."

But let's face it, in 1777, who was concerned about air pollution or chemicals fouling land and waterways? Firing off a dozen plus rockets in a few cities could not have caused much damage anyway (unless you count potential lost fingers or eyes due to misfiring or user error, and this was certainly long before the Consumer Product Safety Commission). But fast forward to today and it's a different story.

Let's start by differentiating between consumer (also known as "personal" or "backyard") fireworks (most commonly bottle rockets and sparklers) and the aerial displays that light up the skies. Firework industry revenues were reported at $900 million in 2006 with consumer revenues representing two-thirds of that amount, according to the American Pyrotechnics Association.

While the use of personal fireworks has increased from 29 million pounds in 1976 to more than 278 million pounds in 2007, the injury rate from personal fireworks plummeted 91% during that same time period, according to the U.S. Consumer Product Safety Committee. The decrease is most likely due to massive education efforts coupled with enforcement of safety standards.

That's the good news. The bad news is that while fewer people are injured directly, there are other areas of concern:

Air quality from smoke and particulate matter. When the air is stagnant, pollution from fireworks may reach dangerous levels. As reported by the Galveston-Houston Association for Smog Prevention, "On January 1, 2003, in the Houston-Galveston, TX area, stagnant air triggered a 'level red' exposure to fine particles that began during the evening hours as individuals set off fireworks in celebration of New Year's day. A monitor recorded pollution levels over 200 micrograms per cubic meter, and averaged about 74 ug/m^3 for the day. It has turned out to be the single worst episode for fine particle air pollution in many years." (To put it in perspective, during the several days after the World Trade Center was destroyed, peak levels of pollution were measured in the 100 to 150 ug/m^3 range, with average levels in the range of 25 ug/m^3.)

Fire. More United States fires are reported on July 4th than on any other day, and fireworks account for half of those fires, more than any other cause. Fires, of course, have an environmental as well as personal cost.

Toxic chemicals. Unfortunately, a mix of toxic chemicals is what brings us the awe-inspiring colors in aerial displays. While the effects of these chemicals on humans and wildlife as a result of fireworks displays have not been extensively studied, it seems like common sense to assume that even beyond the potential problems for people with asthma and other lung problems, exposure to these chemicals cannot be good for people or the planet. When these chemicals are exploded into the air, particles fall to the earth and into the water. While by themselves they cannot at this time be blamed for problems that crop up later in fish, for instance, it's reasonable to consider that they may add to the pollution already present, which obviously is not a good thing.

Child labor issues. China, being the world's principle fireworks manufacturer, is also a source of child labor issues. In 2001, for example, 50 children making fireworks in the classroom for a local business were reported to have been killed in an explosion at their school.

So what's an eco-conscious person to do?

While there are no truly "green" alternatives to aerial fireworks currently available, some strides are being made.

In 2004, Disneyland in Anaheim, California, began launching nightly fireworks shows using compressed air rather than gunpowder. Compressed-air technology reduces smoke to almost nothing at the point of launch, and also reduces noise levels by approximately 60%. According to Sam Atwood, media manager for the South Coast Air Quality Management District (the agency responsible for pollution control in Southern California), air-launch technology combined with low-gunpowder fireworks reduced emissions by 50 to 60 percent. However, it is an expensive proposition and not without its problems, so it has not exactly caught on like wildfire across the world. The Disney corporation itself has been slow to install the system at its other facilities.

A Japanese company, Seikon, has developed a fiber-resin "glue" made of corn starch. This substance holds together rice chaff and sawdust to create a fireworks shell that dissolves in the air or water within 24 hours. When you consider that a large shell normally

FUN ACTIVITY: A RECYCLING BIN DECORATING CONTEST

Provide large cardboard boxes and all the tools to decorate them. During the party everyone can vote for their favorite with the winner getting a choice of treats or treasures. (Check our Halloween chapter or GreenHalloween.org for a list of treasures that work well for prizes for any event.)

made of compressed paper can create almost a ton of debris that can drop on spectators as well as land and water, this certainly can be considered a positive green advance.

According to an article in the *Milwaukee Journal Sentinel*, July 2, 2008, chemists around the world are in the beginning stages of developing a group of new pyrotechnics that rely on high-nitrogen energetic compounds to make fireworks that produce less smoke and soot.

While five U.S. states ban personal fireworks, aerial displays have traditionally been legal in every part of the country except for occasional prohibitions due to weather conditions or drought.

There are people who consider a complete ban on fireworks the only real choice. For those who are more moderate, here are some suggestions and alternatives:

- Talk to the people in charge of your community fireworks displays well in advance of the holiday, and discuss some or all of the following:
  - Apply the 25% reduction rule. Ask them to reduce the display by 25%. This could be in the actual number of fireworks shot off or the length of the display.
  - Ask about the potential for replacing fireworks with a laser light show.
  - Be sure to let officials know that you are concerned about fireworks exceeding the federal Clean Air Act regulations as well as local air and noise pollution standards.
- Do not sit directly under where aerial fireworks are set off or downwind from such a site.
- If you have a lung problem such as asthma, either stay indoors and watch through closed windows or wear a gauze or non-toxic dust mask.
- If you are concerned about noise levels, purchase and use ear plugs for each member of the family.
- Watch fireworks on TV or the Internet.
- Since fractions of firework reaction products also occur in the shells as slag, parents are advised to remove visible residues from yards and playgrounds.

Food
One of the best things about summer celebrations is the fresh, locally grown produce that is available. Even if you live in a city, you're likely to have access to fruits and veggies grown nearby and brought into town to be sold by farmers at weekly markets. Almost

While mosquito repellant, barbeques, and fresh water are often taken for granted, in some places in the world they are luxuries.

◉ Jewish World Watch's Solar Cooker Project is designed to "protect and empower the women of Darfur" by providing women living in refugee camps in Chad with solar cookers. But this project is not about carbon-free cooking. For women and girls fleeing the genocide in Darfur, even the simple task of collecting firewood for cooking can expose them to extreme danger. The Solar Cooker Project enables women to feed their families without having to collect wood and also provides them with income opportunities. To contribute to the Solar Cooker Project, go to JewishWorldWatch. org.

◉ For most Americans, mosquitoes are a mere annoyance, although West Nile Virus is causing some alarm. But did you know that mosquitoes are responsible for the most human deaths worldwide? Mosquito nets can protect people from malaria and other deadly insect-born diseases, but for some, $18 is too much to pay. You can contribute a life-saving mosquito net to a family in need though OxfamAmericaUnwrapped.com.

◉Are you aware that clean water is not an American right? In Hale County, Alabama, one in four homes is not connected to a municipal water supply. Unable to afford bottled water, many families are forced to use sewer-contaminated water. It only takes $425 to provide a family with the water meter needed to bring clean water into their home. Find out more at BuyAMeter.org.

nowhere in the United States is there a need to purchase packaged and preserved items to grace your summer party or picnic table.

If you've never done it before, find a nearby (preferably organic) farm and stop by a week or so before the holiday. Let the farmer know you're searching for some great party meal ideas using in-season veggies and fruits. Be adventurous. Try something you've never eaten before. Open yourself to the possibilities.

Why organic instead of any nearby farm? While locally grown is better than shipped in from somewhere else, studies have shown that organically grown foods actually are better for us. Unfortunately, some of our most common favorite fruits and vegetables are highest in chemical residues when grown non-organically. These include apples, peaches, berries, cherries, apricots, grapes, spinach, sweet bell peppers, and green beans. And while this is particularly true of produce grown in foreign countries and shipped to the United States to satisfy our out-of-season cravings, farms not certified organic in the United States often use many chemicals as well.

A staggering number of different pesticides and other chemicals are layered on our foods, and in most cases even scrubbing cannot get rid of the contaminants. For example, according to the Organic Trade Association, on average strawberries receive a dose of up to 500 pounds of pesticides per acre. Forty-five different pesticides are regularly applied to delicately skinned peaches in conventional orchards. A standard regimen of 35 pesticides is used on conventionally raised tomatoes.

On the other hand, the safest foods (those with the least exposure to chemicals) are asparagus, kiwi, avocado, mango, onion, banana, broccoli, papaya, cauliflower, pineapple, sweet corn, and sweet peas.

This is why it's important to be vigilant even when buying locally. Certified organic farmers must adhere to stringent rules regarding the use of chemicals on their crops. Organic food cannot be produced with conventional pesticides, petroleum-based or sewage-based fertilizers, genetically modified ingredients, or irradiation. Some small farms may not be certified organic but should not be discounted. Check Biodynamics.com for local organic or biodynamic farms in your area.

If you have no choice because there are no organic farms in your area, you might want to educate yourself about the chemicals used. You can simply ask the farmer about his or her use of fertilizers and pesticides if you are concerned. At least with this knowledge you can make informed choices.

And why not consider planting some veggies yourself? Many like tomatoes, lettuce, and spinach can be grown in containers on a sunny porch or balcony. Miniature versions of broccoli, corn, and other veggies have been developed especially for people who don't have the room or don't want to go to the trouble of a large plot. Gardening doesn't have to be a full-time occupation to be rewarding to your family's health. Children love to garden and happily eat veggies they've grown themselves, even when they turn up their noses at store-bought.

Search the web for recipes or spend a few minutes creating a healthier substitute for dishes you might normally buy. For instance, why pay big bucks for a vegetable platter with a small container of dip when you can so easily create your own.

And remember that healthy eating might start with organic, but it also involves making choices like the darkest greens (forest green kale is packed with nutrients that are nowhere to be found in pale-as-a-ghost iceberg lettuce). Also, when making salad for a crowd and providing dressing, offer choices, but watch out. Most prepared dressings consist of little but fat. (If you're going to use them, however, look for organic versions.) Flavored vinegar adds zing without obliterating the variety of subtle tastes found in a mixed salad.

If you live near a fruit farm, start a new family tradition. Just like hunting a Christmas tree, picking fresh organic strawberries, cherries, or blueberries in advance of a party can be a bonding experience.

And at the party, why not have a few ice cream makers handy so you or your guests can churn out fresh strawberry, blueberry, or cherry sorbet?

Thirst Quenchers

I remember when the 4th of July meant jugs of fresh squeezed lemonade set out on picnic tables. These days, ice chests bulge with soda, beer, and bottled water.

Each year Americans buy more than 50 billion single-serving plastic beverage containers. Most plastic bottles, 77% across the country, end up in landfills, streams, and parks as well as along roads where they not only make a mess of the landscape, but can harm birds and animals and will never decompose.

When you're giving the party, why choose to purchase anything at all in plastic bottles? The best idea is to shun convenience in order to diminish the impact of your celebration on the Earth.

Best bet of all? Avoid buying liquids packaged in plastic bottles. Instead, purchase a half dozen pretty pitchers, then fill with made-from-scratch or organic lemonade.

Other wonderfully refreshing summer drinks can be concocted in a blender. Iced tea or coffee can be a real treat and won't get watery if you pre-freeze your choice in ice cube trays, then add to the jug. Or choose Numi's organic iced tea which comes in several flavors like Citrus Black and Tropical White from WorldPantry.com. Santa Cruz's organic juices like white grape are perfect for kids and adults.

Alcohol in glass bottles that can be easily recycled is a better choice than beer in single serving cans because glass takes less energy to produce and recycle than aluminum. And while we're talking beer, organic ales, lagers, and pilsners are increasingly available at local stores. Organic beer sales increased 40% in 2005 over the previous year (the latest year for which statistics are available), tying with organic coffee as the fastest-growing organic beverage, according to the Organic Trade Association. The nation's largest beer company has even jumped on board with two organic beers. This beer is made the same way as any other, but USDA standards require that at least 95% of ingredients, usually barley and hops, are grown without the use of chemicals or pesticides for a beer to be

PRINT OUT THE "THINK OUTSIDE THE BOTTLE PLEDGE" AND INVITE GUESTS TO SIGN (THINKOUTSIDETHEBOTTLE.ORG).

called "organic." Organics cost about the same as other specialty or imported beers. Here are a few to try:

- Peak Organic Brewing Co., (PeakBrewing.com)
- Wolaver's Organic Ale, (Wolavers.com)
- Butte Creek Brewing Co, (ButteCreek.com)
- Wild Hop Lager, (WildHopLager.com)
- Stone Mill Pale Ale, (StoneMillPaleAle.com)
- Santa Cruz Mountain Brewing, (SantaCruzMountainBrewing.com)

Looking to stay local? Check out the "brewing locator" at BeerTown.org/CraftBrewing.

And finally, for those of you who want to whip up your own, BrewOrganic.com.

Other Ideas about Drinks

- If you're going to buy drinks in plastic, buy larger, not individual sizes.

- Before plastic, believe it or not, there was glass. So here's a revolutionary idea: use real drinking glasses. Avoid purchasing throw-away plastic or Styrofoam cups. Guests can keep tabs on their glasses if you tie a piece of raffia around each with a tag and the person's name on it. Or replicate earlier times when guests always arrived with their own dinnerware, cups, and utensils.

Let's talk about bottled water for a moment. The average American drinks more than 26 gallons of bottled water each year. We have become convinced that tap water is not safe to drink. But the fact is, in most cases, we've been sold a bill of goods. Anyone who says that advertising doesn't work only need point to marketers who have us convinced that drinking water from plastic bottles is safer, healthier, and tastes better than water from the tap.

The truth is just the opposite. In taste tests pitting ordinary tap water against bottled water in all price ranges, municipal water right out of the tap continually ranks as well, if not better, than bottled. As for the health benefits, a recent Earth Policy Institute study showed that bottled water is no healthier than plain tap water.

SET UP A FRUITY DRINK BAR

Furnish a blender, a selection of fresh, organic fruits, milk (or milk alternatives), honey, and a supply of ice cubes.

Encourage guests to create their own concoctions and name them just for fun

PREMIUM BRAND WATER— FROM YOUR TAP

In this year's 4th of July party invitation, why not ask your guests to bring their own reusable water bottles and offer to supply as much water as they need. Put out big jugs of ice water and attach our tongue-in-cheek label. To download and print a full color version, visit our website, CelebrateGreen.NET.

Tap Water Regulated by EPA	Bottled Water Regulated by FDA
Cannot have confirmed E. coli or fecal Coliform bacteria.	A certain amount of any bacteria is allowed.
Filtered and/or disinfected.	No federal filtration or disinfection requirements.
Violation of drinking water standards are grounds for enforcement.	Bottled water in violation of standards can still be sold.
Utilities must have their water tested by certified labs.	Such testing is not required for bottlers.
Tap water results must be reported to state or federal officials.	There are no reporting requirements for bottlers.
Water system operators must be certified.	Bottled water plant operators do not have to be certified.
Water suppliers must issue consumer confidence reports annually.	There are no public right-to-know requirements for bottlers.
Costs pennies a day.	Costs $0.80 to $4.00 per gallon.
Contains essential nutrients for the body, such as calcium and iron.*	Natural minerals are removed by filtration.
Chlorine residual in water to prevent bacteria growth.*	No disinfectant present to kill bacteria in bottles.

Chart courtesy of Natural Resources Defense Council Foundation, NDCF.org

*Note from authors: Some ingredients found in tap water such as fluoride and chlorine can be hazardous to your health.

While there is a place for bottled water (for instance, where storms and natural disasters threaten), for most people it's simply a matter of convenience and a habit we've fallen into.

Bottled water is expensive, costing 240 to 10,000 times more than tap water. According to the *San Francisco Chronicle*, for the price of one bottle of Evian, a San Franciscan can receive 1,000 gallons of tap water. They further claim that 40% of bottled water should be labeled bottled tap water because that's what it is!

And consider that bottled water is not governed by the same laws as local water supplies. Every year, for example, San Francisco water is tested more than 100,000 times to ensure that it meets or exceeds every standard for safe drinking water. Bottled water? Few, if any, standards need be met, so none are. The bottles themselves can include

RED, WHITE, AND BLUEBERRY MUFFINS

● ● ● ● ● ● ● ● ● ● ● ● ● ● ● ● ● ● ● ●

Choose local and organic ingredients whenever possible

MAKES 12

INGREDIENTS

2 cups organic brown rice flour
2/3 cup organic sugar
1 stick organic butter
1 cup organic milk
1 cup organic blueberries
2 organic eggs
Dash of cinnamon, baking
    powder, baking soda

DIRECTIONS

Line two muffin pans with
12 (large) muffin cups and preheat the
oven to 400 degrees Fahrenheit.

In a mixing bowl, add the eggs, milk, and butter and blend until smooth. Then add the sugar, baking powder, baking soda, cinnamon, and then slowly add the flour. Turn off the blender. Add 1 to 1 1/2 cups blueberries (frozen or fresh) and mix in with a spoon.

Spoon the mix evenly into the 12 muffin cups, filling each cup around 3/4 full. Bake around 30 minutes until light golden brown on top.

Contributed by Jill Westfall,
WordSmithAndCompany.com

additives like plasticizers, antistatic agents, flame retardants, and heavy metals such as cadmium, mercury, and lead. Do these leach into the water? Do you want to take that chance? And not only is petroleum, a non-renewable resource, used in making the bottles, but add in packaging and shipping to get those bottles into your hands (five trillion gallons of bottled water is shipped internationally each year), and that simple bottle of water becomes an earth-costly extravagance. Just because we can afford to purchase water from Norway and Japan, should we?

One last thought, again according to the *San Francisco Chronicle*, "The rapid growth in the bottled water industry means that water extraction is concentrated in communities where bottling plants are located. This can have a huge strain on the surrounding eco-system. Near Mount Shasta, the world's largest food company is proposing to extract billions of gallons of spring water, which could have devastating impacts on the McCloud River."

MINTY MAKE-AHEAD LEMONADE

Choose local and organic ingredients whenever possible

MAKES ABOUT 3 3/4 CUPS

Before all the choices of drinks we now find in the supermarket, lemonade, orangeade, and limeade spelled summer. You can find many recipes online, but here's a simple one.

INGREDIENTS

4 lemons
1 cup raw brown sugar
3 3/4 cups boiling water
limes
mint leaves

DIRECTIONS

Wash lemons, cut each in half, then squeeze out juice. Place juice and pulp in a bowl with sugar and pour 1 1/4 cups boiling water over. Stir until sugar dissolves. Add lemon halves and another 2 1/2 cups boiling water. Stir well, then cover and let cool. Strain, squeezing out juice from lemon halves.

(Guests can do this part.) Before pouring into glasses, cut a lime in half. Add the half lime plus three mint leaves to the glass. Mash the lime and mint leaves to release the flavor, then add ice cubes and pour lemonade over. If you'd like the lime and mint leaves to be on top, simply pour the mixture into another glass.

Substitute honey for brown sugar if you prefer. And depending on the acidity of the lemons, you may need to tweak the amount of sugar or honey to taste.

At the beginning of the summer, how about purchasing stainless steel water bottles for each member of your family? Bring them with you wherever you go (the bottles, that is, not the family). Remember that single-use bottles should *never* be refilled. The plastic from which they are made may leech a harmful chemical if the bottle develops hairline cracks or dings, which can occur through washing or general wear and tear.

Decorations

The traditional red, white, and blue of July 4th makes it easy to find decorations without spending a dime. We'll bet you already have some objects of these colors lying around the house, to say nothing of your garden. One sure bet is to go on a hunt through your home (get the kids in on this one) and collect anything that is red, white, or blue. While you're at it, how about checking out strings of red, white, and blue lights (LED), or other Christmas decorations? Reusing them for a variety of holidays only makes sense. Or how about taking your family on a red, white, and blue hunt at yard sales or in thrift shops?

Once you've got your items assembled, it's time to start thinking creatively.

Thin lengths of cloth or ribbon can be tied in bows on tree branches, lawn furniture, or even garden tools. Drape larger pieces of fabric over the backs of chairs, make flags, or use them as tablecloths. Small cloth squares could be fastened around pots of red geraniums, used as napkins, or slipped around mug handles to identify them to their users.

And what better to celebrate the United States than to make use of that quintessential fabric, denim. You don't need to know how to sew. Cut up old pairs of jeans to make place mats or clip out back pockets to create cute and useful utensil holders. Let the edges fray.

Pinwheels are easy and fun to make, even for small children. No need to purchase any supplies. Use any recycled paper you have lying around. Color the paper first in holiday shades, cut into the correct size and shape (search the Internet for instructions), then attach to sticks. If you fill some glasses with sand, then stick a pinwheel in each, you've got your table decorations.

Use wool or EcoSpun felt squares (made from recycled plastic bottles and available at fabric and craft stores) to make a series of small flags in red, white, and blue to string along a porch. If you're really feeling green, purchase one or two squares in our favorite color and add them just to let people know you're in the eco-mode.

The color of a tablecloth can make a big impression, so if you can't find appropriate sheets or fabric, consider purchasing organic from AbundantEarth.com.

Partyware

A beautifully set table is the badge of honor for many a host and hostess, even at picnics and barbecues. And gorgeous designs on throwaway tableware make it a snap to set a memorable table. The problem, as you've guessed by now, is the throwaway part. If each United States household replaced just one 40-count package of conventional paper plates this year with 100% recycled ones, we'd save 487,000 trees. Hopefully that kind

MAKE A FOUND OBJECT UNCLE OR AUNT SAM

Put out a pile of wood remnants, sticks, wooden balls, nails, and other assorted hardware. (Invite your guests to bring anything they have that could be used.) Have on hand hammers, non-toxic paint, sandpaper, and glue. Prior to the party, put together a couple of "sculptures" as examples, then let your guests go at it.

of statistic will help you to think creatively about mundane items like plates, flatware, and glasses. Here are some ideas to get you started.

- There's nothing wrong with borrowing from friends or neighbors or asking people to bring their own plates and utensils. Paper and plastics are habits we can choose to break. You might even want to make this a fun aspect of your party. Ask everyone to bring red, white, or blue plates. Guests bringing the same color plates become table mates.

- If you don't want to set the picnic table(s) with reusable dishware, silverware, and cloth napkins, opt for compostable and biodegradable plates and cutlery. Clear Creek's sugarcane and wood-pulp plates are suitable for cold or hot foods, and Nat-Ur forks, spoons, and knives are made from potatoes and corn starch (both at KokoGm.com). Bagasse bowls, made from sugar cane fiber, are available at WorldCentric.org. And lots of choices made from tropical leaves, sugar cane, and other compostable substances, plus utensils made from cornstarch or wood, can be found at SimplyBiodegradable.com.

- Paper napkins are a huge waste. Why not use cloth napkins? You can make them without sewing by simply using pinking shears to trim the edges. Any leftover fabric works fine. Maybe you have a couple of cotton shirts you wore only a few times before they went out of style. Why not turn them into napkins? Another great idea? The humble washcloth. But if you plan to purchase, try Seventh Generation's 100% recycled, chlorine-free napkins, using a minimum of 80% post-consumer waste paper (GreenHome.com). Marcal.com also offers 100% recycled paper products, including napkins, toilet paper, and paper towels.

- After eating, if you've used reusable items, bring a tub of hot water outside where everyone can deposit their utensils and plates, making it easy to clean up. Provide towels to dry off. (Make it fun. How about a dishwashing relay race?)

Activities

Many July 4th parties consist of eating and watching fireworks, but if you want to entertain a crowd for an entire afternoon and evening, games and activities are a must.

Among our favorites:

- **Traditional relay races and games.** Sack race, three-legged race, carry the egg, Red Light-Green Light.

- **Back yard Olympics.** Break up into teams and stage your own events. For instance, long jump, high jump, running relay, obstacle course, jump rope, etc. Make and award medals if you like.

- **Fireworks painting.** Using large pieces of paper and non-toxic paints, let different colors of paint fall in the center of the paper, then use straws to blow out the paint from the center so the finished product resembles fireworks. Add glitter if you like.

- **Recycled newspaper hats.** By checking the Internet you can find instructions for the traditional sailor hat, or go farther afield and create Stetsons, stove pipes, and the ever popular crown (although seeing as this is July 4th, you might want to avoid references to the monarchy!).

- **Recycled coffee can lid twirlers.** Use a nail to poke a hole in the center of a plastic coffee can lid. Draw a spiral that starts a small distance from the hole and extends to the rim. Cut along the spiral line with scissors. Knot a piece of string and thread the other end through the hole. Then hang it and watch it spin (hopefully you've got a little breeze going).

- **Decorate organic T-shirts.** Use non-toxic fabric paints.

- **Potato stamp placemats.** Cut up old fabric or sheets to placemat size. Cut a potato in half. Carve a simple design like a star into the cut side of the potato. Dip the shaped side into a bit of non-toxic paint or a stamp pad, then stamp the shape as many times as you like onto the placemat. When dry, take the mat home and iron it to ensure the colors last when the mat is washed in cold water.

- **Cookie cutter bird feeders.** Why not let the birds have some fun too? Use a cookie cutter to cut stale bread into star shapes. Poke a hole in the point of a star. Thread through some string, then hang from a tree.

MORNING AFTER MESS JULY 5, 2006

MORE THAN 1,000 VOLUNTEERS FROM THE SURFRIDER FOUNDATION COLLECTED AND REMOVED 8,000 POUNDS OF TRASH (INCLUDING THIS COUCH) AND 45,000 CIGARETTE BUTTS LEFT ON A SAN DIEGO BEACH. *Used by permission of Bill Hickman, Surfrider Foundation San Diego, SurfRiderSD.org*

Autumn

Happy Hallogreen®!

Among the holidays that can make our eyes bright with nostalgia, for most Americans, Halloween ranks near the top. There's something about the time of year, the first big holiday of the fall, the dark, crisp autumn night, homes lined with glowing jack-o-lanterns, and of course, the reward for doing absolutely nothing but knocking on doors and shouting the obligatory, "Trick or Treat!"

It's always been a night of fantasy (and a little fear), where we dress up to become someone we're not and set out in search of sugary treats.

Now please don't call us Halloween Grinches (although to be honest it wouldn't be the first time), but we'd like to point out that going green on Halloween absolutely must include, first and foremost, a conversation about greening the treats. But not to fear; we can start this discussion with some good news: in our experience, kids are eager and open to alternatives to traditional candy. It's adults who sometimes have a hard time with the idea of receiving less (or none) of the goodies they so fondly remember as kids.

Although we have yet to do a peer-reviewed study on the issue, in 2007 we met thousands of children (of all ages) and asked as many as we could how they would feel if people were to give them alternatives to conventional candy (some of which we displayed) for Halloween. After scanning the options, how many kids do you think said "no thanks," "no way," or "not a chance"? Answer: not a one. No child of any age, including "impossible" two-year-olds or "incorrigible" teens said they would rather have conventional candy once they saw the choices right there in front of them. And we never threatened anyone with holding their stuffed animal or iPod for ransom. Honest.

Yet, a few reporters (one of whom was adamant that Corey is, undisputedly, not just a green Grinch but *The* Green Grinch), set out to prove that kids would not be open to forgoing their favorite confections in lieu of something healthy by shoving a microphone into a child's face and asking, "How would you feel if you didn't get candy for Halloween anymore and instead got something good for you?" (And believe us, the "good for you" part was said in a way that would make even the sweetest of healthy alternatives sound putrid.)

Of course, the kids they interviewed begged, "Pleeeese don't take away my candy," and whined, "Halloween would be no fun without treats!" You could almost hear the crocodile tears welling up in their poor, deprived eyes and the producers high-fiveing one another. One more do-gooder idea bites the dust, hooray!

But here is why the reporters' methodologies were flawed and why their little experiment proved nothing: they failed to show these children the alternatives. They focused, instead, on what the kids couldn't have instead of on what they *could*, and this breaks a cardinal rule of successfully going green (as well as successful parenting): present desirable alternatives. And here lies the beauty of making eco-friendly choices on Halloween—there are so many great alternatives available.

Which brings us back to the thousands of children who said "Yes! I would love to receive one of those 'other' treats instead of candy." What was so special about them? Nothing. (Well, of course they were all special, but you know what we mean.) Again, we're not scientists, but we hypothesize that unlike when we were kids, candy is no longer a

In October 2007, Corey drafted me to hand out honey sticks at Seattle's Pumpkin Prowl, which brings thousands of families to the Woodland Park Zoo for an exuberant four-night pre-Halloween celebration.

To be honest with you, I have been known to drive a few too many miles out of my way when I'm in the mood for a package of English toffee, so I was a tad concerned about the reaction of little ghosts and goblins who received, instead of a fistful of mini candy bars, a slim stick of honey. Would they cry? Would they tell their moms they'd been cheated? Would I go home with a black eye?

I'm happy to report that I worried for absolutely no reason. Of the hundreds and hundreds of children who passed by, only two or three refused the honey stick. On the contrary, as I held the honey sticks up for all to see and said, "I've got honey sticks," what I heard were what can only be described as shouts of glee. "Honey sticks, I looooove honey sticks," exclaimed a princess. "Me too," agreed her friend, the pirate. "Can I have two?"

very special, occasional treat. Yes, children these days certainly enjoy candy as much as we did, but they're also exposed to it on an almost daily basis, even in homes that don't keep it around. Aside from holidays, today's kids can score sweets at school birthdays (in large classes there can be several a week), special events, and even during trips to the dry cleaners. One first grade teacher we know keeps a bowl of candy on her desk to bribe students to push in their chairs or perform other acts of kindness. Apparently, feeling good about doing right is not enough of a reward. Unless you have a no candy rule and unless your kids are with you 24/7, they're probably getting more sweets than you're aware of, which may or may not concern you.

So why is candy a concern to anyone? Like most things, the issue is not black and white, but generally speaking, candy is an issue when it is made with unhealthy and un-earth-friendly ingredients, when it is handed out and eaten in excessive amounts, and when, as our friends at the Washington Oral Health Foundation would point out, teeth are left unbrushed after consumption. And when you peel back the layers of this question, you might also ask, "What is unhealthy, exactly?" and "What does un-earth-friendly mean?" Taking it a few steps further might mean learning more about how candy is produced, how production affects candy-trade workers, how it is packaged, and how wrappings are later disposed of.

What we do know is that obesity and diabetes rates in the United States are skyrocketing and that common candy ingredients including artificial colors and preservatives can cause behavior problems in some children. We know that while once upon a time receiving a single piece of candy or maybe a small chocolate bar was the norm, today's kids expect (and parents encourage their kids) to receive handfuls of candy at each door on Halloween. We also know that conventionally grown chocolate, in particular, is connected with devastating human and environmental consequences, which we discuss in detail in the Valentine's Day section. All in all, we're confident that there is a better way to keep the fun while losing the undesirable stuff. And surprise-surprise, we have a few ideas on how to do exactly this.

When choosing treats for trick-or-treaters, we suggest that you think back to our introductory discussion of the 3Gs and choose handouts that are healthy, earth-friendly, and/or people-friendly. Don't fret if you can't find items that meet all three criteria, although

Need more ideas for sure-to-please treats and treasures? Visit GreenHalloween.org.

a pat on the back is certainly in order if you do. For example, if you decide to give out stickers this year (which are healthier than candy because they're not, well, candy), but nowhere on the package can you find whether or not they're printed on recycled paper or if the people who made them were receiving fair wages, you can rest easy knowing that stickers are a better choice than the conventional candy you chose last year, which likely would not fit any of the 3G criteria. It's okay to take baby steps. Next year, you can look for a treat or treasure to hand out that is, perhaps, both healthy and eco-friendly.

Also, don't forget the first of the 3Rs–the Big Man on Campus of the green movement: reduce. Reducing the amount of treats and treasures; whether they're people/Earth/community-friendly or not, is the first and best way to help the planet, our kids, and even your bank account. So instead of giving away handfuls of [insert the name of your treat or treasure here], hand out just one. That's right, one. In our experience, something magical happens when you give children just one of something. Do they complain? No! They seem to cherish it more. It may seem to you that we've gone off the healthy and green deep end but we've seen with our own eyes that offering kids one sticker is better than giving them three and giving them one fruit stick is preferable to two. And as a bonus (as if you needed more), allowing children to choose that one special treat or treasure out of a bowl or bag of many somehow adds to the fun. Go figure.

One other thing we've noticed is that children seem to be born with an innate ability to detect cheap, disposable "goodies" and treat them as such. Plastic rings, sticky snakes, and other gumball-machine type toys seems to have the lifespan of a breath before they're lost, broken, or a combination of the two. But when the same child who received the mass produced doo-dad is given an item from nature—such as a seashell, polished stone, feather, or even a handmade item such as an herb-filled sachet or a little gnome made from felted wool—you can watch as these items are transformed into treasures to be played with and cherished for weeks, even months, to come. So try not to replace conventional candy with trinkets that were made in some faraway land (especially if they are not fair trade, even if they were not made by fair trade standards), and will inevitably end up in a landfill after your next trash day. Instead, think about choosing simple treasures that will be prized long after Halloween night. If you can't find or prefer not to

Green Halloween® treats and treasures need not be purchased. Handmade items, especially those made from recycled and natural materials, can be easy and inexpensive, not to mention thoughtful. Books such as *The Children's Year* (by Stephanie Cooper, Christine Fynes-Clinton, and Marije Rowling) and *Earthways* (by Carol Petrash and Donald Cook) suggest loads of ideas for unique seasonal gifts.

We're excited about working with companies to create healthy, affordable, bite-sized versions of their snacks. As these products become available, we'll post them on our website, GreenHalloween.org. If you have suggestions for food products you'd like to see on the list, contact the company directly and let them know about Green Halloween®. As more parents like you demand that the "treats" we give our children are healthy, more health-minded food companies will participate.

Have additional ideas for Green Halloween® treats and treasures? E-mail Corey@GreenHalloween.org with your suggestions and where to find them. We may add them to our website or to our next book.

give out treasures made from natural materials, choosing products made from recycled, recyclable, or compostable materials is the next best idea.

So what alternatives to conventional candy do we suggest?

Our website (GreenHalloween.org) has dozens of suggestions for food (treats) and non-food (treasure) ideas and links for where to find them, but some of our favorites are:

Treats

- Individually wrapped organic tea for kids
- Organic and whole food "bars" or cookies
- Organic fruit leather and sticks
- Boxes of organic raisins and, where available, other organic dried fruits
- 100% raw honey or agave sticks (Note: DO NOT GIVE HONEY TO CHILDREN UNDER THE AGE OF TWO)
- Organic, all natural candy or dark chocolate treats made from fairly traded, organic, shade grown cacao (Look for companies that use petroleum free/compostable packaging.)

Treasures

- Bean bags (homemade are best)
- Bells
- Charms and jewels (lead-free)
- Coins (United States or other)
- Mini cookie cutters
- Crystals or polished rocks
- Fortunes (write them with your kids)
- Glass rings
- Jokes or word games
- Large metallic or compostable star confetti
- Homemade play dough
- Recycled pencils
- Seed packets (organic, of course)
- Sea glass

- Soy or beeswax crayons
- Stamps from foreign countries
- Temporary tattoos
- Tops made from recycled plastic
- Yarn bracelets (an easy make-it project)

THINK KIDS DON'T CONSIDER SOAP A TREAT? GIVE THEM A WHIFF OF A BRAND LIKE COUNTRY MEADOW (COUNTRYMEADOWSOAPS.COM) WHICH OFFERS DELICIOUSLY SPICED LITTLE SLICES SPECIALLY PACKAGED FOR HALLOWEEN.

Party Favors and Prizes (for parties and events other than trick-or-treating)
- Coupons for skating, swimming, kids yoga classes, or the zoo
- Egg shakers and other "instruments"
- Non-toxic face painting pencils—we love Lyra water soluble, cosmetic grade products from Germany
- Play silks
- Halloween-themed toys made from natural materials such as a bat pouch necklace or the adorable "Candy Corn Juicy Bug" from DreamALittle7.com
- Free trade yo-yos
- Jump ropes
- Twig pencils
- A green version (meaning recycled) of the classic Frisbee
- Seed-paper bookmarks

No matter what treats or treasures you decide to hand out, the key is to plan. If you wait until five o'clock on Halloween night, you may find yourself buying the same ten-pound bag of chocolate bars you bought last year. Remember that creating a Green Halloween® means thinking outside the *conventional* candy box, so shopping for treats and treasures doesn't have to take place in a grocery store. Check out a local arts and crafts or gardening supply store, and remember that you can always make treasures yourself. If you are going to buy items and your grocery or natural food store doesn't have what you're seeking, you can always buy goodies on the Internet (check out our website for links), but be sure to account for transit time. If you wait until Halloween eve, it will be too late. Lastly, if you can't find these items on your local store shelves, ask for them. Large chain

Like with traditional holiday treats, many items may be unsafe for children under the age of three. We strongly suggest that parents inspect their children's treat bags before allowing their children to eat or play with any items they receive for Halloween.

supermarkets are starting to carry organic and all-natural goods, but more are needed, and remember that the consumer drives demand.

Our last tip on healthy and eco-friendly treats and treasures is to consider buying in bulk and splitting the bounty with friends (you'll save on shipping costs too). For example, Weisenbach Printing (RecycledProducts.com) sells eco-friendly goodies just perfect for Halloween in quantities of 100–1,000+. Their items are also great for schools, businesses, and anyone else giving away large numbers of treats and treasures, and most of their products can be customized with names and logos as well.

One of the reasons people don't offer healthy or eco-friendly treats on Halloween (or other holidays or celebrations) is because they may not see the point of buying these types of products for other people's children. Why should we care what other people's kids eat? The answer is simple: because the well-being of our nation's children affects all of us.

WHY SHOULD YOU CARE ABOUT HANDING OUT CANDY TO OTHER PEOPLE'S CHILDREN ONE NIGHT A YEAR?

Not only are children our future (and who wouldn't want a nation of strong, healthy citizens?), but when people in our country are unhealthy, we all end up paying the price. Obesity alone costs U.S. citizens $117 billion dollars a year, and cancer, heart disease, asthma, and other illnesses deprive us billions more. Many of these problems are preventable or at least may be less severe in the face of healthy living, including avoiding foods that are known to cause harm. And in addition to money, of course, is the human suffering that comes from enduring the battle with any of these diseases. For example, studies show that the quality of life for obese children is equally poor as it is for children with cancer.

When the fact is that one in three children born today will develop diabetes in their lifetime and when, for the first time in history, children are predicted to have shorter life expectancies than their parents, how can we turn a blind eye and claim that it's none of our business what others' children eat?

Remember that while some healthy and eco-friendly treats and treasures may be more expensive than their conventional counterparts, affordable and nearly-cost-free options are widely available.

Three Eek-o-Halloween Initiatives

Like the orange coin box that has changed with the times, so too has the UNICEF trick-or-treat program which now enables individuals, businesses, and schools to raise money for this child-focused cause through online trick-or-treating. Of course, dressing up and trick-or-treating via the Internet may not have the same appeal as going door-to-door, so if you'd like to collect money for UNICEF the "old school" way, you can always pick up a free, snazzy collection box (check UnicefUsa.org for participating stores) or make your own collection can by downloading a just-as-snazzy label from their website. One other modern development: after collection, you can now bring your coins to any Coinstar machine (located in stores nationwide) and make your contribution to UNICEF there. The machine will even print out a receipt for tax purposes.

SINCE 1950, TRICK-OR-TREAT FOR UNICEF HAS BEEN A TIMELESS PROGRAM BELOVED BY KIDS AND ADULTS ALIKE. CREATED, INSPIRED AND POWERED BY KIDS, TRICK-OR-TREAT FOR UNICEF HAS EMPOWERED GENERATIONS TO DO WHATEVER IT TAKES TO SAVE CHILDREN'S LIVES DURING THE HALLOWEEN SEASON.—UNICEF.COM

Global Exchange's Reverse-Trick-or-Treating is another worthwhile Halloween initiative. In 2007, children in 300 cities in the United States and Canada took part in the program by distributing Certified Fair Trade chocolate information cards (while trick-or-treating) to nearly 47,000 households. Reverse Trick-or-Treating seeks to raise awareness of Fair Trade Certified chocolate and to help end unethical labor practices in the chocolate industry, including forced and abusive child labor. For more information or to take part in Reverse Trick-or-Treating, visit GlobalExchange.org.

Green Halloween® is a community movement to create healthy and earth-friendly holiday traditions, starting with Halloween. Green Halloween® has three primary goals: (1) to educate the public about healthy and eco-wise Halloween options; (2) to increase the number of affordable healthy and earth-friendly Halloween products on the market (by creating new ones or by making improvements to existing ones) and, (3) to raise money

In 2007, Milton Elementary School in Delaware, held a post-Halloween candy swap, sponsored by Bella's Cookies (BellasCookies.com, makers of all-natural, organic cookies and the same company that sponsors Milton's recycling program). In just one day, the students collected 215 pounds of junk candy (that would have otherwise been eaten by the students or their parents) in exchange for a Green Halloween® goodie bag that contained healthy and earth-friendly treats and treasures from local businesses. To participate, children had to bring in at least two pounds of candy each. Sounds like a lot? Not if you consider that the average kid hauls home about ten pounds of candy on Halloween night! Thanks to Bella's (and to the parents, students, school, and businesses that supported the swap), instead of downing ten pounds of junk, children took home fruit, organic pretzels, organic chocolate bites, organic cookies, coloring books and recycled-content pencils, honey sticks, temporary tattoos, stamps, and wildlife stickers.

Would you like to create a Green Halloween® candy-swap? Do you have a Hallo-green story you'd like us to know about? Look for ideas and share your stories with us on GreenHalloween.org.

and awareness for health and environmentally-focused non-profit organizations such as Treeswing, a Seattle-based organization combating the childhood obesity epidemic. Green Halloween®'s website has hundreds of ideas for how to make Halloween the fun, memorable holiday it has always been while putting a green twist on many of the un-healthy and un-sustainable traditions we can all live without. For more information on Green Halloween®, or to bring Green Halloween® to your city, go to our website, GreenHalloween.org.

Eek-o-Friendly Costumes

We once knew a little boy who told his mom he wanted to be a stick for Halloween. "A tree, you mean?" she asked. "No. A stick," he said. And so the mother and son set about finding ways to make him a stick. On brown pants and a brown shirt they sewed little knotholes and a few leaves made of felt, and soon that little boy was transformed into the cutest little Halloween stick there ever was. And not only that; his mom was likewise transformed into the proudest mother-of-a-Halloween-stick there ever was, too! When it comes to costumes, let your child's imagination lead the way."—GreenHalloween.org

The scary truth about store-bought Halloween costumes is that nearly all are made with less-than-natural fabrics and many contain harmful chemicals that are absorbed into the body through the skin, mouth (think Dracula teeth), or through inhalation. In 2007 a slew of news reports documented that some costumes and accessories such as costume jewelry, fake teeth, masks, eyelashes, animal noses, swords, and more were known to contain some top eco-evils such as lead, cadmium, phthalates, formaldehyde, and others, none of which, we'd suspect, are welcome in your home.

An obvious way to avoid exposure to costume-laden toxins (which not only harm children and adults wearing the costumes, but also the environment and the people who are exposed to them during manufacturing, washing, and disposal) is to make your own costumes from natural materials you know to be safe. Remember to consider using fabrics you wouldn't be caught dead wearing on any day other than Halloween, such as burlap (a woven material made from jute, hemp, or flax fiber), which can be used to make all kinds of animal, vegetable, and mineral forms. One year my brothers and I used burlap to become Ewoks (from Star Wars), and on another year the burlap tuned me into a chicken. Sure, it's a little scratchy, but it allows for infinite creativity (not just for costumes but for holiday decorating as well) and therefore, in our book, it receives two thumbs up. Way up.

If you don't want to be a furry biped native to the moon of Endor or an egg-making, feathery cluck-clucking farm animal from Iowa, how about using your creativity to make a costume that parallels your passion for all things green? When creating your own costumes, try to use existing materials you have around the house, or get them used at garage sales, thrift shops, or on the Internet. Always put safety first—and if you are not sure about a product or material, forget about it and find something else to use. Here are some eco-themed costume ideas to get you started:

- **Recycling bin.** Wear brown or black clothes and attach all kinds of recycled materials to them: tin cans, pieces of cardboard, and newspaper, for example. Or, fasten suspenders to a cardboard box from which you've cut out the top and bottom. Cover the outside with newspaper and print "Recycling Bin" in large letters, then fasten items to the inside sticking out from the top.
- **Endangered species animal.** Do some research to find animals that are on the endangered list, then pull together a costume. Wear or carry a sign that says "Help! I'm in danger of going extinct!"
- **Layers of the Earth.** Choose different colors of clothing to represent the four layers of the Earth. Label if you like.
- **Tree.** Choose brown pants and shirt. Either attach leaves to upper body or attach small branches with leaves to arms by wrapping them with twine around the arms. Or you can cut leaves from wool felt and sew or glue them onto the shirt.
- **Cloud.** Wear white clothes. Tear or cut old bed sheets into strips. Tie or sew strips to the arms of a shirt so that when the child waves her arms, the strips will move.

Another option is to organize a costume exchange with friends or neighbors. You can also buy used or rent costumes that have been well worn and washed, as exposure to chemicals will be reduced. But we suggest that you continue to say "no" to costumes and parts made from vinyl, especially if they fit in the mouth or cover the face.

MAKE YOUR OWN PERFECTLY NATURAL FACE PAINTS

A test performed by Washington Toxics Coalition and a Seattle-area investigative reporter found that even children's products labeled as "non-toxic" may be laced with known toxins such as lead. Store-bought, "non-toxic" face paints are no different and can expose you and your children to an array of chemicals and preservatives, including BHA, formaldehyde, kohl (due to lead), phthalates, and parabens, which the Environmental Working Group states, "can disrupt the hormone (endocrine) system, and [in one report] were found in the breast cancer tumors of 19 of 20 women studied." Given that most face paints and pencils contain parabens, your best bet is to make them yourself. You might just save some money doing it this way too.

1 tsp cornstarch

½ tsp water

½ tsp all natural diaper rash cream, such as the California Baby brand (we know, we know, it sounds weird, but it works)

1-2 drops natural/organic food coloring

In a small bowl, mix water and cornstarch. Add baby cream and food color and mix a bit more.

Budget101.com can also help to turn you into a Hollywood worthy make-up and wardrobe artist with their list of do-it-yourself, chemical-free or easy to alter recipes for all your kids' costume requests, from the sweet to the gross and ghoulish.

If you wish to buy new, SarahsSilks.com sells costumes made from all-natural silk while MagicCabin.com sells costumes from silk and cotton velour. Although these are more expensive than conventional costumes, they're sturdy enough to be used as dress-up all year long. (Corey's kids especially love Magic Cabin's unicorn and dog costumes.) For wee-ones, choosing chemical-free materials is even more important, so instead of purchasing a fleece bumble-bee or bear bunting (as cute as they are), we suggest pairing Kee-Ka.com's organic cotton pumpkin or pea-themed romper with an organic cotton "Veggin' Out" vegetable-themed cap from UnderTheNile.com. You could always include Under the Nile's organic stuffed carrot, green bean, or eggplant as a soft, safe, chewable costume accessory. Dress yourself as a farmer!

Trick-or-Treat Essentials

Treat and treasure bags are important Halloween accessories and, ideally, should be just as healthy and eco-friendly as the loot they're carrying and the costumes they accompany. Like costumes, many candy carriers contain chemicals (such as lead, cadmium, and phthalates) that can rub off onto treats and treasures as well as onto the hands that carry them. Try to steer clear of carriers made from plastic (also a non-renewable resource) and instead choose those made from natural materials. Old pillow cases may do the trick (and can be decorated for a pre-Halloween-night activity), but for your princess, how about letting her use one of your evening bags (or finding one used at a thrift store)? Your pirate can make and carry a treasure box, hung from a rope. Your hobo can make a bag out of old scraps of fabric, and your gypsy can carry a hand-made, velvet cotton pouch. Other ideas include used or repurposed carriers such as:

- Baby sling (parent)
- Backpack (mountain climber)
- Bowl (chef)
- Brief case (business woman/man or techie)
- Helmet (football player)
- Large envelope (mail carrier)
- Laundry bag (army guy/girl)
- Loosely woven/webbed produce bag (fisherman/woman or Spiderman/woman)

In addition to something to carry treats and treasures, most trick-or-treaters (or their parents) carry some kind of light for safety and fun. Since glow sticks are used briefly, are disposable, and contain chemicals that are best kept out of landfills, they are an

WHY WOOL WORKS FOR HALLOWEEN COSTUMES

You don't have to dress like a sheep to make your costume out of wool, although we certainly have nothing against the idea. Wool is ideal for Halloween costumes because it is naturally flame retardant and therefore does not require chemical fireproofing (which exposes the wearer to toxins linked to cancer and other ailments). Wool is also biodegradable and compostable. If you're not going to use wool, and your kids' costumes are made out of natural, chemical-free materials, it is safer to stay away from capes and other flowing accessories as these could catch fire when walking past candle-lined walkways.

un-green choice, as are flashlights with disposable batteries. Instead, use flashlights or portable LED lights with rechargeable batteries, or flashlights powered by winding a crank or shaking (kids love these). Light sabers and swords can be made by attaching a roll of paper with cut-outs (with tissue behind the cut-outs, if you'd like) onto to a flashlight.

Hosting a Green Halloween® Party or Neighborhood Bash

Decorations

You might be surprised to learn that Halloween is the second biggest holiday for decorating after Christmas. In 2007, consumers spent almost $1.4 billion on everything from life size plastic witches' cauldrons to strings of lighted ghosts to black throw-away plates and orange utensils.

Having a Green Halloween® does not mean your party has to be decoration-free. Gourds, pumpkins, apples, straw, and other items from nature set the mood as accents on front porches and table tops while also reducing the use of paper and plastics. Decorations such as handmade skeleton streamers and colorful recycled and recyclable tableware add a touch of festivity. Ghosts and scarecrows are easy to make from things you have lying around the house, or the parts can be bought inexpensively from a thrift or salvage store. One hundred percent soy or beeswax candles offer cleaner burning ambiance than petroleum-based paraffin candles and can be purchased in the most important colors of the holiday: black, orange, and of course, green. (Always be sure to keep candles and other open flames out of the reach of kids.) Solar, LED, and solar-powered-LED lights are available in spooky and sweet Halloween styles for indoors or out.

If you're committed to a Green Halloween® party, you'll want to avoid paper or plastic tableware that will be tossed afterwards (unless it can be composted). Instead, opt for your regular tableware, pick up some at a yard sale or second hand store, or best of all, ask your guests to bring their own. Another possibility, if you can find some old glass plates, is to decoupage (glue) Halloween images on the underside. (Only the tops of plates decorated in this way should be washed.)

Witch **party**
should you attend?
Ours of course!

Why?
Because it's a
Green Halloween party
with healthy treats and
treasures for all.
Fun! Games!

Join us
Oct. 31
6-8 p.m.
Our house

If you plan to build a haunted house or other large, exterior decoration, check out the salvage stores. They carry everything from old doors to funky chandeliers to a set of squeaky steps.

Whatever you do, remember the 3Rs and 3Gs in all your decorating choices. With just a little planning, you may even be able to decorate your home (or party) in a way that generates zero waste. Also, be sure to display a handmade or purchased sign for your door, lawn, or window to let trick-or-treaters (and their parents) know that you are proud to be a Green Halloween® home and that you're "thinking outside the conventional candy-box" when it comes to the treats and treasures you're giving away. (You can download the Green Halloween® logo to add to your sign at GreenHalloween.org.)

Food

Consider food edible décor. Before your Halloween party, sit down with your kids and make a list of every food you can think of in Halloween colors: black, orange, and green. Then prepare a menu inspired by these color choices. If you've got tweens or teens, feel free to invent gory, scary Halloween names for your colorful creations. Kids included in planning, preparation, and presentation of food will be more likely to eat (and enjoy) it. Be sure to choose fresh, organic, all-natural, whole, and whenever possible, local foods.

Remember to "recycle" (compost) your unconsumed party food, candy (without wrappers), and "natural décor" including jack-o-lanterns. In some areas of the country, all this and more (including food-soiled paper) can be added to your yard waste bin. Don't pass off uneaten candy to someone else this year (other people can do without the chemicals and bad stuff too); recycle it instead!

Activities, Games, and Crafts

If you're hosting a Halloween party, focusing on fun rather than stuff is a great way to keep things green and to break the stuff-equals-fun association for kids. Laughter and good memories are gifts from the heart that can be enjoyed by all and don't cost a dime or increase your carbon footprint.

TRASH-TO-TREASURE: CANDY WRAPPERS

Whether you eat or compost your candy and other treats, keep wrappers out of the landfill by repurposing them into an eco-fabulous accessory such as a purse. Search Google or another engine for "how to make a candy wrapper purse" to find directions on decoupaging a wrapper purse or weaving one completely out of would-be trash. Or, if your Halloween does not include treats or door-to-door procuring, or if you have the patience and creativity of a worm (but the fashion-sense of a diva), Ecoist.com sells ready-made wrapper bags that look chic enough for the runway.

Search through thousands of Halloween party ideas online. But when choosing holiday and party activities, be sure to consider the developmental age and number of kids present as well as how many adults will be available to help, and always be sure to put safety first. GreenHalloween.org has a list of our favorite Halloween activities, but here's a sneak peek at our favorite.

Conjure Halloween fun with a "progressive party." Coordinate with three or more of your neighbors (in lieu of trick-or-treating, or just before it). With the kids already in costume, start at one house, where everyone does one activity and eats one course of food, and then walk with the whole gang to the next house, where the gang will enjoy the next activity. (For younger kids, limit the number homes so they won't become tired and overwhelmed.) Be sure to let your kids ring the doorbell at each house and shout "Trick-or-Treat!" (or "Trick-or-treasure!" or "Happy Halloween/Hallogreen!"). If you'd like, give each child a Green Halloween® treat or treasure and then invite them in for the next activity and course of food. Here is a sample of what you might do:

House #1
- Activity: Decorate trick-or-treat/trick-or-treasure bags.
- Food: Ants on a Log (celery sticks filled with nut butter and topped with raisins. Use pumpkin butter for a Halloween twist!).

House #2
- Activity: Witch's Limbo (put on some fun music and let the kids play limbo with a broom).
- Food: Spooky Spaghetti (look for 100% organic whole wheat or rice noodles with organic sauce).

House #3
- Activity: Make masks out of recycled paper bags. Have lots of glitter, feathers and recycled/repurposed objects to add. After everyone is done, stage a Halloween parade.
- Food: Date Fingers (chopped organic dates rolled in coconut).

House #4

- Activity: Play "Pass The Pumpkin." Have kids sit in a circle and pass small pumpkins or gourds when upbeat music is playing from live instruments or a CD. When the music stops, the child without a pumpkin is out. Continue until there is only one child left. That child may take the pumpkin home. You may want to later give every child a small pumpkin to take home too.
- Food: Warm apple cider simmered with cinnamon sticks. At this time of year you may be able to find fresh-pressed cider from your local farmer.

FOR MORE EEK-O-FRIENDLY HALLOWEEN TIPS AND TRICKS, INCLUDING RECIPES, DECORATING IDEAS, AND INFORMATION ON HOW TO GET YOUR NEIGHBORHOOD OR COMMUNITY INVOLVED, GO TO OUR WEBSITE, GREENHALLOWEEN.ORG. WE'D LOVE TO HEAR YOUR IDEAS TOO!

Here's to a Healthy and Sustainable Rosh Hashana

The holiday of Rosh Hashana, the Jewish New Year (and the month of Elul leading up to it), is a time for shedding spiritual and relationship baggage. It's a time to open up to new possibilities and be grateful for everything you have. More than anything, Rosh Hashana gives us the opportunity for *tshuva*—to return to our best, most full selves. As we turn inward, we have the chance to ask ourselves what impact we want to have on our communities.

Here are some suggestions so you may welcome Rosh Hashana with mindfulness and joy.

Go apple picking. What could be better than dunking for apples you picked yourself, straight from the tree? Many family farms welcome visitors to pick apples, make fresh cider, and tour their grounds. Needless to say, this is a great activity for the whole family. Find a farm near you at PickYourOwn.org.

Avoid the honey bear. Apples and honey are two of the most recognizable Jewish holiday foods. "Colony collapse disorder" (the mass disappearance of bees from hives) indicates that something is awry in the bee community. (Find out more about the potential causes of CCD by doing a web search.) Meanwhile, the ubiquitous honey bear that sits in most of our cabinets tends to be filled with industrially-produced (and not particularly flavorful) honey. This year, dip your apples in delicious, raw honey produced by a small-scale apiary. Try:

- **Bee Raw Honey.** Recommended by The Jew &The Carrot blogger, Eric Schulmiller.
- **Marshall's Honey.** Raw and certified kosher.
- **Tropical Traditions.** Raw and certified kosher.

Make it Maple. Orthodox maple syrup farmer, Rabbi Shmuel Simenowitz, celebrates the New Year with his family by dipping apples into maple syrup from his own trees. Join him in this sweet twist on traditional apples and honey by switching to maple syrup or, better yet, maple butter (swoon!).

Seasonal centerpieces. Instead of fresh-cut flowers that will wilt after a few days, create a sustainable centerpiece to impress your guests. Place 12 heirloom apples or pomegranates in a glass bowl, or place potted fall flowers (chrysanthemums, zinnias, marigolds, etc.) around the table to add seasonal color.

Eat and Learn. Rabbi Shimon said, "If three have eaten at one table and have not discussed words of Torah over it, it is as though they had eaten of the sacrifices of the dead, as it is written (Is. 28:8)." Ask each of your Rosh Hashana guests to bring a reading (e.g., traditional Jewish texts, Hasidic tales, a favorite poem or scene from a play, children's book, etc.) to share on a particular Rosh Hashana-related theme. Need an example? Try "returning," "scarcity and abundance," or "mindfulness." At dinner, ask your guests to share what they brought.

Highlight local flavors. Rosh Hashana falls at a time of year when it's easy to find fresh local vegetables through your CSA (Community Supported Agriculture farm; see LocalHarvest.org for ones near you) or farmers' market. Search the Internet for recipes that highlight autumn fruits and vegetables, especially local delights you might never have sampled before.

Celebrate non-local foods. Pomegranates are an important symbolic food on Rosh Hashana, but are not necessarily local to most regions in America. Instead of eschewing them entirely, take the moment to recognize why you are including this food and how it fits into your celebration. Ask someone at your dinner table to prepare a few words (a poem or fact sheet) about pomegranates, or whatever other food you'd like to highlight.

Kosher organic wine. Serve your friends and family wines from Hazon's kosher, organic wine list at JCarrot.org. The wines on this list are tasty, *hechshered* (having an orthodox kosher certification), and good for the earth. You'll be able to impress your friends as the world's best sustainable sommelier.

Get outside! Rosh Hashana celebrations have the tendency to fall into the rhythm of pray, eat, sleep, pray, eat, sleep...eat. This year, change up that rhythm by finding some time to get outside and enjoy the crisp fall weather. Go for an early morning walk before synagogue, meditate outside in the afternoon, take a walk on the beach (if you're lucky enough to live by one!), or bring your kids to the park after lunch to sing holiday songs. Whatever way you get there, don't wait until *Tashlich* to get outside.

Cast away cleanup. *Tashlich* is one of the most beautiful moments of Rosh Hashana where we head towards a flowing body of water and toss in bread to symbolically cast away our sins. As part of your Rosh Hashana preparation, take a day in the week leading up to the holiday (and bring your friends and kids) to "clean up" the river or watershed where you will perform the tashlich ritual. Collect any garbage or bottles lying about and walk around to get a lay of the land. When you come back the next week, note if you feel a different connection to the space.

Adapted from *The Jew & The Carrot*: Hazon's blog on Jews, food, and contemporary life (JCarrot.org).

KALE WITH LEMON SAUCE

● ● ● ● ● ● ● ● ● ● ● ●

Choose local and organic ingredients whenever possible

INGEDIENTS:
   1/2 bunch Kale, trimmed and washed, chopped roughly
   2 cloves garlic, thinly sliced into "coins"
   1 stalk celery, thinly sliced
      salt to taste
      1 3/4 cups water
      1 lemon
      1 tsp flour (optional)
   2 tbsp butter

DIRECTIONS
   Over medium high heat, sauté vegetables (celery, onion and garlic) in olive oil. Add kale when celery is bright green and garlic has browned a bit. Sauté for a bit, then add water and juice from half the lemon. Cover and let steam for about 7 minutes. The kale should be wilted and still a bit al dente. Remove the kale from the pan, leaving the juices and the other aromatics. Whisk in the flour and add juice from the other half of the lemon. Keep the heat low and whisk in the butter as it melts. Return the kale to the sauce and stir to coat. Serve immediately with some good bread to soak up the sauce. Simple, yet has a sophisticated taste.

Contributed by Wenonah Michallet-Ferrier

Diwali

Diwali, the Hindu Festival of Lights, celebrates the victory of good over evil. Although legends associated with the five-day festival differ in various parts of India, to all it is a time for joyful as well as spiritual celebration. And while aspects of the celebration such as fire crackers and over-consumption have marred its luster in India, most families in the United States celebrate the holiday in a more Earth- and people-friendly way. Fellowship, food, and gifts form the basis for memorable interaction among generations.

One of the most interesting and beautiful of the Diwali customs is making a rangoli. An exquisite, but temporary, welcome mat (not meant to be walked on), originally found outside of homes, a traditional rangoli is carefully created by hand using rice powder, white and colored with dyes, as well as grains, flower petals, and beads, depending on the artist. Making rangoli once was part of a woman's daily tasks, but now rangoli are mainly reserved for holidays such as Diwali when they serve as a stunning greeting to guests.

Rangoli originally were two-foot squares, but now can be as big as a room. Patterns tend to be symmetrical and geometric with most including items from nature like birds, trees, and flowers, or anthropomorphic figures.

If you have space on your driveway or in front of your home, an engaging family project is to research rangoli designs, then follow the outline or design one of your own in the traditional manner outside.

Before you begin, think about materials. You can color organically grown rice as it was done originally by soaking it in dyes from natural sources like tree bark, leaves, flowers, and such, then allowing it to dry before grinding it up into powder or using the grains whole.

If that sounds like a lot of work, consider pre-colored items you have on hand. You are attempting to recreate the *spirit* of the rangoli, not necessarily match the original materials, so choose what you like. Items such as whole wheat flour, sand, cereals, nuts, beans, lentils, and turmeric or other spices, as well as chopped leaves or pine needles, can all be incorporated.

If you want to make a permanent rangoli, use a piece of paper on which you draw the outline of the design, then cover small sections with a water-based glue. Once the glue is laid, begin filling sections with your choice of materials. For small children, leaves and other larger items will make the project less frustrating. Older kids and adults can take pinches of powders and by rubbing forefinger and thumb together, drop bits onto the paper. Doing it this way is tedious but makes it easier to control where powders land.

Everyone can make their own rangoli designs, or you can download and print out many from the Internet (as well as step-by-step instructions).

Here's a design I created:

Thanksgiving

 My sister-in-law Debbie is hands down the best cook I've ever personally known. Every dish she fashions shimmers with tastes that could ordinarily only be mastered by a Cordon Bleu graduate blessed with an exquisite palate, razor sharp knives, and shelves alive with multihued spices with names the rest of us cannot pronounce. Any meal from her hands, no matter how simple the ingredients, transforms into a masterpiece, something to be savored even by one like me who generally misses the taste of food entirely because I eat so fast. Her pasta melts in your mouth. Homely Brussels sprouts become works of art. But the dish that has me salivating as I write this is her apple pie.

Unlike less generous chefs, Aunt Debbie happily offers up the recipe to anyone who asks and sincerely denies the existence of one or more secret ingredients. But when someone not Debbie attempts to replicate her feat, the resulting dessert inevitably tastes—as a judge in a cable TV gourmet cook-off might decree—inexcusably pedestrian.

So through Thanksgiving meals for more than two decades, we looked forward to (and incredibly, left room for) Aunt Debbie's apple pie. Every once in a while someone would contribute a pumpkin or a mince, but those mostly sat undisturbed as the apple disappeared quicker than David Copperfield's elephant, every last crumb devoured as though none of us had eaten in a month.

But one year, Aunt Debbie, for some reason that still has never been adequately explained to *my* satisfaction, decided not to make apple pie. We showed up as usual, downed the feast like a horde of starving teenagers, readied ourselves for the traditional finish, and sat in stunned silence as some other kind of offering was proffered. (I was so shocked that to this day I have no memory of what was served other than that it was definitely ***not*** apple pie!)

We looked at each other—kids and grownups alike. Then we mutely, meekly, and dutifully eased our forks into the not-apple-pie. We murmured compliments to the chef, no one wanting to hurt her feelings, and pushed away from the table as though nothing had happened.

It was the saddest Thanksgiving of my life.

Now that I've had time to ponder the experience (it happened about 15 years ago), the pain of the moment remains, but I realize my disappointment was not all about the apple pie. After all, Debbie and I are friends. I might have called her anytime and beseeched her to make me an apple pie, and I believe she would have done it.

Cheers to you if you choose to green up your Thursday Thanksgiving gathering. But wait, there's a huge problem Just a few hours later, dawns Black Friday, known as the busiest shopping day of the year. How can that possibly be a good thing for greenies? One day we're thinking hard about how we can lessen our impact on the planet, and the next we can't spend up to our credit limit fast enough.

Here's another idea. This year, pledge to celebrate Buy Nothing Day. Early Friday morning, the day after Thanksgiving, instead of jumping into the car to nab the number one spot in line at K-Mart, join others in your community at a crazily creative event like giving away nothing to shoppers who pass by, or helping put an end to mounting consumer debt by cutting up credit cards. Find information and activities near you by doing an online search for Buy Nothing Day.

The problem was, she'd messed with tradition. We'd always had her pie. We looked forward to her pie. All our feelings of gratitude mixed and mingled and played out in this mythical dessert. Her apple pie tied us together in a way that turkey, cranberry sauce, my green bean casserole, our shared history, and in some cases, even DNA, never could. Aunt Debbie's pie *was* Thanksgiving.

This little crack in our family's traditional celebration happened to coincide with our moving out of state, so I can't entirely blame what happened next on Aunt Debbie's innocent abdication of her apple pie-making responsibilities.

But the fact is that the following Thanksgiving, we went out for Chinese.

BEST EVER!

AUNT DEBBIE'S APPLE PIE

● ● ● ● ● ● ● ● ● ● ● ● ●
Choose local and organic ingredients whenever possible

MAKE A BASIC PASTRY DOUGH USING

2 2/3 cups all-purpose flour
1 cup (2 sticks) very cold butter, cut into
  1" pieces
1 tsp. salt
1/2 cup ice water
  Divide the dough in half, flatten each half into a 6" disc, wrap in wax paper and chill at least 30 minutes before rolling out. When ready to roll out chilled dough, let it soften slightly at room temperature. Roll on lightly floured surface to 1/8" thickness. Fit into pie plate trimming the edge even with the lip. Chill while preparing the filling.

FOR THE FILLING:

  2 1/2 lbs tart cooking apples (5 -7) (Granny Smiths are good. I usually use whatever tart apples we have picked ourselves locally.)

  1 cup sugar
  1/4 cup flour
  1 1/2 tsp. cinnamon
  1/2 tsp. ground nutmeg
  1 T. butter

  Peel, core, and quarter the apples lengthwise. Cut the quarters into 1/2" wedges (you should have about 7 cups.) In a medium sized bowl mix the sugar, the flour, cinnamon, and nutmeg. Add the apples and toss to coat them well. Spoon them into the bottom crust, mounding them in the center. Dot the top of the apples with the butter.

  Preheat oven to 425 degrees. On a lightly floured surface roll out the pastry for the top crust. Place the top crust over the apples and trim the overhang to 1/2". Turn the excess top crust under the rim of the bottom crust and crimp decoratively to seal. With the tip of a small knife, cut three steam vents in the top. If desired the top may now be brushed with lightly beaten egg white and sprinkled with 2 T. of sugar. Bake for 40 minutes or until apples are tender when pierced with a knife through one of the steam vents and the crust is golden brown. Transfer to a rack and cool before serving.

No one has to tell you that Thanksgiving in this country is about two things—food and tradition. I'll get to food in a minute.

We Americans are exceedingly proud of our traditions and uncompromising in our tenacity when it comes to carrying them out in exactly the way they have been since time began (or, in the case of watching Thanksgiving football on TV, since 1962). Whether they are based in fact or fable, we defend them vigorously, and woe unto anyone who suggests that perhaps we could be outside breathing fresh air instead of crammed in an overheated living room bug-eyed before the TV, mesmerized by two-story high Shrek and Hello Kitty balloons tugging their handler's arms out of their sockets as they march down New York's Fifth Avenue in a blinding snow storm on Thanksgiving morning.

 And while personally, I believe that watching television on what I consider the quintessential family holiday is an abomination and that sitting next to each other on a couch, my husband stage-whispering shhhhhh in an exceptionally annoyed voice, as a bunch of overpaid guys who graduated from college without learning to read knock each other senseless does not qualify as "family time," I know I'm in the minority.

My point is, Thanksgiving is a tough nut to crack for the newly eco-sensitive. Even if every member of a family converts to vegetarianism, it somehow seems tantamount to treason to eliminate the bird from the table—hence, the invention of tofu turkey.

So my suggestion with Thanksgiving is to rein in your burgeoning holiday eco-zeal just an eensy weensy bit for the sake of family unity. When you plan to revolutionize tradition, there's no reason to bring out the big guns. Start with a bit of undercover work.

For instance, who needs to make a huge deal out of the fact that you're flying in from out of town for the festivities and you're planning to reimburse the universe by purchasing carbon offsets to "pay for the journey." I'm sure you can guess how Uncle Ike might respond to that heartfelt green action!

But if you do decide to spill the beans, you can suggest that Uncle Ike is simply uninformed. After all, if it's good enough for the Detroit Lions, it's good enough for you. "In 2007," you

Lay a piece of recycled or tree free paper at each person's place at the table along with crayons and anything else that could be used to decorate the page. Ask everyone to write on the lower half of the paper one thing they are thankful for, then decorate the sheet however they'd like. Take a photograph ("head shot") of each person using a digital camera.

Before eating, collect all the papers and ask someone to read them.

Later, scan the pages, upload the photos to your computer, add the correct photo to the correct page, then load everything onto one of the online photo sharing services which makes it easy to turn your pages into a slide show. Everyone will have access to the show and can load it onto their computers, make a DVD, or print on recycled paper if they prefer.

can tell him without a hint of eco-superiority tainting your voice, "the 68th Lion's Thanksgiving Day game was 100% carbon neutral with the assistance of Carbon Credit Environmental Services (CCES) of Detroit (GetCarbonCreditCo2.com), so there." (Well, don't say "so there." Remember that eco-superiority thing? But, you have my permission to think it.)

That should open the door a crack. Let's move on to food.

When it comes to the banquet, while I wish the decision were always simple and easy, black and white, do-it-with-your-eyes-closed, that's just not the case. We who are given the opportunity to choose must, as daunting as it sometimes seems, decide between two or more alternatives, none of which is usually perfect. Darn!

Take turkey, for instance. "Free-range" turkeys are touted as best, but as in many other claims of green leanings that perk up our eco-ears, according to the U.S. Department of Agriculture, the term means little—only that birds have "access" to the outdoors. All other aspects of free-range turkeys' lives can be indistinguishable from those of conventionally raised birds. This means they may be subjected to over-crowding, bred to grow at a lightening speed, and experience an exceedingly short lifespan compared to turkeys in the wild (as well as other gross stuff I really don't want to write about here, but if you're interested, you can look up on the Internet).

In addition, even if a free range turkey happens to be raised on a small farm where it is allowed to roam and slaughtered as humanely as possible, but is flown 1,500 miles to get to your local organic market without stopping at "go" and paying his carbon offsets (as you so willingly did), oops, that's a problem.

But what if turkey remains the heart of your Thanksgiving meal? (You're in the majority here: 98% of Americans partake of this particular fowl on this particular holiday. Farmers sold about $3.86 billion worth of turkeys in 2007, which exceeds the total receipts from sales of products such as rice, peanuts, and tobacco, according to the USDA Economic Research Service.) The answer is to seek out a local farmer who raises turkeys organically, meaning without pesticides, antibiotics, nitrates, or nitrites, in uncrowded conditions where they can graze on natural edibles (i.e., grass, bugs, weeds, acorns, and the occasional bottle cap). In other words, as you and I would like them to be raised (except for the bottle cap) were we inclined to do it ourselves, which of course we're not, so that's the point.

Kosher turkeys are another alternative, especially if they are locally raised and you can visit the farm. According to Kosher laws, animals should be cared for as ethically, and slaughtered as humanely, as possible. However, GoVeg.com and a number of other websites point out that correct Kosher treatment may be the exception rather than the rule, especially in large operations. If this is a concern to you, do your research before making a decision.

You may have heard of "heritage" turkeys (as well as other foods, seeds, and stock). These are not identified as such by the USDA, and the definition varies. According to the American Livestock Breeds Conservancy (ALBC-USA.org, an organization working to preserve rare breeds and genetic diversity in farm animals), heritage turkeys "are defined by the historic, range-based production system in which they are raised." Turkeys must meet the following criteria to qualify as a heritage turkey by their definition: naturally mating, long productive outdoor lifespan, and slow growth rate. For a more thorough description, see the ALBC-USA.org website.

Consumers should be on the lookout for turkeys labeled "heirloom" which may be from older breeds but which, according to the Heritage Turkey Foundation, "can't mate naturally, do not mature like true heritage turkeys, and don't taste as good."

Unfortunately, turkeys raised on farms where they are treated ethically and humanely are more expensive than frozen birds whose short lives were miserable by any standard, and who, once no longer of this Earth, are carted across the country by the freezer-load.

The reason, of course, is that Americans love a bargain, and it's difficult to make huge profits when ethical treatment is more important than money.

But since Thanksgiving is about gratitude, we might want to put a lid on our bargain hunting instincts for once and give thanks that in general, we pay less of our total household income for food than almost anyone else on earth. The exact percentage ranges according to income levels, with the larger percentage spent by those in lower income brackets. But regardless of how it's counted, at under 10% of our expendable income, we have it good

DEFINITIONS AND LABELING FOR TURKEY

NATURAL—Turkey containing no artificial flavor or flavoring, coloring ingredient, chemical preservative, or any other artificial or synthetic ingredient, and is minimally processed (a process which does not fundamentally alter the raw product) may be labeled "natural." The label must explain the use of the term "natural" (e.g., no added colorings or artificial ingredients; minimally processed).

NO ANTIBIOTICS—The term "no antibiotics added" may be used on labels for poultry products if the producer sufficiently documents to the Food Safety and Inspection Service (FSIS) that the animals were raised without antibiotics.

NO HORMONES—Hormones are not allowed in raising poultry. Therefore, the claim "no hormones added" cannot be used on the labels of poultry unless it is followed by a statement that says, "Federal regulations prohibit the use of hormones."

ORGANIC—The Final Rule for the new organic standard was published on December 21, 2000, and it offers a national definition for the term "organic." This rule details the methods, practices, and substances that can be used in producing and handling organic crops and livestock, as well as processed products.

The Final Rule specifically prohibits the use of genetic engineering methods, ionizing radiation, and sewage sludge for fertilization.

This information is provide by the Food Safety & Inspection Service, USDA.

BUT IT SAYS ORGANIC ON THE FRONT OF THE PACKAGE

Part 1

Now that "organic" has gone mainstream, along with the move toward healthier foods, you've probably noticed how everybody from meat packers to Jim down the road has seized on the word as a way to riches. If you are interested in preserving "strict" organic standards, visit OrganicConsumers.org.

Organic with USDA seal=95% organic ingredients

Organic claim on the front of package=70%+ organic ingredients

List of organic ingredients on side panel=Less than 70% organic ingredients

Part 2

You know those labels on fruits and veggies that are so hard to get off? They actually mean something!

◉ A four-digit or (soon, a three-digit number since they've run out of four) means it's **conventionally grown.**

◉ A five-digit number beginning with 9 means it's **organic.**

◉ A five-digit number beginning with 8 means it's **genetically modified.**

The Produce Marketing Association developed this system.

---

compared to Germany (10.9%), Japan (13.4%), Mexico (21.7%). China (28.3%), Russia (36.7%), Indonesia (49.9%), and most other countries, industrialized or not.

And sometimes our infatuation with cheap undermines our best interests. We know for a fact that organically raised foods are healthiest and cause the least harm to us, the environment, and those who grow them, yet we continue to feed our families strawberries layered with pesticides because they cost one-third of what local organic ones do. We argue fiercely that we cannot afford organic foods when we should, perhaps, be arguing that we must.

So how can you manage to pay for a locally raised organic free range turkey? Here are a few possibilities:

◉ Let's say you call up your local farmer and discover that her turkeys sold for $2.50 per pound last Thanksgiving. You're going to need an 18-pound turkey to feed the brood this year. Add a bit for inflation. Do the math. (I'm terrible at that, so I'm not going to do it for you.) Divide the total by the number of months you have until Thanksgiving. Start saving that amount each month. (My guess, even with my limited math skills and the fact that I don't drink coffee, is that your monthly total will amount to less than a daily grande decaf low-fat caramel macchiato medium foam from your drive-through espresso stand.)

◉ If you normally take responsibility for purchasing the ingredients for every dish, consider whether you might eliminate something. Do you need mashed potatoes and roasted potatoes and sweet potatoes and corn? Could you just happen to forget to buy rolls this year? Will someone starve to death before the main meal if you eliminate the chips and dip?

◉ Plan for enough to feed the whole caboodle, with no leftovers. I realize this might sound like an even worse idea than not eating turkey at all, but maybe there's someone out there who doesn't actually *like* turkey all that much and would be willing to forego sandwiches and tetrazzini and settle for some homemade soup from the bones of one heck of a green bird, so I feel it's my duty to at least offer up the idea.

◉ Host a pot-luck Thanksgiving. You provide the turkey and ask your guests to contribute the rest. That's how our family does it, and we've yet to hear one complaint, although we can't deny that this might be because everyone is too busy enjoying the food.

Assuming that you've gone for any one of my genius suggestions and find yourself the proud owner of the perfect eco-gobbler, that's just one part of the challenge. What about the rest of the meal?

Of course, buying organic makes sense. If you need any convincing, there are hundreds of studies available that prove it. I'll share just a few to bolster your argument when you present the idea to your family:

- A peer-reviewed study published in January 2008 showed the urine and saliva of children eating a variety of conventional foods contained pesticides known to cause neurological problems in youngsters. Once children switched from conventional to organic foods, the measurable levels of pesticides disappeared. While pesticides used on "children's foods" were reduced by 57% after the passage of the Food Quality Protection Act in 2006, the amount remains too high according to many scientists.

- Organically grown fruits and vegetables have significantly higher levels of cancer-fighting antioxidants than conventionally grown foods, as demonstrated in a study using corn, strawberries, and marionberries (a type of blackberry), published in the *Journal of Agricultural and Food Chemistry*, a peer-reviewed journal of the American Chemical Society.

- Research published in 2001 showed that conventionally grown fruit and vegetables in the United States have about half the vitamin content of their counterparts in 1963. This study was based on comparing published U.S. Department of Agriculture figures.

- A Danish Institute of Agricultural Research and the University of Newcastle's study showed that cows raised on an organic diet produce milk with 50% more Vitamin E and 75% more beta carotene than conventionally farmed cows. The organic milk has two to three times more of several antioxidants along with higher levels of omega 3 essential fatty acids that provide protection from heart and other diseases.

- The United Nations Food and Agricultural Organization (FAO) stated, "It has been demonstrated that organically produced foods have lower levels of pesticide and veterinary drug residues and, in many cases, lower nitrate contents. Animal feeding practices followed in organic livestock production also lead to a reduction in contamination of food products of animal origin."

WALK IT OFF

Aside from the fact that the food you eat may not be organic, eating too much of it, as you well know, can adversely affect your health. At the very least, prepare to heft yourself out of the chair after the meal and take a walk. Maybe you'll burn off a few calories, but it will take a lot more than a little stroll to equal the intake of a simple holiday feast.

Here, for instance, is what I might eat on Thanksgiving:

6 ounces white and dark meat turkey	340 calories
½ cup stuffing	180
1 roll	110
1 pat of butter	45
½ cup green bean casserole	225
½ cup cranberry sauce	190
Salad with non-fat dressing (stop laughing)	100
1 celery stick with cream cheese	45
1 glass cider	120
1 piece of apple pie	410
Total	1,765 calories

In order to walk off this meal I would need to walk *17.6 miles*.

So I'm thinking that a good incentive to avoid overeating would be to visit the Thanksgiving Calorie Counter (Walking.About.com) *before* Turkey Day and plan out what I want to eat. This way I can choose to consume a little less so I'll have to walk a little less.

Knowing the facts, you may want to buy organic, but your brain and your pocketbook are screaming TOO EXPENSIVE! We talked turkey about this issue, but when it comes to fruits, veggies, and some other foods, fortunately, there are generally far more choices than with the big bird. Most large supermarket chains carry some organic produce, although it may have been brought in by a slow boat from some country you've never heard of half way around the world. One way you can help local farmers is to ask the manager of your market whether they carry locally grown organic produce, and if not, would they consider doing so.

If we were paying for actual food, the price of what we eat would be reduced by as much as 80%. Between 1990 and 2000, consumer spending for food increased by 37% with marketing costs responsible for almost all of the increase. As some farmers have pointed out, the packaging for the product costs more than they are paid for the ingredients.

Other ways to save money while shopping organic:

- Create your own co-op to buy in bulk. See if you can strike up a deal to buy a few bushels of organic squash. Split the bounty among family and friends, and be sure to offer your famous Thanksgiving recipe for butternut squash casserole or ask the farmer from whom you've purchased for his tasty suggestions. This works whether we're talking produce or bulk organic packaged food from a warehouse. Buying in bulk always makes financial sense as long as the food is eaten and not left to rot in the bottom drawer of the fridge.

- Plan to freeze it yourself. All that bounty bought in bulk can be frozen. So the week before Thanksgiving, assemble a group, and while they're cutting up green beans, carrots, cauliflower, or turnips in anticipation of the big day, why not make use of their time and knife skills to load up your (and their) freezer? At other times of the year, ask your local farmer what preparation is necessary for freezing. And if sterilizing jars sounds like a fun way to spend your time, you just may be ripe for some old fashioned canning or jam making. This could be another shared, pre-Thanksgiving activity. Homemade apple sauce is a great treat, is easy to make, and can be frozen. Just wash organic apples well, slice (I leave the skin on), toss into a pot, add a little cider or water, then let the boiling begin. Stir, pop in a bit of honey and/or cinnamon to taste. If you like your applesauce smoother, whirl it in a blender before freezing. Let cool, then freeze in batches.

- If you are not buying every bit of your Thanksgiving meal locally and plan to use some canned or packaged items, many supermarket chains now carry store brand organic items that are likely less expensive than name brands. And if you can't find frozen or organic canned, regular canned fruits tend to have less pesticide residue than those same fruits do when fresh. Since fruits for canning don't have to look perfect, farmers can use fewer pesticides, and the fruit is usually washed several times before processing.

◉ Ignore that warning in your head, *You will die if you eat an apple that is not perfectly red, round, and as free of blemishes as America's next top model.* We're a nation of bratty food wusses, trained to purchase only flawless fresh fruits and vegetables. Blemishes generally don't impact the safety or healthfulness of foods. Know the exceptions, such as green potatoes or anything slimy or, other than mushrooms, moldy (that's a joke). But in general, if you find a bruised or spotted specimen, ask for a discount and you just might get it. Then cut around any area that looks suspicious or cook well to kill off the potential for sending you or your Thanksgiving guests to the hospital, which would do nothing for your reputation, much less ours.

◉ Just like with every other shopping trip, take a list and stick to it when stopping at a farmer's market. Be strong, be tough, sing a few verses of "I am woman, hear me roar," if you have to, but never, ever, ever pick up an eggplant just because it's so shiny you could use it for a makeup mirror or an heirloom tomato because its aroma seduces you the way your husband used to.

◉ Watch for coupons, both online and from your local organic market. Sign up for e-newsletters which sometimes contain recipes and valuable money saving ideas, along with great advice. Speaking of which, what are you going to do with all the money you'll save taking these hints? Think about it. Hey, maybe you can buy a free range organic turkey and contribute it to your local food bank!

◉ Be aware that items that have just come into season will be more expensive. Wait a week and see if the price comes down. If you absolutely, positively, cannot wait, buy a single one and delight in it.

◉ Purchase the most of what is least expensive at the moment. Eat the way our recent ancestors did, before refrigeration allowed us to hold onto lettuce until it melts into goo. In cold winter climates, this means buying veggies like organic potatoes, sweet potatoes, beets and other root vegetables, carrots, or leafy greens. Of course, if you live in Hawaii, California, or Florida, "local" usually offers many more choices year 'round.

- Join a local food co-op. You may be able to work off the cost of your turkey in just a few hours.

- My final, and if I must say so myself, brilliant money saving tip has nothing to do with actual food. It has to do with memory and cars. Come on now, let's admit we all know the routine. We hop into the SUV and head to the farmer's market, stock up on squash and potatoes for T-day. Once home, we realize we've forgotten the cinnamon and butter. Send someone to get 'em. Later that day we open the fridge and oops, no flour for the gravy. By the time we're done, we've made three or four trips, and thus added embarrassingly to the green house gas situation. Might as well have bought everything at once at the big box store down the street. So while we may not be saving money on the actual food, by making only one trip instead of four, we're saving money on gas, wear and tear on the car, and greenhouse gas emissions which in turn means we should have more money for organics or at least a clearer conscience.

In case you've been asleep in the aisle of your local grocery and are oblivious to the trend, the most recent food craze, aside from organic, is buying local. While the concept makes a lot of sense when you realize how far supermarket food travels to get to us, the question remains, what exactly is local? No definitive (or USDA sanctioned) definition may exist, but it seems to me this is question is of the common sense variety, akin to wondering whether a pie can be called blueberry if it's made of pears!

"Local" first of all means my backyard. I plant the seeds, water, and watch as my food grows. Local. (The added benefit, of course, is that I know for sure that it was raised without unpronounceable stuff sprayed all over it, and besides, nothing matches the flavor of an heirloom tomato warm from the vine, even if it's the only one that ripens—the others fall off way before their time when I happen to be out of town and can do nothing but let them lie and become one with the soil.) Next would be neighborhood farms, let's say within huffing and puffing distance for me. With no access to those, I'd say five to twenty miles. Many people define "local" as having been farmed no more than 100 miles from the

WHAT A SHAME!
According to a study by the U.S. Department of Agriculture, we waste 96 billion pounds of food in America each year. That turns out to be:

- 263,013,699 pounds of food wasted each day...

- 10,958,904 pounds wasted each hour...

- 182,648 pounds wasted each minute...

- 3,044 pounds of food wasted in America each second!

market or taking no more than one day to reach market. Sounds reasonable. Whatever the definition, local is good for the planet.

For instance, the Leopold Center for Sustainable Agriculture compared what it takes to haul food from other states into Iowa with semi trailer trucks versus hauling by small light trucks within the state. Simply upping the in-state number by 10% would result in an annual fuel savings ranging from 294,000 to 348,000 gallons and yearly emissions reductions ranging from 7 million to 7.9 million pounds.

And last year, the University of Washington predicted that if *half* of all King County's approximately 1.8 million residents ate a locally grown Thanksgiving dinner instead of an "imported" one, they could avoid contributing to emissions equal to 2.4 million vehicle miles.

In addition, are most of us are aware that those grapes we use to garnish our Thanksgiving dessert may have spent two weeks traveling to get here before being placed in bins where they might languish another few days before we select the lucky ones and bring them home? Fresh, they're not.

The main constraint on shopping at your local farmer's homestead is the time of year. Unless you live in a temperate climate or are blessed with a heated greenhouse, obtaining fruits and vegetables locally 12 months a year means that at some point in the summer you may be inundated by zucchini and by January you're beginning to hate turnips with a passion usually reserved for politicians. Not sure what's in season and available in your neck of the woods at the end of November? Find out by checking 100MileDiet.org or LocalHarvest.org.

IF THERE'S SIMPLY NOTHING TO SATISFY YOU LOCALLY AS YOU PREPARE FOR THANKSGIVING, GO FOR THE NEXT BEST THING, PACKAGED ORGANIC.

◉ Although carbon footprint is an issue with shipping, you can order organic via the web no matter where you live. DiamondOrganics.com and AzureStandard.com are two alternatives. (Like many other online food vendors, Diamond Organics offers nationwide free shipping.) Even Amazon.com has an "organic and natural" section which often offers discounts on specific items.

- Check out local bakeries for organic rolls.
- Organic dried fruits make a lovely hostess gift as well as a nice addition to the T-Day meal.
- How about trying organic quiche from DiamondOrganics.com for an appetizer?
- Organic seasonal apples, pears, vegetables, and gift baskets can be ordered nationwide from companies like Callie's Organics (CalliesOrganics.com).

Q: When are turkeys thankful?

A: When the cook is vegetarian.

When I became a vegetarian at the age of 15, I received a lot of funny looks and derogatory responses. Most people probably thought I'd adopted vegetarianism as mindlessly as I had the white lipstick I sported at the time. And while my lip color probably changed a dozen times before I graduated, I've been a vegetarian for almost 20 years.

It wasn't as though I woke up on my fifteenth birthday and announced my new dietary proclivity. Even as a three-year-old, I sometimes refused to eat meat. (One day my mom saw that I wasn't eating a piece of chicken and asked, "Are you going to be a vegetarian when you grow up?" "No," I replied, "I'm going to be a nurse.")

In any case, as a vegetarian, Thanksgiving has always presented a challenge, not for me, but for people around me. "What on Earth are you going to eat?" they ask in dismay, overlooking a table bursting with sweet potatoes, green beans, salads, and rolls, not to mention apple pie. Meat eaters often treat my decision not to eat turkey like epicurean treason. I've been told more than once that I just don't get what Thanksgiving is all about. Funny; I thought it was about being thankful.

Actually, I have more of a connection to Thanksgiving than many people because my great-great-great-great-and-so-on-and-so-forth-forever-and-ever-amen grandfather was William Brewster, the minister on the Mayflower (of course, by now he probably has hundreds of thousands of descendants, so maybe you're one too). But my point is that I'm here to assert that a having a vegetarian Thanksgiving is a valid option, and I'd like to use my Thanksgiving bloodline to leverage my case: Thanksgiving can be celebrated just as well without dining on our feathered friends.

Q: What's the key to preparing a reduced footprint, low-carbon Thanksgiving meal?

A: Go turkey-free.

According to a 2006 United Nations Food and Agricultural Organization report, the livestock sector is responsible for 18% of all carbon emissions, whereas transportation accounts for just 13%. Further, a 2005 University of Chicago study demonstrates that making the change from a meat-based diet to a plant-based one would reduce your carbon footprint as much as swapping an SUV for a sedan.

Where to Find Your Choice Turkey

	Commercially Grown Frozen Turkey	Commercially Grown Free-Range	"Locally" Grown	Organic (USDA accredited)	Heritage	Kosher
Where to find	Local supermarkets	Local supermarket and on-line	LocalHarvest. org, TheDailyGreen. com	LocalHarvest. org, TheDailyGreen. com	Heritage Foods USA. com	Local kosher markets or online

Q: What to do if you don't eat turkey?

A: Adopt one instead.

Okay, perhaps the thought of inviting a turkey to sit next to Uncle Fred at this year's Thanksgiving dinner is a little unappetizing, and maybe it's true that adopting a turkey won't make a significant dent in global warming, but if you're going to go veggie, why not start a new family tradition and support an organization working hard to save turkeys from becoming someone else's meal? For more information, go to AdoptATurkey.com.

Drinks

- If you can't locate local organic eggnog or would like to add some spirit to what you purchase, try Papagayo organic white rum, imported from Paraguay and distributed through MaisonJomere.com.

- Organic cider is generally non-alcoholic. But if you're craving something stronger, how about artisanal cider, an alcoholic beverage fermented from 100% freshly expressed apple juice made from apples which have been sourced from the same geographic region where the cider is produced. Find a local provider by doing an online search.

- To finish the meal, try organic Fair Trade coffee from the WomensBeanProject.org which teaches job readiness and life skills through employment in a gourmet food production business. Or check out Caffelbis.com for shade grown, organic, Fair Trade coffee from an all-women consortium of growers trying to break the cycle of abuse.

CAN'T BE "BEET!"

BEET HUMMUS

● ● ● ● ● ● ●

Choose local and organic ingredients whenever possible

SERVES 10

This brightly colored dish can be an exciting alternative to a regular hummus appetizer. It's packed with flavor as well as healthy antioxidants and also offers a nice source of protein.

INGEDIENTS:

2-3 large beets (about a pound)*
1/3 cup sesame oil
1 medium onion, chopped
1 tbsp ground cumin
1/8 tsp cayenne pepper (optional)
14 oz can white cannellini beans
1 tablespoon tahini
1/3 cup plain yogurt
3 garlic cloves, chopped
¼ cup lemon juice
½ cup vegetable stock
Salt and pepper to taste

*In a time crunch, 2 cans of canned beets can also work

DIRECTIONS

Place beets in a pot of boiling water and cook for 30-35 minutes until soft. In the meantime, sauté onions with the cumin and cayenne pepper in the oil for 5 minutes until soft and slightly clear.

Place cooked and peeled beets in a food processor with onions, beans, tahini, yogurt, lemon juice, garlic, and stock until smooth. Add any remaining oil and process until all ingredients are combined. Place in refrigerator and serve at room temperature. Serve with whole wheat pita slices or hearty grain bread.

Contributed by Mary Purdy, certified nutritionist and registered dietitian. Seattle, WA, www. NourishingBalance.com, adapted from a recipe by Kay Scarlett

Thanksgiving Three Ways

This chart offers some ideas for evolving from your traditional holiday meal to one that is better for you and the planet. Want to try something organic? Here are some (not all, that's for sure), suggestions. And if you'd like to bring in some new flavors, why not try a choice from the third column. To tempt your palate, you'll find the recipe for beet hummus in this book. The rest of Mary Purdy's scrumptious alternatives are on our website, CelebrateGreen.NET.

Traditional	Organic	Healthy Alternative
Dips and chips	Make "chips" from organic veggies including potato, sweet potato, and carrots, or use fresh, raw veggies. Make dip base from organic yogurt, sour cream, or tofu.	Beet Hummus on whole grain pita wedges
Turkey	See the previous discussion on turkey.	Tempeh (a form of tofu) Croquettes with Mushroom Flourish
Gravy made with pan leavings, flour, and canned stock	Organic ingredients available, or buy ready-made organic.	N/A
Sweet potatoes with marshmallows	Use organic sweet potatoes and leave off marshmallows, or make marshmallows from scratch using organic ingredients, where available.	Sweet Potato and Parsnip Whip
Canned cranberry sauce	Use fresh whole and organic berries.	Cranberry apple relish
Green bean casserole: frozen green beans, canned bean sprouts, canned mushroom soup, canned water chestnuts, cheddar cheese, canned fried onions	Fresh, organic beans and sprouts. Organic canned soup and water chestnuts. Organic cheese. Fry organic onions yourself in organic grapeseed or other high heat oil, or leave off.	Zesty Green Beans with Triple Nut Topping
White rolls with butter	Organic wheat, spelt, or rice flour with organic butter or coconut butter.	Whole Grain Orange Raisin Bread
Eggnog	Organic available ready-made.	Spicy Chai Tea
Apple pie with ice cream	Organic ingredients or ready-made available.	Gingerbread with Lemon Coulis and Winter Fruits

Winter

Christmas Traditions

dECOrating Tips

Close your eyes and think about your favorite holiday. What comes to mind? What do you see? What do you hear? What do you smell? For many of us, the atmosphere and ambiance that surround life's special occasions ignite fond memories. Decorations can play a large role in our family traditions, setting the mood and enhancing our experiences. Putting the green in Christmas decorating, like every other holiday, can be simple, affordable, and fun for the whole family (not to mention beneficial and wise).

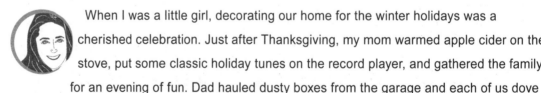

When I was a little girl, decorating our home for the winter holidays was a cherished celebration. Just after Thanksgiving, my mom warmed apple cider on the stove, put some classic holiday tunes on the record player, and gathered the family for an evening of fun. Dad hauled dusty boxes from the garage and each of us dove in searching for our favorite holiday decorations: a delicate heirloom glass ornament, a wooden reindeer mom had bought on a trip to Hawaii when she was a teenager, droll little mice she'd handcrafted, or a worn copy of *The Night Before Christmas*. Within hours our desert abode transformed into a winter wonderland where Santa would soon make his annual visit (somehow managing to expertly steer his flock of reindeer away from our roof's solar panels).

Decorations were rarely purchased new, although some, like ornaments, were given to us as gifts. And contributions made in school by my brothers and I, no matter how pitiable they might look in others' eyes, were displayed proudly. We learned to cherish decorations not because they were expensive or store-bought, but because they held significance.

Whether decorations were purchased, received as gifts, or handmade, all of our décor was saved and reused. The more these decorations aged, the more cherished they became, until at some point a few reached celebrity status. One such decoration, Elfie the elf, became the stuff of legend. Elfie couldn't help but make us giggle with his plump belly, pointed hat, cream-colored face, painted eyes, and cloth-covered wire arms and legs. Despite his scraggly appearance, Elfie was so revered that each year, instead of a star, this impish sprite clung to the tip of our Christmas tree. Elfie was venerated because he had been topping trees since my father was a little boy. Elfie is now celebrating the holidays with his third generation of children. Every December he gazes benignly from his place of honor, and if I have anything to say about it, he will continue to forever. Elfie's story illustrates why reducing and reusing are not only eco-wise, but meaningful as well.

3 R's Decorating

During the winter holidays, Americans throw away 25% more trash than they do the rest of the year. Aim to go zero waste with your holiday décor this year by saying no to anything disposable. Instead of buying decorations that can't be reused, recycled, composted, or consumed, look for décor that is earth- and people-friendly. Applying the three green Rs to your holiday decorating choices is also easy to do and can inspire creative family traditions that will be remembered for a lifetime.

Let's briefly check the 3Rs and see how they can be applied to Christmas decorating.

Reduce

Reduce the number of decorations you acquire by focusing on *quality* décor that will be meaningful and make impressive contributions to your family's traditions year after year. Instead of filling your shopping cart with items boasting the life span of a fruit fly (and that will most likely end up in a landfill), consider investing in or crafting a small number of decorations that make a visual impact and mean something to you and your family. Make a ceremony of packing them away and preserving them so they can be used over and over. Try also to reduce the number of decorations you buy that are made with petrochemicals (unless the items are recycled) and other unsustainable materials. Lastly, keep in mind that decorating in a simple and uncluttered fashion can look modern and sophisticated.

Tips:

- Make that decorating list and stick with it. Whether you like to stock up before the holidays or during the sales following, you'll save money and the Earth's resources by buying only what is on your list.
- The same is true of shopping online. Try to avoid "trolling" your favorite sites unless you are looking for a specific item. You might even want to take yourself off store e-mail lists to avoid being tempted with items you'd love to have, but don't need.
- Be willing to make a long-term commitment. Will the item you're buying last and play a role in future holidays? If you're not sure, leave the store without the item. Still want it a week later? You can always go back.
- Reduce waste and save money by just saying no to disposable decorations.
- If you have the option of buying two similar decorations, choose the one with less packaging.
- Before purchasing an item, ask yourself if you could substitute something you have at home or make a similar stand-in for a more personal (and most likely much less expensive) solution.
- Reduce your eco-footprint and support your local economy by buying decorations created by local artisans. Farmer's markets and street or holiday craft fairs are great for finding affordable, unique, and locally made treasures.

Reuse

Reusing is one of the best methods of staying green and decorating for your holidays, and it offers ample opportunities to find creative uses for items you already own. Refurbish older decorative items that have lost their charm or repurpose objects that are generally used in other ways. Before you toss it in the trash or give it away, consider whether it could be turned into an inspired decoration.

Why buy a new cheese tray for your Christmas celebration when you can make new use of an extra piece of tile or a wood cutting board? Wreaths fade and grow dusty after awhile. Pick a new theme and reuse the basic form, selecting whatever items you'd like and attaching with wire. Add a bright fabric bow cut from an outdated clothing item or table cloth and you've made something old new again.

Tips:

- Rent or borrow decorative items instead of buying new ones. If you are going to purchase decorations, check out eBay.com, Craigslist.org, Freecycle.com, garage sales, and thrift and consignment stores before buying new.
- FamilyFun.com has some great ideas for making decorations out of previously used materials nearly everyone has around their home. Check out their "Grocery Bag Gingerbread Folk" and "Pie Plate Ornaments" for starters.
- Arrange a decorations exchange with friends or family. Those stuffed snowmen that used to charm you, but now appear as exciting as worn out shoes, could be a hit with a family that feels the same about their Santa collection.

 Once you've chosen a color scheme for the holidays, look through your house and gather all the items with those colors in them. Whatever could add color, regardless of where it currently resides in your home, can enhance the festivity without costing anything. Search for pillows, art, fabric, towels, clocks, candle sticks, pieces of paper, utensils, etc. In our house, I use a red wool throw, red towels and wash cloths, and green vases. I've even been known to take red shirts and button them over throw pillows and clip a small evergreen sprig, tie it with a ribbon, and fasten to the shirt's pocket. Instant celebration!

Recycle

When you're thinking about ways to support recycling with holiday decorations, remember to use or buy items made from recycled materials instead of those containing only virgin resources. Also, consider giving priority to decorative products that can later be recycled if they cannot be reused. This way, you're including recycling before, during, and after your celebration.

As a child, I remember making great use of the greeting cards our family received. We created all kinds of things from them, but one winter we made placemats from holiday cards we'd collected over the years. We gave some of the placemats to a local retirement home and kept others to use for our own holiday celebrations. We reused those recycled Christmas card placemats for years, and it will come as no surprise to you that they are still being enjoyed by my own kids. The mats are now part decoration and part family history. It's hard to imagine that any store-bought placemats, as beautiful as they might be, could create the same degree of joy and excitement these cardboard heirlooms do each December when they are unearthed and laid on our table.

Tips:

- If you're buying decorations, look for those that are made from recycled materials such as paper, plastic, rubber, and glass. Eco-Artware.com has decorative items made out of recycled tea bags, vinyl records, and Scrabble tiles.
- Acquaint yourself with what can and cannot be recycled where you live, and be sure to check the labels for items you're planning to buy.

DIY Decorations

One green mantra you know well is, "Go local!" So when you're thinking about holiday decorations, who could be closer to your home than you? DIY (do-it-yourself) projects offer the opportunity to utilize local talent and reduce, reuse, and recycle while at the same time encouraging your creativity.

 Finding ways to incorporate recycling into holiday décor can be a family activity that children of all ages will fondly remember. When I was a kid, most of my family's decorations for every holiday, but especially Christmas, were made by hand by my mom who was both frugal and creative, a winning combination for green decorating. From holiday-themed table cloths to centerpieces to seasonal throw pillows, my mom made it all, often from found objects, scraps of fabric, and recyclables. Better still, she found ways to engage us kids in the creative process, and we loved decorating the house with our own handiwork.

If you'd like to make decorations for an upcoming holiday or event but don't feel particularly inspired, take a look at magazines or watch a decorating show on TV for ideas, then replicate them with recycled materials and eco-friendly alternatives. Have you ever seen those shows where experts take a room expensively decorated for Christmas, then find ways to echo the look and feel for pennies on the dollar? You can work the same magic with holiday decorating by applying green principles (such as the 3Rs) and a little creativity to the decorative process.

Do you own a gold lame dress you won't wear again in 100 years? Cut it up and use the fabric for placemats or a designer-look tablecloth. Has your mom offered to lend you her silver pieces and china? Fantastic! Can banners, place cards, and wine or cheese menus be fashioned from recycled or reused materials such as paper, fabric, or ribbon? Excellent. You're well on your way. Whatever your choices, if they incorporate actions taken to reduce some impact on the planet, you've done an excellent job. And when your friends and family ooh and ah over your decorations and ask where you got them, you *might* just consider going DIY for all of your holiday décor.

Like many busy people, though, you may not have the time or inclination to create your own Christmas decorations, or you may want to purchase items to accent handmade creations. Why not join the global effort to help people and the planet by purchasing products made by other individuals? According to BuyHandmade.org, "The accumulating environmental effects of mass production are a major cause of global warming and the poisoning of our air, water, and soil. Every item you make or purchase from a small-scale independent artist or crafter strikes a small blow to the forces of mass production." On their website, you can join the pledge to buy only handmade during the holiday season and find links, such as to Etsy.com, where you can choose from thousands of handmade products including decorations for holidays and celebrations year-round.

Tips:

- For some easy and child-friendly Christmastime do-it-yourself decorating projects, consider making gingerbread houses, stringing popcorn and/or cranberries chains (or making chains from recycled or tree-free paper), or ornaments from objects in nature and from around the house. These traditional and festive family activities create invaluable memories and contribute to your home's holiday "look" without taking much away from the planet.

- Imagine the possibilities with silk. DIYers can dye their own silks for use as decorative table cloths, runners, and more. A wonderful aspect of this is that you can choose any color scheme you like. You're not locked into the "Christmas look of the year." Seek out Peace Silk (humane) options from AuroraSilk.com.

- Early in December, get together with friends and choose an eco-friendly DIY decorating project from a book, magazine, or the Internet.

- Use DIY techniques to turn ordinary objects into decorative accents or gifts. Picture frames are great for this and can be used for more than just holding pictures. Tiny ones can be painted, decorated with buttons or beads, and used as place cards at a party table. Medium sized ones given similar treatment can display colorful seasonal cards. Very large ones, with the simple addition of two handles and some colorful paper or photographs slipped beneath the glass, can serve as trays.

- Paper is probably the cheapest resource for decorating. Learn the magic of origami and fold dozens of flowers for the tree or table. Various types of chains can be made by folding the paper in different ways. (Check online for directions.) Use magazine and catalog pages, recycled or recyclable papers, and string the chains inside and out. Paper placemats are fine for a holiday party when you make them yourself and can recycle the paper or take them to a copy store and have them laminated for many years of use.

Going au Natural

Items from nature, especially those found near your home, make perfect eco-friendly decorations and are often free. Collecting and adorning porches, table tops, and mantles with natural found items can be a fun family activity and a great way to save money and precious resources. Seasonal items like pinecones, acorns, gourds, apples, pomegranates, nuts, and evergreen boughs are ideal in fall and winter. Driftwood and polished and found stones are perfect year around. As a bonus, when you no longer need these items for your decorations, most can be consumed, composted, or returned to their original homes. Be sure to collect natural items legally. In an effort to preserve

---

If your DIY holiday projects call for glue, "non-toxic" just isn't green enough. In the future, craft glues made from resources such as soy may become widely available, but in the meantime, we love low VOC EcoGlue in recyclable packaging (EcoGlue.com). You can also make craft-worthy glue with plain tapioca powder or corn/wheat flour.

habitat, many national forests and beaches have rules against taking anything at all, and of course, respect private property rights.

If you live in a locale where decorative items from nature are hard to come by, or the nature that surrounds you does not offer articles with quite the look you're seeking (i.e., the cactus centerpiece is starting to irk you), OrganicBouquet.com has an extensive selection of organic wreaths, herb swags, garlands, and floral arrangements that are sure to add just the right decorative touch to your holiday or celebration. Look also for Christmas and seasonal-themed coconut fiber doormats, available at Whole Foods Markets or online.

Using live greenery, in addition to or instead of floral arrangements, can be an ideal decorative option, especially at Christmastime. Live greenery such as potted plants and herbs are beautiful, fragrant, and useful (herbs like rosemary, for example, might be displayed in the kitchen and snipped into holiday dishes as well.) Incorporating live greenery (including Christmas trees) also improves your indoor air quality and reduces the risk of fire (as compared to cut greens that can dry quickly). When your holiday or celebration is over, live greenery may be planted or replanted outside (depending, of course, on your climate). Smaller plants also make charming and thoughtful party favors.

◉ Decorate your tree with consumables such as cookie ornaments and strings of popcorn and berries. After Christmas, feed them to the birds or compost them in your garden (or through your yard waste company, where available). Centerpieces can be made of consumables too.

◉ Where consumables are not an option, choose items from nature. (Imagine all you can do with a pine cone!) Or choose sustainably and ethically sourced items from gifts to garlands by shopping online, at craft fairs or in eco-considerate brick and mortar stores.

IN THE WINTER MONTHS, REMEMBER TO DECORATE YOUR HOME'S ENTRIES AND DOORWAYS WITH LOTS OF MISTLETOE. ACCORDING TO GREENPEACE, "THIS WON'T REALLY HELP THE ENVIRONMENT...BUT MORE KISSING HAS GOT TO BE GOOD FOR WORLD PEACE."

Consumable and compostable candle holders, such as fruit and vegetables, make a sensible addition to holiday décor. Bring in a bit of Christmas in Hawaii by using a pineapple or two. Just carve out room for a taper candle and voila! Or choose an apple or clove-pressed orange for a more traditional feel.

Lighting

Great Christmas décor not only looks nice, it sets a holiday mood. But as any filmmaker or photographer will tell you, the secret to making décor shine, as well as establishing ambiance, is lighting.

If you're reading this book, chances are you already know that the use of incandescent bulbs is a major source of greenhouse gases and contributes to global warming. Incandescent bulbs are such an eco-no-no that some countries are opting to phase them out. But this does not mean that earth-friendly holiday decorations must be lit by sun- or moonlight alone (although these are certainly good options where available). A festive and eco-friendly atmosphere can be created by using old and/or new technology. Let's start with the old.

Fire sets a mood and creates a feeling of elegance, mystery, or reverence. Lit candles bathe your holiday event in a warm glow while at the same time preserving energy and ozone. Candles used in green décor should always have lead-free, cotton wicks and be made of 100% natural materials. Petroleum-based candles (such as paraffin and gel candles) and leaded wicks, release toxic chemicals such as lead, benzene, and toluene into the air. Humans and pets breathe this air and the chemicals may linger in the environment with temporary and longer-term repercussions. Soot from petroleum-based candles also is unhealthy and, over time, can grey walls, ceilings, and furniture. Candles made with natural ingredients such as hemp, soy, vegetable oil, or beeswax (which has very little drip and smells like honey as it burns) create significantly less soot, burn longer, and are better for the environment because they are made from sustainable resources. Natural candles come in all shapes, sizes, and colors and can be purchased in numerous stores such as Whole Foods Market or online. For more on candles, see Valentine's Day.

Having a fire in your indoor or outdoor fireplace should not be overlooked as a decorative, mood-setting option, but when doing so, be sure to choose your fire source wisely and use it in moderation. Burning wood causes pollution inside and outside, but products such as Java-Logs and Duraflame are made from petroleum-free materials (like recycled coffee grounds or other renewable resources) and promise to reduce emissions

by up to 80% when compared to burning chopped wood. Java Logs even crackle like the real thing.

A gas fireplace burns cleaner than wood but still calls on a non-renewable resource, so be sure to use wisely. Burning wood logs in a fireplace or wood-burning stove should be done in accordance with local laws, and remember that wood should be seasoned to reduce smoke.

LED lighting is fast replacing incandescent and CFLs as the savvy choice for several reasons. First, LED lights use 80%–90% less energy than traditional lights, are more than twice as energy efficient as CFLs, don't contain mercury, and are cool to the touch, so they are safer for people (and Christmas trees) too. Lasting longer means that you'll save money and that the planet's resources will be conserved as they will not be used to create, package, and deliver additional lights. LED lights are available in a variety of colors and styles including icicle-Christmas lights, ribbons, bows, and screw-in styles that change colors.

Another green decorative lighting option is low-watt, low energy, or fluorescent lights, available in a variety of colors and styles including bulbs and tubes.

But for outdoor lighting, the green cream of the crop is solar, which can be used even in winter (assuming you have at least some sun) and is available in everyday and holiday styles (including string lights and wreaths), none of which cost a cent to operate or use a drop of electricity, yet provide the mood and ambiance of traditional lights.

So what to do with the un-earth-friendly Christmas lights you already own? It's a real green conundrum, for sure, but generally speaking, it is best not to buy new lighting products, even green ones, until your existing lights are damaged, deemed unsafe, or ready to be replaced. Relegating them to a landfill or passing them off to someone else who is going to use them are not preferred choices even when newer, more eco-friendly options are available. But when your lights are ready to go, send them to HolidayLEDs.com for free recycling (and get a discount on your purchase of new LED holiday lights). Or check with your local recycling center or trash pick-up company to see if they will take the cords. If so, remove the bulbs and use them for craft projects if you like, then bundle the cords and tie up the ends so they don't hang loose and get caught in the recycling machinery.

Regardless of your lighting choice, be sure to select less lighting over more and keep lights on a timer. Unless you're using solar, leave lights on for no more than six hours each night. (For a normal home use, this will cost about $0.50 if you have LED lights as opposed to $30 for incandescents. (Data from 2007.)

People-Friendly Decorating

Although being earth-friendly is great, being earth-friendly *and* people-friendly is even better. Traditional holiday decorations are often made by people in other countries who may be underage, working in unsafe conditions, and/or making substandard wages. Big name suppliers of inexpensive holiday décor are able to sell products at such low prices in part because the people making them are pitifully paid. Being earth- and people-friendly go hand-in-hand, so start by looking for holiday décor that is American made or associated with the Fair Trade Federation (FTF) or Co-op America's Fair Trade Program. Visit FairTradeFederation.org for a list of fairly traded or ethically sourced products near you, or check out some of these sites for great holiday decorative and gift items such as wreaths, stockings, ornaments, and more that are also made fairly:

- AngelsAgainstCrime.co.za
- CrossroadsTrade.com
- eShopAfrica.com
- EthicalShopping.com
- EticaFairTrade.com
- GiftsWithHumanity.org
- GreatGreenGoods.com
- Ilala.co.za
- Lucuma.com
- OneWorldProjects.com
- Orenoque.com
- TenThousandVillages.com
- TaraLuna.com

Note: When you are unable to find ethically sourced décor at your favorite stores, don't be shy. Let management know that you prefer to purchase items that are made with people-friendliness in mind. If enough people ask, change will come.

GREAT HOLIDAY DECOR INCLUDES OUR OLFACTORY SENSE

Forego unhealthy synthetic air fresheners and potpourri which release toxins into the air and instead try simmering apple cider with cinnamon. Or why not use fresh cut flowers or herbs, or place a few drops of your favorite essential oil on dried flowers, pinecones, or other items from nature. Burning pure beeswax candles will fill your home with the sweet scent of honey.

You can also tie cinnamon sticks around a natural votive candle or bake fresh gingerbread cookies to evoke the warm and unforgettable fragrances of winter.

The Tree

While it might seem like artificial Christmas tress are the green way to go because they're perpetually reused, studies show that most aren't. The average time people keep their artificial tree is a surprising four years, before adding it to a landfill where it will spend centuries. On top of that, fake trees take a significant amount of energy to produce, package, and ship (most come from China), are petroleum based, and are usually made of polyvinyl chloride (PVC), a highly toxic substance that creates dioxins during production. Artificial trees also off gas for a period of time while they are in your home. Many contain lead, a powerful neurotoxin that can flake off onto the floor, gifts, or hands that touch it. Not healthy for your family or for the Earth, nor for the people who make the trees (and who typically make low, sometimes unfair, wages). If you are going with an artificial tree, save one from a landfill and buy used. There is one more eco-faux option: vintage aluminum trees (aluminum is a non-renewable resource).

Still, most tree-loving people find it hard to buy a tree that's been cut down until they consider that trees, just like any other crop, are grown by farmers who constantly replant to replenish their supply. And as the trees grow, they make oxygen and absorb carbon dioxide while at the same time making a home and offering protection for wildlife as well as stabilizing soil. Using farmed trees also gives you a chance to support your local farmers. If you do use a cut tree, be sure to recycle it after Christmas by chipping it into mulch, composting it, or, if it's allowed in your area, tying it to a sand dune (to slow erosion), or placing it in a pond or lake where it can become habitat for fish.

Note: Conventional Christmas tree farmers typically make heavy use of chemical pesticides and fertilizers, and even certified organic growers may use some approved chemicals. Ask questions of your grower such as, "How do you deal with pests such as mites?" and "How do you control ground cover?" If possible, buy your tree directly from the farmer or ask if the store you buy from does their own tests for pesticide residues. Look for certified organic farms or buy from farmers who utilize Integrated Pest Management (IPM), which incorporates natural and mechanical means to control pests, reducing the need for chemicals. Also, if you live in a part of the country where salmon habitat is threatened, seek out trees that are certified Salmon-Safe. You can learn more about being an eco-conscious Christmas tree consumer through the Coalition of Environmentally-Conscious Growers, a not-for-profit organization seeking to promote consumer education and sustainable tree growing practices.

Like any other products, decorative items can contain hidden dangers. Even natural objects, such as holly, can be poisonous when consumed by people or animals. But Earth and human toxins such as lead, cadmium, PVC, and phthalates are commonly found in painted and plastic items including Christmas tree ornaments. Generally speaking, you're safer to go with petroleum-free products made in the USA, but even the widely-used term, non-toxic, means very little. If you are unsure whether or not a particular item is safe, ask. If you still cannot be sure that the item is acceptable, err on the side of caution and go without, look for a healthier alternative elsewhere, or make the decoration yourself with materials you can trust from retailers or websites such as EcoArtworks.com and GreenEarthOfficeSupply.com.

For those who can't bear the thought of buying a cut tree, live, potted evergreens can be enjoyed indoors and then planted after the holiday. (Imagine if you planted a new tree every year—after a quarter century, you'd have grown a forest of memories.) If you do go this route, however, you'll want to plan in advance and speak with your local nursery about how to prepare for and address your tree's needs, taking into account temperature changes (from inside to outside), size and species of the tree, ground hardness, and dirt temperature. For more details visit RealChristmasTree.org.

- For eco-friendly tree farmers near you, check out LocalHarvest.org or GreenPromise.com.
- To find tree recycling near you, go to Earth911.org.
- In some areas of the country, live, potted trees can be rented! Ask your local nursery, check out LivingChristmasTrees.org, or use an Internet search to find out if this option is available near you.
- Contact your local forest service and ask about permitted Christmas tree cutting in areas that are deemed in need of thinning or where trees will be replanted.
- If you've got a few years to wait, you can purchase Christmas tree seedlings through TreeInABox.com or HerbKits.com.

Tree Ornaments/Decorating

A Christmas tree without ornaments is naked indeed, so avoid any unnecessary embarrassment and dress your tree in what it really wants to wear: eco-friendly décor. Start by reusing ornaments you already own or can acquire from others, unless they are unsafe (many ornaments, especially those made in China, contain lead which can flake off and be inhaled or ingested by wee ones). Tree décor made from consumables or natural materials are almost always the best choice because they're the safest for you and the planet and are compostable/biodegradable. Using found or made natural décor will also save you money over buying from a store. As with all products, when buying online, at markets, at fairs, or in brick and mortar stores, look for ornaments that were created by people who were paid and treated fairly.

Here are additional ideas for greening your tree décor:

- Instead of throwing something out, make it new again. For example, used incandescent lights can be painted and hung as ornaments.
- Use a baby shoe or old toy as an ornament, adding the child's name and date.
- Use popcorn and or cranberry strings (feed to birds or compost after use).
- Make origami ornaments out of colorful repurposed paper.
- Hang cookie cutters from ribbon or string.
- Use memorabilia—concert tickets, lift passes, or airline tickets from a special vacation (use Modge Podge to secure them to wood scraps if desired).
- Make ornaments from found or acquired objects such as pinecones, buttons, antique silverware, ribbons, shells, etc.
- Make cutouts from last year's Christmas cards.
- Use wool felt, scraps of fabric, or yarn to create, sew, knit, or crochet elves, birds, stars, or trees.
- Create photo ornaments by gluing pictures onto small rounds of found wood or on lids that would have otherwise gone in the trash.
- Cut out pictures from magazines or holiday cards and glue onto plastic lids. Decorate with beads, buttons, or jewelry and punch a hole and hang with string or yarn.
- Make gingerbread people or reindeer ornaments from repurposed brown paper bags.
- If you're buying ornaments, choose lead-free, Fair Trade, or ethically sourced options from stores or websites such as
  - CrossraodsTrade.com
  - Lucuma.com
  - TenThousandVillages.com (also in stores nation-wide)

For lots more ideas, visit our website, CelebrateGreen.NET.

Stockings

 I still remember the magic of waking up Christmas morning to find the stocking that I had left empty the night before, bursting with goodies. That sense of surprise always meant more to me than the gifts themselves, no matter what they were. My kids experience that same joy and excitement using stockings created by their grandma from fabric scraps. (I would have handed down my

According to the U.S. Department of Commerce, Bureau of Census, #22 on the list of "Top 30 Imported Products from China" are "entertainment articles," all of which, except three, are Christmas décor items such as ornaments, nativity scenes, and artificial Christmas trees.

own stocking to one of them, but Santa still uses it for me.) Stockings, like ornaments, don't have to be fancy or expensive to become meaningful traditions. Using them year after year adds to their uniqueness, and they never need replacing unless they've been irreparably damaged.

If you don't have an heirloom stocking or hand-me-down and don't want to sew or knit your own, look for gently used but still serviceable stockings at thrift shops, garage sales, or on eBay.com. If you don't know how to sew, how about decorating on old rain or snow boot? Buying new? Look for stockings made from recycled materials (such as wool sweaters) or organic cotton or wool, or support artisans by buying one from a co-operative or fair trade store, either online or in person.

Holiday Cards

We all know it's not polite to go right for the gift when there's a card to be opened first. This year, how about making your gifts' first-impression a tree-friendly one by committing to one or more of these alternatives:

- Purchase recycled-content cards. Ideal choices are 100% recycled from 100% post-consumer waste. (Also, look for companies that use soy based inks.) GreenFieldPaper. com sells a set of 100% junk mail Christmas cards with the world "Joy" on the front—the "o" is a recycled symbol. BorealisPress.net claims to sell "the greenest cards you can buy," with the selection ranging from humorous to touching.

- Go tree-free by choosing cards made from any number of alternative materials including coffee, garlic, or hemp. If you can't find just the right look, buy a generic tree-free note card and embellish it yourself.

- Buy or make a seed embedded card that can be planted (and enjoyed) after the holidays. KidBean.com is sells a variety of holiday-themed Grow-A-Note® card sets.

- Create new cards from old materials. Last year's cards are the most obvious choice, but seasonal images from magazine ads, calendar pages and catalogs are easy to find as well.

CUT HOLIDAY CATALOG WASTE

Another way to cut waste is to say NO to holiday catalogs. Instead, utilize the Internet or cancel all but the one or two catalogs you just can't live without. When you're done, reuse or recycle them. To find out more, visit EnvironmentalDefense.org, or to eliminate all or most of your holiday catalog waste, go to:

- GreenDimes.com (charges $20 to stop your junk mail and plants 10 trees on your behalf)

- CatalogChoice.org (a free service)

◉ Go zero-waste by using free or for-fee e-cards. SmileBox.com allows you to send holiday themed and personalized photo, video, or music greetings to family and friends. We plan to offer e-cards on our site as well, so be sure to stop by and see if they are up yet on CelebrateGreen.NET.

◉ Although it's made with paper, a fair trade foldout "Merry Christmas" card from TenThousandVillages.com is a human-friendly option. The card doubles as a banner.

◉ Save this year's cards for next year's use as cards, tags, or place-markers ,or repurpose them now by turning them into placemats, ornaments, garlands, and more.

GIFTS
Go less: less lights, less gifts, less wrapping, less waste.

According to a survey by Deloitte & Touche, nearly one in five consumers expected to buy "eco-friendly" products during the 2007 holiday season, and 17% said they would be willing to spend more money to do so. Another independent study found that more than two-thirds of consumers felt green gift giving was important. A third poll found that 58% of Americans wanted to receive green gifts, and Pricegrabber.com discovered that 71% of respondents felt buying earth-friendly was the way to go. This is all good news for Mother Earth since Americans spend about $9 billion a year just *decorating* for the holidays, and much of that money is spent on inexpensive, disposable products that are bound for the landfill.

Other shopping trends include reduced use of disposable bags, the popularity of hybrid vehicles and electronics/appliances sporting the Energy Star seal, and the explosion of new eco-friendly online stores catering to green-focused consumers.

Still, between Thanksgiving and Christmas, people throw away one million tons of trash per week, which is not a surprise since 20% of the year's retail sales are concentrated in the holiday season. Excessive packaging and millions of shoppers driving from store to store are hard enough on the Earth, but when you consider that about 30 million Americans return gifts at the end of the season, it might lead one to ask *what's this all for*?

There's a new movement to decrease our holiday footprint called "Buy Nothing Christmas," and as untraditional as that might sound, according to polls, many people agree: good memories and love are more important than things. BuyHandMade.org is another organization encouraging people to step off the mass consumerism train by making meaningful gifts themselves or by supporting others who do (you can take the handmade pledge through their website). But when planning your holiday gift list this year, remember that it's not all or nothing. There are plenty of ways to give gifts that will be cherished and that don't damage the Earth. Visit WasteFreeHolidays.com for ideas or give some of ours a try:

When gifts of time, creativity or contribution aren't what you're looking for, you can still be an eco-conscious gift giver by buying products that have the least amount of impact on both people and the planet. Remember to consider the lifespan of the products you're choosing by thinking about:

- Where they come from
- How they got here
- How they will be used
- How long they'll be used
- Where they'll go after they're used and how long they'll be there.

In addition, be sure to consider not only the product itself but also the relationships among

- The product
- The planet
- The people who grew or made the product
- How the product is packaged and transported

- Give gifts of yourself using your time, talents, and energy.
- Give consumables that can be enjoyed without adding to landfills or that can be composted later (such as gingerbread cookie ornaments).
- Give experiences like massages, classes, or tickets to events, museums, or activities such as ice skating.
- Give gifts from the heart like poems, artwork, or photo-collages.
- Give something handmade. For ideas, check out DIYNetwork.com.
- Give gifts that you know will be used or cherished. Money and gift cards are great choices because your giftee can choose exactly the gift they like. Gift cards themselves may not be recyclable although more are being manufactured from bioplastics (potato, sugarcane, etc.) and are biodegradable and compostable.

Gifts that Give Back

- Carbon offset gift cards from CarbonCounter.org
- Support artisans and animals by buying through CraftersForCritters.com. Proceeds go to animal rescue organizations.
- Cell phone ring tones featuring the sounds of an imperiled species (from the Center for Biological Diversity.) Free, but donations are accepted.
- NetworkForGood—choose your charity; gift cards available
- SaveASnowman.com—adopt a snowman or family and help stop global warming
- Adopt a more traditional endangered creature such as a polar bear (most popular) or a stingray (least popular), or join the Endangered Species of

the Month Club (and receive a different plush animal each month) through WorldWildlife.org.

- ChangingThePresent.org—you choose your cause
- JustGive.org—your giftee can choose the cause
- GiveMeaning.com—charitable e-cards from $5 and up. Your giftee chooses the charity they'd like to support.
- FEED1Bags.com Reduce disposable bag use while providing a year of meals to one hungry school-aged child. Bags are made in audited and certified fair labor facilities from organic, rapidly renewable burlap (raw jute), and will decompose naturally.
- Buy used or new books through BetterWorld.com and help fund literacy. The company also participates in carbon offsetting.
- Book offsets. For $1, EcoLibris.net will plant one tree to offset the impact of one book you're buying. Buying ten books this holiday season? Buy ten offsets to help reduce the impact of trees lost.
- Shop from stores such as Gap and Target at NonProfitShoppingMall.com and choose the charity you'd like to support.
- ABCHomeAndPlanet.org contributes to causes that help people and planet

Here are some green gifts (and stocking stuffers) everyone on your list can enjoy:

Babies
- Sustainably harvested wooden toys such as rattles, blocks, or rocking horse
- Eco-Me Baby Kit—everything you need to make your own healthy and safe baby products (Eco-Me.com)
- Soft, colorful, organic cotton and wool music box from LaLaNatural.com

Children
- 100% recycled fabric monsters from CottonMonster.com
- Ecologically themed cooperative games from EcoToyTown.com
- Earth Friends dolls from TheEarthFriends.com. A group of nine girls and boys made in the USA with natural and recycled materials like organic cotton, hemp, and recycled plastic. Each comes with accessories that include a backpack and a Hope Tree Planting kit.

TOXIC TOYS

Toxic toys are a great concern to many parents, but how to know if the products your child is playing with are safe? From lead in children's jewelry to phthalates in rubber duckies to parts that act like GHB (the so called "date rape" drug) when swallowed, toys, it seems, are not as innocent as they look. Although government-level action is brewing as this book goes to press, we suggest that you do your own research before allowing your children to play with toys that cause you concern. This can be tricky during the holiday season when your children receive gifts from well-meaning but uninformed friends and family, but considering the risks, you may feel some awkwardness is worth it. Whatever approach you take, get to know the organizations working to keep toxic toys out of children's hands, and be sure to frequent the recall database at CPSC.gov to stay abreast of toys that have been deemed unsafe. Whenever possible, give preference to toys made of natural materials. They are not only safer for your kids, but healthier for the planet as well.

Resources:
- SafeKids.org
- HealthyToys.org
- ToxicFreeLeagacy.org
- EcoCenter.org
- WAToxics.org

- Stocking Stuffers for Children
  - Wool and natural material Christmas elves, animals, robots, pouches, sets and "Juicy Bugs" (like those decorating these pages) from DreamALittle7.com
  - Recycled and recyclable Preserve Jr. toothbrushes from Recycline (supports the National Wildlife Federation's efforts to save and protect endangered animals)
  - Fair trade instruments (JamTown.com)
  - Kleen Kanteen water bottle
  - Sustainably harvested wood cars, trucks, boats, trains, and airplanes
  - Eco-friendly posable animals (Anamalz.com)
  - Xeko trading cards, made and packaged with 100% recycled paper/stock, printed with soy inks, four percent of the sales are donated to Conservation International

Teens

- Organic and 100% natural lip balm or zero-waste Cargo Plant Love Lipstick (in a compostable corn-based lipstick case made from corn and a plantable seed embedded box)
- Tree-free journals made from elephant dung (MrElliePooh.com)
- Sustainable tees on a mission at TeesForChange.com
- Messenger bag made from repurposed billboards (EcoLogicDesigns.com)
- Hip key chains and belts made from tires or bottle caps
- 100% recycled Jimi wallet
- Body Glove's 100% petroleum-free "Eco Wetsuit" made by using 1/10th the energy used in the production of typical wetsuits. Logo printed in organic, water-based ink.
- Sustainably sourced snowboard or skateboard from ArborSports.com
- Stocking Stuffers for Teens
  - All natural Peelu Gum or Glee Gum
  - Hemp beading kit from LaLaNatural.com
  - Makeup from IAMAPeacekeeper.com ("Eyelashes get along, why can't we?")

Adults

- Membership to BetterWorldClub.com auto club
- All-weather Sun Jar that uses solar cells, a rechargeable battery, and LED lamp
- Recycled chopstick art from ChopStickArt.com

- Eco-design game from PlayReThink.com
- Organic fruit-of-the-month club DiamondOrganics.com
- Bamboo LCD TV (and other electronics cased in bamboo rather than plastic)
- Solar-powered Bluetooth headset
- Laptop cased in corn-based plastic
- USB rechargeable batteries
- Upscale handmade gifts from Guild.com
- EcoPod home recycling center
- Eco-savvy starter kit from GreenSender.com (or compiled by you)
- Products (i.e. business card holder, money clips, cuff links) made from recycled computer and electronic components from EcoArtware.com
- Whisky barrel speakers

Pets

- Spike's biodegradable "Business Bags"
- Eco-me kits for cats and dogs containing everything you need to care for your pet, naturally
- Hemp dog leash

Green Gift Resources

For places to shop visit:

- 3RLiving.com
- Eco-artware.com
- eConscious.com
- Gaiam.com

- NovaNatural.com
- PlanetHappyToys.com
- PristinePlanet.com
- VivaTerra.com

… or use green search engines or similar sites:

- EcoEarth.info
- EcoSearch.org
- EcoSeeker.com
- GreenGiftLinks.com

- GreenLinkCentral.com
- GreenMaven.com
- LiveGreenOrDie.com
- TheFindGreen.com

Three Simple Gifts from Nature that will Surprise and Delight Anyone with an Outdoor Space to Decorate

Here are three items to make that require very few supplies and are fun and simple to make. If you are not collecting materials from your own property, always be sure to ask for permission. In many state and federal parks, it is illegal to collect shells, branches, pine cones, and even rocks.

Driftwood/Found Wood "Pile" Sculpture or Mobile

I happened to be at a beach last spring where collecting drift wood was legal, so my husband and I gathered two armloads. When I got home, I found a piece of rebar, grabbed the drill, and drilled holes a little bigger than the diameter of the rebar in each piece. I pushed the rebar into the dirt, then threaded on pieces of driftwood and faced them in different directions.

Having almost half the driftwood left, I decided to make a mobile. This time I drilled much smaller holes, just big enough to thread through fishing line. First I tied on a wooden bead, then I began alternating adding pieces of driftwood with beads until I'd used up all the wood. I made a loop a the top and hung it up.

You could do the same thing with a variety of twigs and branches if you have no access to drift wood. (For a photo of the driftwood sculptures, see our website, www.CelebrateGreen.NET.)

Rock Plant Markers

Having the memory of an amoeba, I can rarely remember what I've planted where. These markers can be placed wherever you've put seeds or bulbs. I used a permanent ink stamp pad and they stand up very well to the weather. I've packed them in a wooden box along with seeds I've collected as a very personal gift for gardening friends.

Amusing Garden Signs

Signs like these can be purchased at garden shops and craft shows, and they're not cheap. But they are easy to make and you can personalize them to your own take on gardening. For instance, my yard boasts one that speaks to my frustration with the grazing habits of native four-legged creatures: *Deer will be composted!* (Only kidding, although after they have nibbled through my roses and yanked out tomatoes, I admit to pondering this dreadful thought.) Other signs I've painted or sayings that could be used:

- All suckers will be removed from this garden
- Bugs need not apply
- Funny farm

- Garden 'o weedin'
- Grow darn it!
- NOT the Garden of Eden
- Vegetables in training

Use any piece of wood you might have lying around. Wood can be old or new, smooth or rough. You can paint the background or leave it natural and paint or stamp on the words. Hang your sign from twine or wire threaded through a couple of screw eyes. Add more screw eyes at the bottom if you want to attach embellishments like twigs, bits of ribbon, or recycled buttons.

Wrapping

There's no denying it: unwrapping a mysterious gift hidden inside layers of paper can bring great delight. You don't have to abandon this tradition all together if you don't want to; there are plenty of alternatives available that don't require buying a product made of virgin trees that will shortly become waste or require recycling once the gift is opened. Alternative gift wraps include:

- Repurposed items or other would-be-waste such as newspaper, comics, calendar pages, catalogs, wrapping paper, tissue paper, wallpaper scraps, magazine pages, blueprints, maps, sheet music, posters, old photos, grocery bags, playing cards, coloring book pages, instruction sheets, aluminum foil, and more. If needed, tape or glue items together and decorate or customize with crayons, paints, or anything else you might like to use.
- Wraps that are gifts themselves such as scarves, hats, clothes, or antique linens, table cloths, decorative boxes, functional boxes (like a jewelry or tool box), luggage, pillow cases, kitchen containers or cookie jars, aprons, pockets, baskets, or reusable shopping bags. Link the gift to the wrapping you use; for example, bamboo salad servers can be "wrapped" inside of an organic cotton oven mitt or hemp dish towel.
- Cloth wrap that may be used for countless future occasions such as:

- Each year, $5 billion dollars worth of gift wrap winds up in landfills.

- If every family wrapped just three gifts a year in something reused or repurposed, 45,000 football fields of paper would be saved.

- If every household reused just two feet of ribbon, enough ribbon would be saved to tie a bow around the entire planet.

- According to Robert Lilienfeld and Dr. William Rathje's *Use Less Stuff*, using one less Christmas card per person would save 50,000 cubic yards of paper.

- Fabric remnants
- Drawstring bags (Love the variety of sizes and fabrics offered by the splendidly named www.CelerateGreen.com.)
- Furoshiki cloth (Furoshiki.com)

If you're open to creating a new tradition of wrap-free or wrap-reduced gifts, how about trying these options:

- Just tie a repurposed bow or some raffia around the gift itself.
- Give gifts that don't need wrapping such as gifts of your time, talent, or creativity, or experiential gifts.
- Instead of wrapping gifts, how about hiding them? Even adults love a good treasure hunt. Use hints, clues, or riddles for a twist.

Other tips:

- Pack gifts safely in air-popped popcorn, biodegradable/compostable starch packing peanuts, previously used peanuts, air-filled bags, or repurposed packing materials such as shredded or crumpled paper. Even pine needles, real peanuts, or straw can do the trick if you don't wrap too much in advance. (A surprise you don't want when your child opens his present is a bunch of bugs greeting him.)
- When buying paper, make it 100% recycled or tree free.
- Make gift tags from previously used holiday cards, wrapping paper, business cards, calendars, or other thick paper stock that would otherwise have been bound for the recycle-bin. Cut and glue onto paper or the gift itself, or use a hole punch and secure with reused ribbon or raffia.
- Avoid buying metallic wrapping paper and cards. They're difficult to recycle.
- Cellophane is often touted as an earth-friendly choice. Although it is biodegradable, the process used to make it (and the by-products created as a result of the process) are polluting.
- For bows and ribbons, think reused or reusable such as scarves, neckties, shoe laces, or even a measuring tape!
- Attach reusable items (such as ornaments, cookie cutters, or small toys) and items from nature (such as pine cones, cinnamon sticks, sprigs of evergreen, or dried flowers) for a final touch.

Wrapping Resources:

- WrapSacks.com sells multi-use gift wrap bags; the bag's journey can be tracked from giftee to giftee via their website.

- Luxurious silk dupioni furoshiki from VivaTerra.com or furoshiki made from recycled plastic bottles from Furoshiki.com.

- Learn how to make your own amazing gift boxes from everything from toilet paper rolls to cereal boxes at ReadyMade.com.

Clothes

Okay, so now your house and gifts are looking eco-chic, but what about you? Green divas and divos (why not?) who are hosting or attending holiday parties know that looking good and feeling good go hand-in-hand. Think that green fashion is all about recycled tire flip flops and hemp ponchos? You'll be amazed at how the fashion world—like most other industries —is beginning to go green. Always buy sweatshop-free and look for designers in your area. Here are a few of our favorite resources to help you look eco-gorgeous this Christmas:

EcoDiva

Website	What They Offer
BlissWorld.com	Check out Sworn Virgins' sexy black sleeveless v-neck dress with silk tie, made of bamboo
MoralFervor.com	Upscale, eco-funky clothes
LaraMiller.net	See her holiday collection
DeborahLindquist.com	Our favorite is her vintage tweed and wool baby doll dress with recycled cashmere templar cross appliqués
LoyaleClothing.com	Organic cotton vegan faux fur coat
MyCorset.com	Organic, sustainable, Fair Trade clothing, including outerwear
Guild.com	For natural fiber, handmade shawls and scarves that look like works of art
Ecoist.com or Novica.com	Metallic clutch or shoulder bags made entirely of post-consumer recycled aluminum pull tabs by women artisans

EcoDivo

- OrganicAvenue.com (cruelty-free Peace Silk shirt in "black sand")

- Rawganique.com (check out their sexy Eco Couture Collection)

- ClothingMatters.net (hemp/silk dress shirt)

As a child, my favorite holiday decoration was a handmade green checked fabric calendar that Mom hung on a wall every December 1st. Each day of the month was represented by a felt square featuring a different folk art symbol. Tucked under every square, a special message awaited. Most announced we'd be engaging in a family activity. Ice-skating, baking gingerbread, tree selection, and caroling were some of my favorites. Every year of our childhood, my brothers and I eagerly awaited the unveiling of the calendar. After I became a mom, my parents gave it to me in the hope that the tradition begun with a piece of cloth and good intentions would continue to flourish. (Go to our website, CelebrateGreen.NET, to get ideas for making your own calendar.)

Shoes

- MooShoes.com (vegan dress and casual shoes for women and men)
- TerraPlana.com (eco-responsible shoes for men and women)

Kids

- KateQuinnOrganics.com (organic cotton duds, perfect for the holidays)
- KidBean.com (organic cotton velvet fleece sweater vest for boys and organic cotton dresses for girls)
- Sternlein.com (organic cotton and organic wool tights)

Your Eco-Christmas Checklist

Here's a list of ideas to help inform your holiday choices. Remember that these suggestions are ideals and may not work or be appropriate for your family. If you're green at being green, choosing just one option is a great place to start, but if being eco-savvy is old hat for you, you may be up for the challenge of ensuring that tips are checked off the list.

- ☐ *Trees:* Christmas trees are live or come from local, pesticide-free, sustainable farms, and are chipped or composted after use.

- ☐ *Lights:* Christmas lights are ideally LED, fluorescent, or solar, are on a timer, and used conservatively. For older-style lights, use only the ones with small bulbs (small bulbs=less wattage), and purchase eco-friendly lights when they need to be replaced.

- ☐ *Ornaments and décor:* Decorations are hand crafted, purchased locally, made by artisans earning fair wages, and/or made with 100% natural materials. Look for products that are recycled and recyclable, reused or reusable, or consumable/compostable. Watch out for non-recycled plastics and products that may contain lead, phthalates, and other toxins.

- ☐ *Tableware:* All tableware (plates, glasses, utensils, napkins, tablecloths, etc.) is non-disposable. Instead, go reusable. If you don't have enough, borrow from friends or family, rent, or find the items used.

- ☐ *Ornamental crafts:* Favorite earth-friendly Christmas crafts include making "snowflakes" from recycled or reused paper, wreaths and centerpieces from collected tree trimmings, pop-corn (non-microwave) and cranberry garlands, gingerbread houses, ornaments from reused or repurposed materials, candles from beeswax or soy, and stockings out of natural fabrics (or scraps) or knit from natural fibers.

- ☐ *Cards:* Send Christmas letters and invitations by e-mail (or use services like Evite.com). Cards and thank you notes are made from recycled, reused, or tree-free materials, and inks are soy-based.

- ☐ *Gifts:* Handmade, activity-based, consumable or charitable donation gifts are ideal. For other gifts, look for items made by fairly paid and treated artisans from natural, sustainable, reused or recycled materials. Avoid gifts that are over-packaged, mass-produced, disposable, come from unknown origins, require a lot of additional components, and won't last long or are cheaply made.

- ☐ *Wrapping:* Gift wrap and packaging are reused or reusable and made from repurposed, recycled or tree-free materials (or not used at all). Ribbons are reused, repurposed or made from raffia. To ensure the safety of items being shipped, use real air-popped popcorn, old newspaper, biodegradable starch packing peanuts, or previously used packing materials in reused boxes.

- ☐ *Food & Drink:* Holiday meals are made from local and organic foods which contain healthy, natural, non-genetically modified ingredients. Drinks, including alcohol, are organic, and wine bottles come with real cork stoppers. Food scraps are composted or included in yard waste bins (where available).

- ☐ *Clothing:* Holiday attire is reused, borrowed, rented, or made with natural materials including organic cotton, silk, wool, hemp, or recycled fibers.

- ☐ *Parties:* Strive to make yours a zero waste party by saying no to disposable packaging and décor. Use only products and items that can be consumed, reused, recycled, or composted.

FEELING ECO-ANXIOUS DURING THE HOLIDAYS? YOU'RE NOT ALONE.

People feeling uneasy about their impact on the Earth and about what to do about it can seek help from someone specializing in **ecopsychology**. According to EcoPsychology.org, ecopsychology "is situated at the intersection of a number of fields of enquiry, including environmental philosophy, psychology, and ecology, but is not limited by any disciplinary boundaries. At its core, ecopsychology suggests that there is a synergistic relation between planetary and personal well being; that the needs of the one are relevant to the other." But before you run out and consult someone to help you with your eco-angst, note that a license in ecopsychology does not exist, so we suggest that you see someone licensed or credentialed in a valid psychotherapeutic field. Check out EcoPsychology. org for a list of practitioners—you'll be surprised by how many there are!

Hanukkah

Healing the Earth: The Green Menorah Covenant

The Green Menorah is the symbol of a covenant among Jewish communities and congregations to renew the miracle of Hanukkah in our own generation: Using one day's oil to meet eight days' needs: doing our part so that by 2020, United States oil consumption is cut by seven-eighths.

There are three aspects of the Covenant: hands-on action by congregations and congregants to reduce CO_2 emissions on their own; infusion of Jewish festivals, life-cycle events, prayers, and education with eco-consciousness; and advocacy for change in public policy.

Just as the Menorah at the Holy Temple was rooted in the image of a tree, its branches, and buds, so we need to renew the sense that our earth calls on us to light the Planetary Menorah by reducing our use of oil.

Actions to Heal the Earth through the Green Menorah Covenant

There are three levels of wisdom through which Hanukkah invites us to address the planetary dangers of the global climate crisis – what some of us call "global scorching" because "warming" seems so pleasant, so comforting.

We can encode these teachings into actions we take to heal the earth each of the eight days.

1. The Talmud's legend about using one day's oil to meet eight days' needs: a reminder that if we have the courage to change our lifestyles to conserve energy, it will sustain us.

2. The vision of Zechariah (whose prophetic passages we read on Shabbat Hanukkah) that the Temple Menorah was itself a living being, uniting the world of "nature" and "humanity"—for it was not only fashioned in the shape of a Tree of Light, as Torah teaches, but was flanked by two olive trees that fed olive oil directly into it.

3. The memory that a community of "the powerless" can overcome a great empire, giving us courage to face our modern corporate empires of Oil and Coal when they defile our most sacred Temple: Earth itself.

We are taught not only to light the menorah, but to publicize the miracle, to turn our individual actions outward for the rest of the world to see and to be inspired by.

So we invite you to join in The Shalom Center's (ShalomCtr.org) Green Menorah Covenant for taking action—personal, communal, and political—to heal the earth from the global climate crisis.

After lighting your menorah each evening, dedicate yourself to making the changes in your life that will allow our limited sources of energy to last for as long as they're needed, and with minimal impact on our climate.

No single action will solve the global climate crisis, just as no one of us alone can make enough of a difference. Yet, if we act on as many of the areas below as possible, and act together, a seemingly small group of people can overcome a seemingly intractable crisis. We can, as in days of old, turn this time of darkness into one of light.

Day 1: Personal/Household. Call your electric-power utility to switch to wind-powered electricity. (For each home, 100% wind-power reduces CO_2 emissions the same as not driving 20,000 miles in one year.)

Day 2: Synagogue, Hillel, or JCC. Urge your congregation or community building to switch to wind-powered electricity.

Day 3. Your network of friends, IM buddies, and members of civic or professional groups you belong to. Connect with people like newspaper editors, real-estate developers, architects, bankers, etc. to urge them to strengthen the green factor in all their decisions, speeches, and actions.

Day 4. Automobile. If possible, choose today or one other day a week to not use your car at all. Other days, lessen driving. Shop online. Cluster errands. Carpool. Don't idle engine beyond 20 seconds.

Day 5: Workplace or College. Urge the top officials to arrange an energy audit. Check with utility company about getting one free or at low-cost.

Hanukkah, the Jewish Festival of Lights, commemorates the victory of a small band of Jews over the Greek-Syrians more than 2000 years ago. The menorah, a nine-armed candelabrum, is central to this holiday celebration. It represents the miracle of the oil—the fact that one day's worth of oil burned for eight at the temple's rededication after the triumph.

Some families are fortunate enough to own a menorah that has been handed down for generations. Artists have crafted menorahs that sell for thousands of dollars. But whether the family proudly lights a menorah that has glowed through 100 Hanukkahs or one glued together by their children, the spirit that illuminates the room is the same.

Menorahs can, and have been, fashioned from almost any items. And what more perfect way to establish a "green" tradition at Hanukkah than to make your own from found, recycled, or just plain "green" materials.

Day 6: Town/City. Urge town/city officials to require greening of buildings through ordinances and executive orders. Creating change is often easier on the local level!

Day 7: State. Urge state representatives to reduce subsidies for highways, increase them for mass transit.

Day 8: National. Write your public officials, urging them to push forward

on new laws and policies to radically reduce fossil-fuel use and greenhouse-gas emissions. Check The Shalom Center's Website for the newest information on public policy.

Make our planet's Hanukkah a happy one!

- - - - - - - - - - - - - - - -

Kwanzaa

Kwanzaa, Swahili for "first fruits," has been around for only forty-two years. But like every other celebration, this African-American tradition has already evolved and is still evolving as individuals find their personal ways of integrating the ideas and principles into their family lives and community events.

Each night for a week, a group celebrating Kwanzaa may come together, light a candle, and discuss one of the seven principles: unity, self-determination, collective work and responsibility, cooperative economics, purpose, creativity, and faith.

Activities such as games, reading, or crafts that illustrate the principles often are a part of the evenings.

Here's a project that not only speaks to every one of the principles, but also promotes earth-friendly, people-friendly, and community-friendly ideals. Everyone can join in the fun and feel great that they have celebrated by making a real contribution to children in need.

Make and Contribute a Doll for the Uthando Project (UthandoProject.org)

In South Africa's KwaZulu-Natal region live one quarter of South Africa's children. Two in every three is raised in poverty, and 1.5 million are younger than six. HIV and AIDS have orphaned many, and thousands are infected. Facing hardships that would devastate most adults, these children are deprived of their childhoods. Play is a word without meaning.

To support caregivers and their children in discovering the joys and richness of play, Uthando Project (Uthando is the Zulu word for "love"), distributes dolls in KwaZulu-Natal.

Instructions for sewing, knitting, or crocheting dolls are on the Uthando website. But in keeping with our desire to support people- and earth-friendly projects, we offer the list below to help you make eco-friendly choices for materials you'll need to produce the dolls.

While it's true that you may spend more money purchasing organic and eco-friendly supplies it's a meaningful way to live your values, especially at Kwanzaa.

- **Fabric for doll bodies.** There are a number of choices. Recycle items made from any shade of brown material. Or, if you choose to buy new, you might want to purchase EcoSpun felt made from recycled post consumer plastic bottles.
- **Hair.** Unravel a sweater or look for other items of clothing that might be reused as hair. Organic wool yarn in natural colors, Soysilk yarn, eco-cotton, or Tencel yarn (made of wood pulp cellulose) are all good choices. You may even be able to find yarn made from milk or corn!
- **Doll's clothing and accessories.** Again, recycled fabrics (especially in bright colors) are the best, but if purchasing, look for organic cotton colored with natural dyes, not synthetic or chemical. In fact, another fun activity for Kwanzaa might be to dye your own fabric using natural dyes. Lots of information on how to do this is available on the Internet, or see this book's Easter section.
- **Stuffing.** According to the instructions on the Uthando site, it's best to use real stuffing and not small pieces of fabric. However, if you choose to be more earth-friendly, avoid polyester fiber fill and reach for kapok, eco-wool, or hemp fibers.
- **Sewing.** Organic cotton thread is a good choice, as is Tencel .

If you've made a doll or two during the week of Kwanzaa, you might enjoy creating a naming ceremony on the last night. Check out Uthando.com for a list of Zulu names and their meanings. Then, in remembrance of the ideals of Kwanzaa, send the doll off to a child far away who will welcome it with open arms.

New Year's

On New Year's Eve 2007/2008, the world bid farewell to the landmark Times Square New Year's Eve ball. But not a tear was shed.

Why? Because that night the newer, *greener* Times Square New Year's ball was unveiled—a brighter, more colorful, innovative orb made of artisan-cut crystals and about 10,000 LED lights (as compared to the previous 9,576 halogen and incandescent bulbs). The "Let There Be Light" ball (by Waterford Crystal) is so energy-efficient that its use requires roughly the same amount of energy as ten toaster ovens. (For those of us who are electrically challenged, that's not much.)

Traditions such as the dropping of the ball on New Year's are meant to continue over time. But as we become more informed about what it means to actually create that sustainability, some of our traditions may need tweaking (i.e., keep the ball, lose the energy-draining lights). Yet a few traditions were created to be sustainable in the first place, even if this was not the original intention, or are focused on people rather than things and on healthy, local, and seasonal foods. In many countries around the world, the new year is saluted with a nod to nature, the idea of renewal, and wishes for good luck. But traditions had to start somewhere, so why not take the opportunity this New Year's to create an eco-friendly tradition or two? Here are some ideas:

- Plan a group outing like a hike or, weather permitting, a bike ride to a nearby park. Name it the Eco-Resolution Ride. Plan fun events at the park and pack a healthy picnic.
- Or, use an outing as an occasion to remember someone who has passed away the year before. Plant a tree or create a garden plan to initiate when spring comes.

- Use New Year's Day as an opportunity, as many do around the world, to sweep out the old. This could mean checking your medicine cabinet and jotting a date on your calendar to take expired prescriptions to a doctor's office for disposal, or examining dates on emergency supplies including stored water to ensure they are still fresh. You might take a look at your cleaning supplies and note which can be replaced by more earth-friendly choices when you run out.

- Make a journal in which to write during the upcoming year. Creating one from materials you have on hand can be as simple as stapling pages together, or more complicated—painting, sewing and/or embellishing. If you're unsure about how to bind, search the Internet, and if you prefer to purchase a journal, look for one fashioned of handmade, recycled, or tree-free materials. If each member of the family makes a journal, you might want to read from them the following New Year's Day. You could also make a family book that you keep handy so that anyone can write in it during the year, then read the entries together on New Year's Day.

- Play an **Eco Q&A** game with your family or group you might have over for a holiday meal. Make up a list of questions for each person to answer (depending on the age of family members). A few examples:
  - What habit did I change last year that impacts the environment?
  - What is the most important thing I learned last year about living green?
  - What people inspired me last year to live a more eco-aware life?
  - What am I most proud of when it comes to living my life in an eco-friendly way?
  - What is the fondest memory I have about living green?

- Get out a calendar and fill in dates for fun eco-activities throughout the upcoming year. Whether you want to volunteer to help clean up a stream or go on a tour of a wildlife refuge, noting a target date can help make it more of a reality. At the same time, plan ahead to celebrate occasions in a greener manner by noting when, in advance of each celebration, you need begin to gather supplies, make or purchase games or gifts, and plan activities. As we've said throughout this book, planning is key to any successful green celebration.

The first New Year's Eve we spent with my in-laws, my husband's mom, True, showed off her personal tradition. She climbed onto a chair at one minute before midnight, and when the clock struck the magic hour, she leapt off "into the new year." Where this tradition came from, I never knew or don't remember, but she continued performing it into her nineties (with help, of course, from one of her slightly nervous sons). This little antic offers a glimpse into Grandma True's impish personality, and as long as we are around, how can we fail to remember her with a smile every New Year's Eve?

Traditions, whether silly or meaningful, birthed out of habit, handed down through generations, or tweaked to make them personal, help connect us to those who came before. When we invent or change them in ways that reflect our personal beliefs and values, we become a part of the celebration's ongoing evolution.

Promises for the New Year

Traditional New Year's Resolutions	Corey & Lynn's New Year's "Ecosolutions"	Check Off Your Resolutions
Lose weight/eat right	Eat organic, whole foods and be aware of your portions.	☐
Pay off debt/save money	Reduce consumption and pay off debt, or pad your nest egg with money saved.	☐
Get a better job	Find or create work that is fulfilling for you and that contributes to the betterment of the world, however large or small the scale might be.	☐
Get fit	Ride your bike or walk for transportation.	☐
Get a better education/be constantly learning	Educate yourself about issues that affect you, your family, your community, the global community, and the planet we all share. Strive to learn one new fact every day and share what you know with others. You could also take a class in biodynamic gardening, or even earn a Green MBA.	☐
Drink less alcohol	Drink less alcohol, but if you do consume, buy organic/biodynamically grown and give preference to glass bottles over aluminum.	☐
Quit smoking	Quit smoking and donate the money you previously spent on cigarettes (and/or the equivalent of time you spent smoking) to an organization that is working to prevent cancer.	☐
Reduce stress	Pamper yourself with products you make with organic food, herbs and oils, and only buy beauty products that are free of toxic chemicals (Frequent CosmeticDatabase.com). Patronize organic and eco-friendly spas.	☐
Take a trip	Take an eco-vacation as close to home as possible (and buy carbon offsets for travel).	☐
Get organized	Reduce the amount of "stuff" you acquire (and accumulate). Take care of what you own and find ways to reuse or recycle everything else. Buy only high-quality, eco-friendly products that won't need replacing, and clean your home only with homemade or non-toxic products from trusted companies.	☐

Resolutions that don't need updating
(Use freely in their as-is conditions)

- **Volunteer to help others**
- **Enjoy more quality time with friends and family**
- **Find a soul mate** (assuming you're not already married)

NEW YEAR'S DECORATING TIP
Use outdated calendars taped together to make a unique New Year's tablecloth

Eco-Bubbly & Green Drinks

What's in your glass this New Year's Eve? Is it something mixed, shaken, or stirred; straight up, on the rocks, or blended; icy, hot, room temp; or some combination of the three? No matter how you like it, turn all your drinks an eco-friendly green by following these guidelines:

- Only buy organic wine and champagne. They're now widely available and are better for you, the people who grow the ingredients, and the planet. Not only does drinking organic wine help you avoid exposure from up to 250 different types of chemicals found in some conventional brands, but organic wine also has fewer sulfites, so a January 1st headache may be averted by going pesticide-free. Ask at your local store for organic alcohol or look online. You'll be impressed with the variety available, and most won't break the bank. See sidebar on page 160 for definitions of organic wines.

- If you live in a salmon sensitive part of the country, look for wines that are certified Salmon Safe. Go to SalmonSafe.org for a list of certified wines.

- Try to buy wine with real cork stoppers, and preferably stoppers that are approved by the Forest Stewardship Council. If your favorite organic or BD wine comes only with a plastic stopper or metal screw top, ask the winery to consider changing to cork. The World Wildlife Federation (WWF), a global conservation organization, says that cork is a sustainable resource and is "a vital source of income for thousands of people [and supports] one of the world's highest levels of forest biodiversity, including endemic plants and endangered species such as the Iberian Lynx, the Iberian Imperial Eagle, and—symbol of the Maghreb—the Barbary Deer." For details on why supporting the cork industry is imperative, go to the WWF's website, Panda.org.

- Whenever possible, buy alcohol in glass. It does not leach phthalates into your drink (as some plastics can) and takes fewer resources to recycle than aluminum. Karma Champagne comes in mini bottles that are recycled *and* recyclable.

- Ensure that whatever you're adding to your alcohol (fruit, mixes, etc.) is organic.

- Look on LocalHarvest.org for vineyards, breweries, and more that are organic and nearby.

For the real deal in organic beverages try:

- ○ OrganicVintners.com (organic, biodynamic (BD), and vegan wines, as well as club and wine of the month programs)
- ○ FreyWine.com (America's oldest organic and BD winery)
- ○ LoftLiqueurs.com (tree free bamboo labels)
- ○ SkySaddle.com (organic and BD wine)
- ○ ModMix.com (organic cocktail mixes)
- ○ SouthernWine.com (Liquid Ice organic vodka)
- ○ DiamondOrganics.com (organic champagne)
- ○ OrganicWineJournal.com (e-magazine for organic wine connoisseurs)

Non-Alcoholic Beverages

- ◉ Try organic sparkling beverages in champagne-style bottles. Flavors like sparkling lemonade, limeade, and tangerine from Santa Cruz Organic (SCOJuice.com) pack some citrus-filled punch.
- ◉ Make your own sparking drinks from freshly squeezed or bottled (glass preferred) organic juices and mineral water. Consider using organic, sustainably harvested juices like pomegranate, açaí, or blueberry. These are bright, festive, and packed with antioxidants.

Confused about organic and non-organic wine labels?

So is the wine industry. As we were researching this section of the book we spoke with owners of wineries, organic wine shops, and representatives from government and consumer agencies (see how far we'll go for you?), but it wasn't until Corey contacted Tom Hutcheson of the Organic Trade Association (OTA) that we understood the cause of the confusion—semantics. Until now, some of the finer points of labeling rules have been open to interpretation. According to Tom, the USDA has on their "to do list" the clarification of several policies, specifically regarding foods that do not contain 100% organic ingredients (and whether or not certain ingredients, such as yeast, can even qualify as organic). Until these issues are hashed out, what you need to know of wines in the organic category is that the biggest difference is whether or not sulfites and other ingredients are allowed to be included. Here's the scoop:

Made with Organic Grapes:	Wines not Labeled as Organic but Use Organic Ingredients:	100% Organic; Organic:	Biodynamic wine (BD wine):	Conventionally Grown Wine:
Wines that use organic grapes. May have added ingredients and sulfur dioxide (not to exceed 100 parts per million——less than allowed in conventional wines).	Wineries that are not (or not yet) certified organic may include organic grapes in their wine, **but cannot note this on the label**. In this case, the organic ingredient(s) will be noted only in the ingredient list. Sulfites may be added.	Wines that are produced with certified organically grown grapes. No sulfites may be added (although naturally occurring sulfites may exist less than 20 ppm).	Ingredients are farmed with techniques that utilize the vineyard's natural resources without the use of synthetic chemicals of any kind. Certified BD vineyards typically meet or exceed the standards and regulations for organic certified farming. May add sulfites (not to exceed 100 ppm).	Made with grapes that may have been farmed with chemicals. Grapes top the list of foods with the highest pesticide residues. Sulfides are usually added.

Other Tips:

If you've had too much to drink (even if *you* don't think you have) but you can't spend the night where you are because you just can't sleep without your Al Gore doll, call a green taxicab. Many cities now offer alternative fuel taxi services, most of which use hybrid cars and vans. So even if you're a tad hung-over in the morning, at least you can feel good about how you got home—safe, sound, and green.

Five Compelling Reasons to Drink Organic Wine

Did you know that grapes are one of the most heavily sprayed fruit crops? If that's not enough, here are five more reasons to go organic:

1. **Better Flavor and Taste**

   Organic farming starts with nourishing the soil, which eventually leads to nourishment of the planet, and ultimately, our palates. Perfectly ripened, organically grown grapes offer pure flavor and great fruit intensity.

2. **Keep Chemicals out of Your Glass**

   Two-thirds of all pesticides on the market are not registered under current EPA health standards. Many EPA-approved pesticides were registered long before researchers linked chemicals to cancer and other diseases. Now the EPA considers 60% of all herbicides, 90% of all fungicides, and 30% of all insecticides to be potentially carcinogenic. The bottom line is that pesticides are poisons designed to kill living organisms and can also be harmful to humans. In addition to cancer, pesticides are implicated in birth defects, nerve damage, and genetic mutation.

3. **Support Organic Farmers and Their Health**

   Most organic wineries are small, independently owned and operated family vineyards, concerned primarily with the environment and its entire life-chain. Farm worker health is a major concern. A National Cancer Institute study found that farmers exposed to herbicides had a six times greater risk than non-farmers of contracting cancer. An estimated one million people are poisoned annually by pesticides.

4. **Protect Groundwater Quality**

   Organic farming protects and conserves water resources. According to EPA estimates, pesticides are contaminating the groundwater in thirty-eight states, polluting the primary source of drinking water for more than half the country's population.

5. **Prevent Soil Erosion**

   Soil is the foundation of the food chain in organic farming. Due to our history of conventional farming methods, we are suffering from the worst soil erosion in history.

   —Printed with permission from Town Hall Coalition's *Organic and Biodynamic~ Wine and Vineyard List* available at TownHallCoalition.org.

Alcohol-Free New Year's Drink Recipes

WOW!

POMEGRANATE NOT-TINI

● ● ● ● ● ● ● ● ● ● ● ●

Choose local and organic ingredients whenever possible

SERVES 4

This festive non-alcoholic cocktail is a perfect addition to your holiday meal for the kids, non-drinkers in your guest party, or as an offering at your post New Year's Eve brunch.

INGREDIENTS

1 cup pomegranate juice
1/4 cup lime juice
2 1/2 cups soda or seltzer water
5 ice cubes
Pomegranate seeds for garnish
Pomegranate rind sliced into 4 1-cm by
   1-inch pieces for garnish

DIRECTIONS

Combine pomegranate juice with lime juice and soda water and ice. Shake or stir very gently for 1 minute. Strain out ice and pour drink into 4 martini glasses. Sprinkle each glass with 5-10 pomegranate seeds which will float atop the drink. Slice a small opening into the middle of pomegranate rinds and secure on the rim of each martini glass.

Contributed by Mary Purdy, certified nutritionist and registered dietitian. Seattle, WA, www. NourishingBalance.com

JUST LIKE A VIRGIN MOJITO

• • • • • • • • • • • •

Choose local and organic ingredients whenever possible

MAKES 4-5 CUPS

This tasty cocktail is perfect for a hot summer day or a celebratory occasion.

INGREDIENTS

1 tbsp water
1⁄2 cup lime juice
1⁄2 cup mint, finely chopped (leave a few sprigs for garnish)
2 tbsp agave nectar (a natural sweetener made from cactus)
Crushed ice
Soda/seltzer water
1/2 tbsp bitters

DIRECTIONS

Combine lime juice, water, agave nectar, chopped mint, bitters, and ice to a shaker or container with a lid. Shake for 30 seconds to fully combine all ingredients. Pour into 6 glasses. Add enough soda/seltzer water and several ice cubes to fill the glass. Garnish with lime and mint sprig.

Contributed by Mary Purdy, certified nutritionist and registered dietitian. Seattle, WA, www. NourishingBalance.com

CRANBERRY GINGER CIDER

• • • • • • • • • • • •

Choose local and organic ingredients whenever possible

MAKES 4-5 CUPS

This simple and refreshing beverage is excellent served hot on a brisk winter's eve or chilled with ice for a spicy summer thirst-quencher.

INGREDIENTS

2 cups real cranberry juice (try to avoid "juice cocktails" which can have added sugars or highly processed high fructose corn syrup)
3 cups apple cider
2 tbsp minced fresh ginger
1 Cinnamon stick (you can use more for garnishes if desired)

DIRECTIONS

Place all ingredients in a sauce pan and place on medium heat for approximately 20 minutes, allowing for the flavors to mingle. Strain out ginger and cinnamon stick and serve hot with a cinnamon stick as a garnish/stirrer, or place in refrigerator for an hour to cool and serve with ice.

Contributed by Mary Purdy, certified nutritionist and registered dietitian. Seattle, WA, www. NourishingBalance.com

Valentine's Day

According to a 2008 National Retail Federation report "**Consumers Opt for Quality Time with Loved Ones Over Traditional Gifts This Valentine's Day,**" for the first time ever, gifts of togetherness, such as dinner or weekend getaways, now rank higher on a list of popular Valentine's Day gifts than any other except greeting cards. Gift cards, a good green choice because they don't require wrapping and because they reduce the chance that a purchased gift will be unwanted and therefore discarded, are also rising in popularity, while the mainstays of V-Day—candy, flowers, jewelry and cards—decreased in popularity this year.

Move over red; Valentine's Day has the potential to be the greenest holiday. Can you guess why? Come on, say it with me, **love doesn't cost a thing**.

Although the history of Valentine's Day is debatable, it's actually been around since before Hallmark was a twinkle in J.C. Hall's eye. Way back in the year 496, Pope Gelasius declared that February 14th was to be celebrated in honor of Saint Valentine, and over time, the day evolved into the holiday of love. And even though Valentine's Day is now an almost $17 billion industry, showing your loved one that you care does not have to cost a dime or use up precious resources. Valentine's Day provides an opportunity to recognize that what each of us really, truly wants deep down inside is to be loved and appreciated. And while flowers, chocolates, and gifts are certainly nice, they aren't required. Expressing your love in authentic and creative ways will beat even the best "off-the-rack" gifts every time.

 Every Valentine's Day, my husband writes me a poem. Because he doesn't write poetry on a regular basis, nor is he a particularly emotionally expressive guy, receiving a poem is incredibly special. I'm so moved by his words and touched by his efforts because I know that he puts his whole heart into this gift. And even though on more than one occasion I've had to ask gently, "What does this mean?" I've loved every single one of my poems because they remind me of how much I am loved and cherished.

In 2005, according to the Los Angeles Times, Hallmark set out to discover which Valentine's Day card was the most popular and assumed that the answer would vary by locale. But much to their amazement, they found that one particular card ranked highest everywhere. The card, by designer Marcia Muelengracht, read, "For the One I love" on the card's front and on the inside stated, "Each time I see you, hold you, think of you, here's what I do ... I fall deeply, madly, happily in love with you. Happy Valentine's Day." To me it's not a shocker that people like this card. Who wouldn't be entranced by these sentiments? We all want to know that someone in the world loves us so much that it hurts (in a really feel-good kind of way, of course).

So our green suggestion for Valentine's Day is to place most or all of your efforts on showing your love in ways that will coincidentally show your love for the planet by reducing the resources that would have otherwise gone into material gifts.

Options for free (or low-cost) and green love expressions are infinite. For example, you could write your love a heartfelt letter, take him on a moonlight hike, enjoy a tandem bike ride, or prepare a picnic at the site you first met each other or where you first fell in love. You could create a video-montage of fun times you've spent together, or collect some quotes and poems that remind you of all the reasons you fell in love and continue to care. Or how about writing a song, giving a full body massage, or taking digital pictures of yourself in various locations holding signs that say, "I love you!" Be silly, be creative, but most of all, be thoughtful, and your gifts will be treasured.

Here are a few more ideas:
- Cut a bunch of old photos into heart shapes, punch a hole in each, then thread them onto a piece of yarn. Hang the strand above the bed.
- Write her a book of love. Each page might have a single sentence telling her why she is wonderful. Decorate pages with hand drawn hearts. Doesn't matter that you can't draw. This is one of those situations in which the thought really does count.
- Make a book of coupons, each one good for a massage, bubble bath, or cleaning the house, clothing optional.
- Get some cookie cutters that spell out **LOVE** (Beau-Coup.com) and make some sugar cookies together.
- Have a candlelit dinner with two twists:
  1. You cannot speak (laughter exempt).
  2. You have to feed each other every bite.
- Offer an admittedly hokey, but sweetly romantic gift like:
  1. Two pears with a sign that says: We're a perfect pair
  2. A recipe book with a card inscribed: A recipe for love
  3. A pancake turner with a card that says: My heart flips for you
  4. A light bulb (LED) with a sign that says: You light up my life

"WE SHOULD CARE [about the use of pesticides to grow flowers in other countries] because those poisons don't stay inside the [floral] tents. They drift out, they walk out on the clothes of the workers, they enter the bodies of their children, filter into groundwater, work their way up the tropical food chain, at the top of which are songbirds whose return we await up north every spring. Some of those chemicals attack the ozone layer that stretches over and protects us. Some evaporate and fall as rain or snow anywhere from the North Pole to New England. We are materially connected to those flower farms, as we are connected to all the circulating flows of the planet. Not as intimately as if we were eating the flowers, but strongly enough to care.**"**

Donnella H Meadows (1941-2001), former director of the Sustainability Institute and an adjunct professor of environmental studies at Dartmouth College

Valentine's Day 164

Kids can spread the love too. Instead of handing out store-bought cards that are not necessarily all that thoughtful or earth-friendly, encourage your children to make cards using recycled materials. (My daughter's class did this over a year ago and the cards were so special that she still keeps them in her bedroom.) Origami, paper airplane, or "fortune" cards can be made from junk mail or magazines and are a fun twist on the conventional valentine. Or, here's a sweet idea: banish paper cards altogether and instead give away edible cards by making healthy cookies or cup-cakes that say "Be Mine," "I ♥ U," and "Friends Forever."

If you're not convinced that your love will admire your eco-savvy-thoughtfulness and you want to take greening your V-Day a little more slowly, we can help you there as well. Let's start by talking about flowers, a top-selling Valentine's Day gift. Then we'll move on to chocolate, another Valentine's Day favorite. After that we'll explore cards, then candles, and later, romantic getaways. Finally, we'll tie up this discussion with a list of green gifts your sweetie pie is sure to love. If you're still yearning for more, throughout the chapter we'll even toss in a few resources for further reading.

Flowers: Only organic will do, my love.

Flowers are a staple of the Valentine's Day tradition, popular as gifts for both sexes. Roses are the preeminent symbol of love and the most popular type of flower sold on this holiday. But while a dozen roses or a bouquet of mixed flowers may make your sweetheart swoon, the truth about this crop is less than rosy.

In order to get that picture perfect look, flower farmers from all over the world commonly resort to heavy use of chemicals (such as insecticides, fungicides, and growth regulators), some of which have been banned in the United States because they are known to be toxic to people and the environment. But since most cut flowers sold in America are imported (many from countries where these chemicals are unregulated) and since the United States requires that all imported flowers be insect-free, toxic pesticides, fertilizers, and other chemicals are widely used, causing flowers to arrive at your sweetheart's door with similarly toxic residues. Even conventionally grown American flowers may contain pesticide residues up to 1,000 times greater than in food products. And while you and your love may not be eating the flowers (although certain kinds are certainly edible), exposure to toxins is possible through touching and smelling alone, although the Society of American Florists (the trade association representing the United States floral industry and "the face and voice of a strong, unified floral industry"), cites evidence stating that exposure to chemicals through residue is not proven to be harmful to consumers.

But while the debate rages over whether or not pesticide residue on flowers is dangerous for consumers, few can deny that the chemicals used in the flower biz pose risks for the hundreds of thousands of people who grow, pick, and prepare conventionally grown flowers. Numerous studies show that floral workers around the globe, most of whom are poor women of childbearing age, are exposed to chemicals day in and day out, and as a result of this exposure many suffer from ailments such as headaches, fatigue, infertility, or miscarriages, while their babies are at greater risk of being born with birth defects or other problems. In one study, nearly 60% of the floral workers in Ecuador suffered signs of pesticide poisoning. In a Costa Rican study, 50% of the workers did. Greenhouses are of special concern because people who work in them are exposed to at least 127 different chemicals while in a confined space. Certain pesticides are also known carcinogens. Floral workers are exposed to chemicals through inhalation as well as their skin, and because pesticide residue sticks to clothing, the chemicals are transported home with the workers where their children and other family members are exposed. Lastly, floral workers are often paid unfair wages and treated unethically, forced, for instance, to work overtime during holiday rushes. Workers from companies that are Fair Trade Certified, however, receive protective gear, training on safe handling of agrochemicals, fair wages, childcare and schooling for their children, paid maternity, vacation and sick leave, and financial and educational advancement opportunities.

Of course, the Earth and its non-human inhabitants suffer from pesticide use as well. Chemicals used in floriculture leach into soil, wells, and waterways (as revealed in a 2003 *San Francisco Chronicle* investigation near a California lily farm utilizing conventional farming practices) and are integrated into the food chain when animals consume sprayed plants, leading to death and/or contamination of their predators and offspring. Some portion of chemicals also evaporates and later returns to Earth in snow and rain. Other common chemicals deplete our ozone layer. All of this in the name of perfect, pest-free flowers.

Some of the most popular flowers for Valentines day, including carnations, chrysanthemums, and orchids, are extremely difficult to grow without chemicals and (at the time of this writing) are therefore not available for sale as organic or pesticide free.

And let's not forget that buying imported flowers impacts the planet as well. According to Cynthia Barstow, adjunct professor at the University of Massachusetts and author of *The Eco-Foods Guide*, "From stem to store, flowers travel an average distance of 1,500 miles, adding significantly to global warming and pollution. Every three hours, one 35-ton cargo plane departs Colombia, jetting flowers around the globe."

Although there are ongoing local and worldwide floriculture campaigns to ensure human and environmental health and well being, the very best choice you can make when buying cut flowers is to buy Certified Organic, Fair Trade Certified, VeriFlora Certified, biodynamically grown, or "transitionally grown" flowers (from farms undergoing the switch from conventional to pesticide-free), or to buy organic flowers at your local farmer's market. You can also pick your own flowers—and give your valentine a custom arrangement—from your own organic garden, from an organic flower farm, or from flowers growing in the wild, although these may not be viable options in February. You could also buck tradition altogether and give your love potted or plantable plants, or the seeds or bulbs to grow them. You could enjoy a picnic in a flower garden or, through Kiva.org, make a contribution in your sweetheart's name to an individual or family trying to generate the resources needed to open an organic flower farm.

For a cold winter's night when *eating* chocolate is just not enough, how about cozying up with your love and a shared cup of hot cocoa? Try these organic and Fair Trade brands:

- Cocoa Camino organic, Fair Trade, shade-grown (CocoaCamino.com)

- Lake Champlain organic, Fair Trade (LakeChamplainChocolates.com)

- Equal Exchange organic, Fair Trade hot chocolate (EqualExchange.com)

Online retailers:
- OrganicFlowers.com
- CaliforniaOrganicFlowers.com
- DiamondOrganics.com

Where to find local, organic flowers:
- LocalHarvest.org/organic-flowers.jsp
- Certification and floriculture resources
- TransfairUSA.org (information on Fair Trade Certification)
- Veriflora.org (all about the VeriFlora Certified Sustainably Grown program)
- Demeter-USA.org (information on biodynamic growing practices and where to buy)
- EcoBusinessLinks.com/organic_flowers.htm (resources for organic flowers)
- AboutFlowers.com (general information about cut flowers by Society of American Florists)

International green floral resources (Seventy Percent of cut flowers sold in the United States, especially on Valentine's Day, come from other countries.):

- FirfFowers.de (German based green seal "Flower Label Program")
- Floverde.com (Columbian green seal flower program)
- ExpoFlores.com (Ecuador's green seal flower program)
- FairFlowersFairPlants.com (European "initiative to stimulate the production and sales of flowers and plants cultivated in a sustainable manner")
- My-mps.com (information and certifications for international floriculture industry)
- LaborRights.org (International Labor Rights Fairness in Flowers Campaign)

Grow-Your-Own

- SeedsOfChange.com (everything you need to create your own organic bouquet)

Chocolate (It's Bittersweet)

Chocolate is a beautiful thing. Aside from the fact that it tastes good (which is a pretty big bonus indeed), chocolate—especially dark chocolate—contains a dizzying mix of over 300 naturally occurring chemicals and compounds including high concentrations of flavonoids, which are plant-based pigments that act as antioxidants, decrease inflammation, and lower blood pressure and cholesterol. Chocolate is also known to make us feel less depressed (thanks to substances that stimulate a pleasure center in the brain) and more alert (due to a substance often confused with caffeine). Throughout history it has gained almost mythical status as a powerful aphrodisiac. With all this in mind, it's no wonder that Americans spend billions of dollars on chocolate each year, about $323 million of which is for traditional Valentine's Day treats.

But while dark chocolate, in our humble option, should be nominated as a wonder of the world, or even better, for a Nobel Peace Prize (if you've ever been a young, hormonal woman living in a college dorm with other young, hormonal women, you'll know exactly what we mean), chocolate has a dark side that's important to know about.

For all the good and healthful qualities chocolate touts, it is also a major contributor of terrible offenses including deforestation, loss of wildlife habitat, massive pesticide use, and labor injustices such as forced slavery and child labor. While some of the major chocolate companies in the United States claim to recognize these issues, few have made

WHAT IS THE DIFFERENCE BETWEEN CACAO AND COCOA?

Cacao is the tree that produces the cacao pods which house cacao seeds which becomes cocoa powder from which we make hot chocolate and other treats..

The good people at Global Exchange (GlobalExchange. org) have created some fun ways to celebrate the day of love while spreading love to those who grow and make the products we enjoy on this day. Their Fair Trade Valentine's Day Action Kit includes a heart-shaped box of Fair Trade, organic individual chocolates, 30 Valentine's Day cards (with a Fair Trade message, of course), an Amore/Love banner, and an I Love Fair Trade iron-on, all sold in an recycled paper bag for just $15 (contents and price may vary). The website also sells an array of holiday and everyday gift items and has lots of ways you can get directly involved with the Fair Trade Chocolate Campaign and other issues related to global labor practices.

strides to ensure that the cacao (cocoa) they source and use in their chocolate products is grown ethically or by ecologically sound methods.

Why Sustainably Grown Cacao Matters

Cacao growing naturally in the rainforests of Central and South America as well as Africa has been cultivated for thousands of years. In its ideal form, cacao grows in a rainforest under a canopy of shady trees that are home to birds and other species of animals and insects including midges, small flies responsible for pollinating cacao. While some cacao is still grown and harvested traditionally, many forests have been cleared in order to grow sun-loving hybrid cacao plants that have higher yields and are better able to meet the massive and growing worldwide demand for chocolate. Deforestation is just one part of the problem, however; when trees are gone, so too are cacao-dependent aviary habitats, as well as the environment in which midges thrive. Without the shade, cacao trees are exposed to the elements and therefore weakened, leaving farmers to resort to heavy spraying of pesticides, which, of course, are harmful to farmers, animals, the Earth, and for you, and may contribute to pesticide resistant pests and diseases.

According to *The Green Guide*, "Pesticides used by cocoa growers include chemicals, such as paraquat, that are extremely hazardous to workers, and others, such as lindane, that are suspected of causing cancer and disrupting hormone functions and reproduction. Once sprayed, pesticides inevitably wind up in groundwater, air, and in the chocolate itself." To make matters worse, the hybrid cacao plants need constant replenishment in new soil, leading to more and more deforestation. All in all, growing cacao outside of its natural state upsets the entire ecosystem in which it is found and threatens the well being of animals, farmers and consumers alike.

The human toll of conventionally grown and harvested cacao is also alarming. In 2000, the U.S. State Department released its findings that 15,000 children from the Ivory Coast in Africa (the world's biggest supplier of cacao beans) had, in recent years, been sold or tricked into slavery for cacao, cotton, and coffee farming. In addition, the International Institute of Tropical Agriculture found that almost 300,000 children working in West African cacao farms were coping with dangerous working conditions. In 2001, two members of congress took note of the issue and asked plantation owners, traders, and manufacturers to agree to the Harkin-Engel Protocol, which asked the chocolate industry to develop certifications that would ensure chocolate to be grown and harvested without the use of child slaves. Unfortunately, the Harkin-Engel Protocol expired in 2005, without an industry-wide certification being implemented. In addition, the industry continues to struggle with additional labor issues that affect adult workers such as unsafe, unsanitary, and unfair working conditions. Individuals, governments, organizations, and companies are making strides to improve the lives of plantation workers and their children through education, training, and financial assistance. But unless the chocolate you buy to satisfy your love's sweet tooth is certified Fair Trade, the bitter truth is that it may have been grown unethically.

So this Valentine's Day, when purchasing chocolate, cast your vote (and flex your consumer power) for people-, animal-, and planet-friendly practices by seeking out chocolate that is Certified Organic, Fair Trade Certified, and Certified Shade-Grown (look for the Rain Forest Alliance Certification). And remember that more is better when it comes to third-party certifications. The ideal, of course, is "triple certified" chocolate, such as Rainforest Relief's ForestChocolate label that denotes all three of the above mentioned categories. And if the label on your chocolate doesn't mention organic, shade grown, or Fair Trade practices? Call the company to inquire. But chances are, some or all of its cacao has been grown or harvested at the expense of people, animals, and/or the planet.

Organic, shade-grown, and/or Fair Trade chocolates make up a tiny percentage of the market, yet demand is on the rise. The sale of organic chocolate, for example, is growing annually by 70%, and sales are expected to remain strong.

Fortunately for all you gift givers and chocoholics out there, dozens of companies are now moving into the organic, fair-trade arena. Many sell not only bars, but also chocolate powder and "chips" for baking, as well as specialty items like chocolate sauces, syrups, and samplers. We list many on our website, CelebrateGreen.NET, but here are three that offer organic, Fair Trade, and shade grown alternatives.

- Sjaak's Organic Chocolate (Sjaaks.com)
- Theo Chocolates (Chocleteer.com)

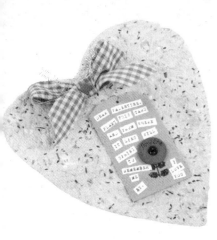

- Rainforest Friendly (RainforestFriendly.com) uses some or all **uncertified** shade grown cocoa.

Cards

Every year, consumers buy enough holiday cards to fill a football field 10 stories high. That's 2.65 billion paper greetings that mostly come from virgin trees. Valentine's Day is the second biggest holiday for card sales, so this year, show your love for the planet and your love by going tree-free (use alternative paper sources), making cards from materials you have lying around your home (just about anything can be a 'card' if you think outside the box), or using e-card services. Likewise, you can make your own paper using a blender, some screen, and some scraps of just about anything; you can even make biodegradable seed paper that later can be planted.

Candles

I thought choosing candles as a gift, not to mention a romantic accessory for a Valentine's eve, would be a no-brainer. I love them—the flickering light, the fragrance, the ambiance created when a half dozen are burning on the window sill. According to the National Candle Association, I'm not alone. Retail sales of candles are approximately $2 billion annually. Ninety-five percent of candles are purchased by women. Nearly half of women say they use candles as part of their decorating scheme.

So what's the problem?

In the 1850s scientists discovered how to separate and refine a waxy substance in petroleum into what we know as paraffin. Petroleum, of course, is not a renewable resource, and burning petroleum products produces volatile compounds (such as formaldehyde), which contribute to poor indoor air quality and, on a larger scale, global warming. Obviously, lighting a paraffin candle alone is not going to melt the glaciers, but if, like most candle aficionados you burn them once a week or more, your health could be the greatest issue.

At one time, candle wicks were stiffened with lead wire. After studying potential risks, in 1976 the U.S. Consumer Product Safety Commission warned consumers and religious groups that they might be subjecting themselves to airborne lead through use of candles

MIND YOUR BEESWAX

Beeswax candles need contain only 51% beeswax to be called beeswax candles, and soy candles can include as little as 20% soy wax. When buying candles, check for additional potentially harmful ingredients.

containing the substance. But it was not until 2003 that the CPSC voted to ban the manufacture and sale of lead-cored wicks and candles containing them after determining such candles could present a lead poisoning hazard to young children.

Today, it is likely that candles manufactured in the United States are free of lead, but many are made outside of the United States in places where lead is commonly used. Similarly, while metal core wicks made in America and manufactured from tin or zinc are thought to be relatively safe, the same product made elsewhere may not be so healthy.

A third issue for candles is that they can contain toxic ingredients masked under the name "fragrance." Candles should only be scented with essential oils (EOs) because synthetic fragrance often contains chemicals and materials that are cited as triggers of asthma, allergies, and headaches and may disrupt hormones and the nervous system. Fragrances can also accumulate in breast tissue and are secreted in breast milk. Even a 2002 article in the peer-reviewed *Flavour and Fragrance Journal* states that, "With this increased usage and exposure there are increased anecdotal and clinical accounts of fragranced products causing, triggering, and exacerbating health conditions. Further concerns relate to the bioaccumulation of fragrance chemicals in human tissue and the long-term impact. In addition there are environmental concerns as fragranced products add to both air and water pollution." If you enjoy the smell of fragranced candles, choose those that contain EOs or select our favorite, beeswax, which naturally emits a warm, honey scent.

Candle-Safety.org questions candle manufacturers regarding product safety and processes used in production. They don't test individual candles, but you can use their database to check whether or not a candle you purchase is likely to meet safety standards.

Although vegetable oil candles are available and are a better choice than paraffin, many contain palm oil, the second most popular oil in the world (after soya). Palm oil is ever present in food and cosmetics (including those made by self-proclaimed "natural" companies), but is controversial because some palm plantations have been created at the expense of rainforests and animals (most notably the orangutan) as well as indigenous

How about going 100% zero impact by memorizing a poem and reciting it for your love, writing your message in the sand, or sculpting it with food you can later enjoy together.

If you absolutely must buy your sweetheart a card, look for one made from 100% recycled paper that is at least 30% post-consumer waste. Recycled and tree-free cards can be found in stores or online. The Organic Consumer Association (OrganicConsumers. org), a non-profit "focused exclusively on promoting the views and interests of the nation's estimated 50 million organic and socially responsible consumers," sells beautiful Valentine cards printed on Hemp Heritage tree-free paper. Sales of the cards support OCA's ability to "deal with crucial issues of food safety, industrial agriculture, genetic engineering, children's health, corporate accountability, Fair Trade, environmental sustainability, and other key topics."

- Whether making or buying candles, be sure they are made from beeswax, organic soy or palm-free organic vegetable oil. Buying Certified Organic supports sustainable farming practices and ensures that you're not supporting the sale of genetically modified organisms (GMO's).

- Use only lead-free cotton wicks.

- Use beeswax candles or candles scented with EOs.

- Look online for directions on how to make your own candles by dipping or rolling and for ideas on decorating them as well.

- Consider a rechargeable, glass, or LED candle instead.

peoples. There is no certification for rainforest-, animal-, or people-safe palm oil, so until there is, it's best to avoid its use or choose organic palm oil.

The best bet is to stick with unbleached (non-white) candles made with 100% soy, or better yet, beeswax. Beeswax has many benefits over traditional candles including the fact that when compared to paraffin candles, beeswax burns cleaner, causes less soot, lasts longer, purifies the air, leaves little to no wax, has a brighter glow, and smells *divine*. Soy is a less expensive alternative to beeswax and, like beeswax, produces fewer toxic byproducts and is long-burning. Although we've never had to clean a soy candle spill, we've also heard that soy cleans up well with just soap and water. One hundred percent soy and beeswax candles also are renewable and biodegradable, and both can be made at home or purchased in natural food stores and online. When buying soy candles, look for those made from 100% organic, American-grown soy. We especially like the 100% beeswax candles from Seattle's Big Dipper Wax Works.

My dearest love,

This Valentine's Day, let me whisk you away to a romantic resort where we will enter our room after stopping to admire the recycled flip flop welcome mat made in the U.S.A. by a home-based mother of six. We'll be overwhelmed by the simple elegance of furniture fashioned from recycled or sustainable lumber and cork. Surprisingly, when we inhale, we'll breathe nothing but fresh air unpolluted by sanitizers, deodorizers, or carpet cleaning chemicals. It will be odd at first, to be free to open a window that has not been permanently shut using paint that off-gasses VOC's, but I promise, we'll grow to love it.

We'll jump joyfully into the geothermal pool, just off our xeriscape patio, then emerge to dry ourselves with bamboo towels before slipping into hemp robes and felted slippers made from the wool of sheep who are held only for shearing once a year, but who otherwise live a life of luxury feasting on herbicide-free alfalfa . Next, under the faucet that shuts off automatically after three minutes, I'll lovingly, but briefly, wash your hair using non-toxic soap from a dispenser and later massage you with 100% pure lavender oil while we are warmed by heat from stored solar cells on the roof which, by the way, can barely be seen because they are hidden by dozens of trees that help to lower the resort's temperature in the summer by at least 10 degrees. We'll dim the Energy Star qualified compact fluorescent bulbs, then slip beneath sheets made of organic cotton for a brief nap. We'll dream of the day when we have saved enough money to buy a Prius by fashioning all our necessities (and gifts for a swiftly diminishing list of friends) from naturally occurring molds and dust bunnies.

In the evening, we'll dine from corn-based plastic plates on free range chicken and kale so dark green we will be able to actually see ourselves growing healthier with every bite, along with three melt-in-your mouth spelt quinoa ravioli topped with tofu cheese. The finest organic wines will accompany the incomparable cuisine and the meal will conclude with a mix of locally grown fruit pulp molded into the shape of a Greenpeace ship, surrounded by Fair Trade dark chocolate hearts. I'll lovingly brush crumbs from your lips using a cloth napkin and together we will walk, hand in hand in the moonlight, carrying the remains of our feast to the composter.

In the morning we'll hug each other joyfully when we realize that no newspaper has been unthinkingly delivered to our door. Before leaving, our arms entwined, we will read the informational pamphlet printed on 100% post consumer waste paper, on being good green guests, and attend a thrilling class about turning lint into stationery on which to write and thank the management for our earth-friendly stay. Finally, we will agree to load up our car with sheets, towels, table linens, furniture, carpeting, window coverings, appliances, bedspreads, etc. that are no longer useable or useful to the property so we can donate them for reuse to a homeless shelter. As we leave, we'll receive a friendly wave from the gardener, so happy to be using gray water to keep the flowers blooming in their biodegradable pots without chemicals with scary names like methyleneurea.

Imagine, my love, a getaway without guilt. I know we are going to enjoy an unforgettable getaway, made even more romantic by the knowledge that together, our carbon footprint will be the size of a newborn babe's.

Love,
Me

Romantic Green Getaways

We hope you've had a bit of a laugh with our writer (Thanks, Lynn!), who maybe went a bit over the top in the pursuit of the perfectly green getaway, but interestingly enough, many hotel properties and B&B's around the world are jumping on the environmental bandwagon.

If you go to EnvironmentallyFriendlyHotels.com, you can enter the city or zip code where you'd like to vacation and receive a list of properties that claim various degrees of environmental awareness and action. There's a handy list of measures that the site uses to judge the "greenness" of each venue. These include the items mentioned in the letter, and additional ones such as educating staff about green practices, placing recycling bins in guest rooms, and promoting "green" in their PR. Only two hotels on the list (at the time of publication), own the coveted seven trees ranking, but 92 have a five-tree rating which means they received between 23-26 "Yes" check marks in green attributes.

Low-impact resorts and camp grounds, even youth hostels (OK, they're not exactly the best for romantic getaways), are starting to pop up around the world. If you happen to live in or will be visiting England or Scotland, check out The Green Tourism Business Scheme (Green-Business.co.uk) where you can find more than 1,400 tourism businesses in England and Scotland that have been certified regarding water and energy use and the purchase of local, organic food.

All this talk about environmentally acceptable places to stay is exciting, but the problem is that unless you live close enough to walk, ride a bike, or take public transport, getting there can ruin your best eco-intentions.

The greenest way to weekend is to stay as close to home as possible. For a couple, flying is the worst choice, then driving. (A car loaded with a family can actually be less environmentally impactful than going by plane. You can also purchase carbon offset credits to reduce the impact of your travel, whatever your transport mode.) Explore the train alternative too. But if you can find a romantic place to stay right around the corner, grab it. And if there is no local green choice, think outside the box. How about a home exchange? Or, if it's warm enough in February where you live to camp, you could rent a yurt or snuggle in a tent.

BUYING CARBON OFFSETS FOR TRAVEL?

Check with Green-E.org, the country's first program to certify that products sold to offset flying and driving have been verified in a number of areas including no double selling of emission reductions and appropriate disclosure to consumers.

If you choose a hotel that is close, but non-eco friendly, do your best to mitigate your own impact by following some simple suggestions.

- Ask that your bed linens and towels not be changed during a two-night or longer stay. Or bring your own. Many people travel with their own pillows, so why not pack a towel too? And rooms don't need to be cleaned every day unless they are in hospitals.
- Bring your own toiletries and soap. Do not use the "sample" sizes provided by the facility unless you know leftovers will be recycled.
- Ask about recycling. If the facility does not recycle, you might want to take home newspapers and empty bottles to dispose of them properly.
- Keep air conditioning off unless absolutely necessary and heat as low as possible.
- Stay away from the mini-bar and forget the bottled water. (See the 4th of July section to learn why.)
- Request that a newspaper not be dropped at your door.
- Keep the lights off whenever possible. Turning them low for romantic effect unfortunately has no impact on their environmental cost.

Green Valentine's Day Gifts

CHECK OUT THE BOOK *FODOR'S GREEN TRAVEL: THE WORLD'S BEST ECO-LODGES AND EARTH-FRIENDLY HOTELS.*

TIPS

- Spread the love and do your shopping on NonProfitShoppingMall. com. Don't see your favorite charity on the list? Add 'em!

- As an alternative to paper, use a cloth wrap from Furoshiki.com or VivaTerra.com, a cloth bag from CelebrateGreen.com, or wrap your love's gift with you (wink, wink).

In addition to trips and chocolate, candles and flowers, meaningful, romantic gifts are widely available in eco and organic, too.

Gifts for Her
- Lingerie
  - Looks like our friends across the pond (in England, that is), are way ahead in developing new fabrics for lingerie. There are designers who've come up with bras made from silk, hemp, bamboo, organic cotton, or Lenpur, a biodegradable fabric made from white pine tree clippings. Sounds rough on the skin, but its silky texture wins raves.
- Organic herbal slippers contain hot/cold packs to ease aching feet

I LOVE YOU WITH ALL MY HEARTS

- Heart shaped boxes made from natural or recycled materials. Inside, place a love note or two (on recycled paper, of course).
- Ethically sourced, eco-friendly jewelry (see Mother's Day section for details)
- Linda Loudermilk's "Too Hot to Handle" pink tank top (a percentage of the sale price is donated to StopGlobalWarming.org)
- Chocolate Bar accessories: purse, coin pouch, or bracelet made from repurposed, recycled content chocolate wrappers from organic, Fair Trade company (ChocolateBar.com)
- Organic heart-shaped cookies (EcoExpress.com) or all-natural, heart-shaped lollipops (NaturalCandyStore.com)
- Organic cotton, Ingeo (plant-based down alternative), or Pure Grow Wool (organic and humane) blankets

Gifts for Him
- Organic cotton, bamboo, or hemp boxers
- A pair of sustainably harvested wood sun glasses (TheGreenLoop.com)
- A love message bean. Water it, and the bean imprinted with the word love grows (TansuStyle.com)

For a Romantic Evening Together
- Alpaca throws, great for snuggling under (AlpacaUnlimited.com)
- Rainforest bath crystals and soaps (EcoExpress.com)
- Hot heart massage kit (FairLightCosmetics.com)

"...THERE'S A LOT WE CAN DO TO MAKE OUR SEX LIVES GREENER."—TREEHUGGER.COM

Valentine's Day—ahem—Activities

You might have already noticed, but doing good feels good. But did you ever wonder why? Recent scientific studies reveal that giving—*in the philanthropic sense*—creates hormonal reactions in the brain similar to those of food and sex. So while "benevolence glow" may not be a household term, we think it should be, and what better way to engage in glow-producing activities than on the holiday that celebrates love? Remember that being generous of spirit doesn't have to cost a dime; so while financial contribution might be one path to feeling good, so too are donating your time and talents. For Valentine's

Day, you could also consider doing good alongside a person you love; you'll make others feel happy while reaping the rewards together.

So if being charitable makes you feel like you're making love, does making love make you feel like being charitable?

While the jury is still out on this one (perhaps because researchers are having a hard time finding non-rabbit participants), you *can* incorporate eco-friendliness into your love life for Valentine's Day and beyond. Showering with your partner, rather than alone, is fun and saves water and energy (although *extended* showers won't). Making love with the lights out and generating your own heat are also favorites. For a complete lesson in green love, check out EarthErotics.com or TreeHugger.com. Search for "How to green your sex life."

GIFTS FOR HIM OR HER

- Have some organic handkerchiefs embroidered with a fun, but loving quote.

- If you have a special drink you share, empty and clean out the bottle, then write him a message about how much you love him or describing a favorite memory and give him your message in the bottle.

- Go to the website TheRomantic.com/kissing, and write out the list of ways to kiss (or compile your own). Tell your partner you are going to spend Valentine's Day experimenting to see which kind of kiss is best.

Baby Showers

Nothing sends a woman's credit card careening toward its limit faster than the thought of a newborn baby. There's something about thumb sized booties, caps that tie under the chin, and hand knit blankets that ignites our shopaholic tendencies.

The funny thing is, there is no time in our lives when we require less "stuff" than in infancy. Think about it: What does a newborn really need? To be nursed, to be held, to be warm. No baby comes out screaming for a $40 onesie, even the cutest one ever made that proclaims "Green Babies Rule!"

Does this mean we cannot ever buy a single thing or that we should stop welcoming babies to the world with a party? Nope! It means applying eco principles in our buying decisions and when planning a baby shower. It means before we are inexorably drawn into the vortex of Babies-R-Us or even GreenBabyCo.com, that we pause, take a breath and consider the options.

Greening Up the Baby Shower

So much of the 'stuff' that accompanies baby-focused parties is not only un-earth-friendly, it can also be potentially harmful to the pregnant mother or child. Who wants to risk that?

Throwing a green baby shower is, in many ways, the same as giving any party. For starters, you'll want to practice the 3Rs and 3Gs (see intro for explanation). When making party choices, you'll be considering not only the health of mother and baby, but also the planet and the people who grow, make, or manufacture the products you're using. Sustainability, of course, is the goal. For instance, you may choose to deliver hand made, seed-embedded invitations to your guests, line tables with beeswax candles in reused glass baby food jars, or feature a "Welcome Tree Hugging Trainee" sign made from colorful, repurposed paper.

Once you've decided to green up the shower, it's time to consider the traditional aspects. So many showers involve eating and maybe playing a game or two. The bulk of time, though, is spent opening gifts. How about shifting (not eliminating) the focus to the parents, especially the mom?

Whether she's still pregnant, is going to adopt, or the baby beat the shower date and has already arrived, any mom or mom-to-be cannot help but be overjoyed at getting a bit of extra attention. And if dad is included in the festivities, there's no reason he wouldn't appreciate being "showered" with a bit of consideration as well.

Some ideas:

- Gift mom with a shawl (preferably hand knit by someone she knows). Give it to her at the beginning of the shower, then have her unwrap a matching baby blanket later.
- Bring slippers or knit socks along with some essential oils to lend calmness and warmth.
- Have some beautiful music (or womb sounds!) playing in the background.
- Ask each guest to write down a prayer, words of encouragement, or advice that the parents can read at the shower as well as later when they're feeling "challenged."
- Offer the mom a rosewater footbath. Both parents might enjoy a hand or neck massage. Hiring a massage therapist to give everyone present the same is a great idea.
- Ask everyone to think about and share what they think the mom and dad will bring to their child's life or why they will be good parents.
- Have everyone bring a single bead with a hand-written note about why they chose that particular one. At the shower, have the mom string them. The resulting bracelet or necklace could be worn at the birth or kept for the baby to show later on how much he was cherished even before he arrived.
- Offer some all natural "Womb Lollipops" from SoothingTheWomb.com.

- Have everyone bring a stone from where they live. Add them to a pot in which a small live tree has been planted. If appropriate, parents can plant the tree with the stones around it as a reminder of the day when friends and family gathered.

- For expectant mothers or mothers awaiting the birth of a soon-to-be adopted baby, ask everyone to sit in a circle. Give a ball of wool yarn to the person sitting next to the mom-to-be and ask that person to share a prepared poem, wish, or positive thought about the upcoming birth or adoption. Then ask that person to hold onto one end and pass the ball of yarn to the person sitting next to her. That person shares some positive words, holds onto the strand, and passes the ball to the next person. This process continues until everyone in the circle has given the mom gifts of supportive words and the group is holding the string together, in a complete circle. When the expectant/new mom receives the ball, she can say whatever she wishes. She is then invited to wrap the string around her wrist. Scissors are sent around the circle and each person cuts enough yarn to form a bracelet. Everyone will wear their bracelets until they receive word that the new baby has been born. As a final gift to the mom, once her baby comes home, the host of the shower can present a keepsake baby cap or blanket knit from the same skein of yarn as the bracelets were made.

- If the parents of the expectant parents have planned ahead—way ahead—a shower is the perfect time to unveil clothing, toys, blankets, and baby books that once belonged to the new parents and that the grandparents-to-be have been saving. See below for safety note about previously owned toys.

Gifts

When choosing gifts for a green shower, you'll want to ensure that they are made from healthy, sturdy, sustainable materials.

Clothing

- A newborn's thin skin readily absorbs chemicals that come into contact with it, including those that are transmitted via conventionally grown cotton or petroleum-based fabrics. Instead, choose clothing made from organically grown fibers such as organic cotton, hemp, organic wool, bamboo, or silk with no finishing agents and, if you like, colored with eco-friendly dyes. But remember that when it comes to colorful clothing, it's the parents you're pleasing, not the baby.

- Wool is an ideal material for baby clothing, hats, and bedding. It helps moderate a baby's temperature, is naturally fire- and dust-mite retardant, naturally anti-microbial, and biodegradable/compostable.

- Used and handmade clothing are great choices (some eco-savvy parents are now asking that all their gifts be pre-owned).

- Find inspiration to create a gift yourself in the book *Nature Babies: Natural Knits and Organic Crafts for Moms, Babies, and a Better World* by Tara Jon Manning.

- Recycled cashmere booties from SoothingTheWomb.com.

- Hats with large brims and flaps that protect the back of the baby's neck from the sun. Look for ones made from eco-friendly fabrics.

- Organic hand crocheted baby shoes from ZiaAndTia.com.

- Have guests sign an organic T-shirt or onesie.

- Purchase plain organic T-shirts from AmericanApparel.net in a variety of sizes, then embroider on phrases like:

  - ★ Eco babies rock
  - ★ Eco geek in training
  - ★ I'm sustainable
  - ★ Loco for eco

  - ★ My mom's greener than your mom (picture of a frog)
  - ★ Nature girl/nature boy

  - ★ Organically grown
  - ★ Protect my environment. Please.

Toys

- Too many toys contain hidden dangers including lead (a neurotoxin) and phthalates (a hormone disruptor), as well as other toxins that can harm babies in the short- and long- term. The safest toys are made of natural, pesticide-free materials such as organic cotton, hemp, wool, silk, or untreated wood. Look for products made in America and buy quality items that will last and won't need upgrades, batteries, or replacement. PlanetHappyToys.com labels toys for health, sustainability, and human-friendliness (Fair Trade). They'll even tell you where in the world their toys originate.

- Do a search on the Internet for organic or eco-toys and you'll be drowning in cuteness. Even mainstream stores like Target are carrying some, but be sure to check the labels to ensure what you are buying is the real deal. Amazon offers a darling anteater made of organic cotton and stuffed with pure wool.

- If you are buying used or gifting a treasured toy from your own childhood, be sure to look it over for loose parts. Also, heirloom toys including painted rattles, small cars, and blocks are likely to contain lead. Older plastic toys also can contain chemicals that are especially susceptible to breaking down in heat (leaching of the chemical Bisphenol-A from plastic baby bottles into milk has raised serious concerns and may be removed from new bottles prior to this book's printing, but be careful of older ones), so if plastic toys were put away in an attic, they may not be safe. See what you can learn about a particular item by searching online, but when in doubt, do not pass the item on. It can be kept in a sealed cabinet, but should never be played with or given to a child, especially one fond of putting everything in her mouth.
- Organic cotton or wool crocheted baby blocks and balls.

Furniture and Bedding

- Choose bedding (including pads) made from organic cotton, wool, silk, bamboo, or hemp. See "clothing" for explanation of why this is important.
- Furniture should be made from natural materials (no composites, plywood, or particleboard) and preferably finished with beeswax or vegetable-based wax or oils. If this is not available, no-VOC/water-based paints and stains should be used. Look for furniture that is made from sustainable wood, preferably FSC or Greenguard certified.
- Wood or bamboo rockers, changing tables, potty chairs, feeding chairs (high chairs), bowls, and step stools are ideal.
- How about a rocking chair created from webbing sourced from surplus stocks of automotive seat belts from GreenAndMore.com.
- Think long-term use. If a crib can be converted into a toddler bed, it's a better choice. Moses baskets have become popular (look for ones made from organic materials) for infants and can be used later as a "bassinet" for your child's baby dolls and stuffed animals.

Other Goodies

- Give gifts of yourself such as preparing healthy meals for the new family, babysitting, doing laundry or housecleaning, or offering to rent a flick and prepare dessert for a "new parent movie date."
- Gift certificates for baby massage classes or mommy and me yoga.

- Books on parenting such as *The Green Parent* by Jenn Savedge
- Items that encourage bonding between parents and child like slings made from organic materials or organic pillows to support baby's head when she is nursing.
- Depending on the parents' taste, fun, cute or inspirational drawings, paintings, or photographs, framed in natural wood, or if you're a photographer or artist, offer to capture an image of the new family.
- LED night lights
- Organic cotton or bamboo towels and wash cloths
- Babies generally don't need all the powders and lotions we foist on them, but if you select these items as gifts, be absolutely sure they are natural, organic, made for infants, and that they are free of parabens. If you don't know, don't buy. Also check for natural, low-impact laundry wash such as that made by Bi-O-Kleen or Seventh Generation, and cloth (organic cotton or hemp) or chlorine-free disposable baby wipes that are also paraben-free.
- A metronome or heart-beat CD. Sometimes helps when baby can't be next to mommy's heart.
- Diaper bag made from recycled materials
- Natural rubber duckie
- Hand made mobile. Not for over baby's crib, but nearby where he can watch.
- A necklace with the baby's name on a charm made from recycled silver in sizes for dad as well as mom.
- Make or purchase the baby's first initial in wood. Decoupage with photos of the baby's parents or paint to match the baby's room. Add a ribbon for hanging.
- Cruelty-free wool car seat cover from LaLaNatural.com
- Donations made to an organization in the baby's name. A few of interest:
  - KidsInDanger.org—Works to protect children by improving product safety
  - LaLecheLeague.org—A mom-to-mom network to support breastfeeding mothers and their babies
  - ChildrensEnvironment.org—Part of New York's Mt. Sinai hospital, "seeking definitive answers about the relationship between toxic chemicals and health so we can protect our children, now and in the future."
  - Treeswing.org—Aims to be a catalyst for curbing childhood obesity

BABY BONNET

Make a simple baby bonnet from a handkerchief that baby can wear home from the hospital or at its christening. Mom can tuck it away until her child is grown and ready to get married. On that day, with a ceremonial snip of a single stitch, the hat returns to a hankie which can be presented to the bride (by her mother or the groom, if the hat belonged to him) and pinned under the bride's wedding dress for good luck or for "something old." Look for directions on the web.

- MarchOfDimes.com—Dedicated to improving the health of babies by preventing birth defects, premature birth, and infant mortality.

Wrapping

The best choice for wrapping is one that generates zero waste. What better to wrap a gift for a newborn than something that the baby (or parents) can later use or enjoy? One idea is to use organic cotton baby clothes, cloth diapers, or silk play cloths. Another is to ask all the guests to wrap gifts in gently used clothing, blankets, or other fabrics that will be sewn into an eclectic, keepsake quilt.

For more about raising an eco baby (or to support a family who is):

- TinyFootprints.org
- HealthyChild.org
- AskDrSears.com

Graduations

At a Washington state middle school, children raise coho salmon hatchlings that are released into an on-campus stream.

Elementary kids in Minnesota work at prairie restoration as part of their curriculum.

A private Long Island, New York school relies on geothermal energy to assist its air conditioners, and an early childhood center in Massachusetts not only boasts its own wind turbine, but also purchases solar and wind power.

Hundreds of educational institutions around the United States, from preschools to college level, have begun building (or rebuilding) to green standards, serving local food, recycling, using eco-sensitive procurement policies, and/or focusing resources on pesticide reduction. Waterless urinals, low-flow toilets and fixtures are no longer oddities in these buildings.

College students, always among those on the forefront of change, are demanding green dorms, recycling everything from film to furniture, handing out compact fluorescent bulbs to incoming freshmen, lobbying hard for alternative fuel use (students at Middlebury College in Vermont pushed through a biomass plant), and encouraging carbon offsets to equal out the toll that campus-sponsored events take on the planet, among many other eco actions.

In 2007, graduating students at more than 100 universities took sustainability pledges promising to recycle and conserve resources. Many affixed a green ribbon to their gowns as a public display of their commitment to a sustainable future.

A growing number of school districts and state legislatures are mandating sustainable design for future construction projects. Schools at all levels, seeking an official "green school" label or certification, or are working to make it onto a well-publicized list like the Sierra Club's annual top ten green college campuses or TheGreenGuide.com's top ten environmentally-committed K-12's.

All this to say that eco awareness and action have taken hold in educational institutions. From preschool to grad school, public, private or religious, schools today play a major role in the green movement. So when celebrating an educational milestone, it only makes sense to honor students by paying homage to this increasingly significant aspect of their education.

All of the usual green actions, of course, apply to graduation parties. Whether borrowing rather than buying, putting out recycling bins, or purchasing from local farmers, there are dozens of ways to put your green stamp on the celebration. (See other chapters for specifics.)

Another aspect of life that most graduates share (well, once past preschool anyway), is a desire to use what they've learned to help others. This may be especially true among those college graduates who take the sustainability pledge, students who attend fully committed "green schools," or those with an emphasis on caring for each other as well as the environment.

That's why graduation is the perfect time to gift green-minded grads with something that appeals to their eco altruism. Here are some ideas:

- Put the graduate's values to work by purchasing shares in a socially responsible investment fund. You can find both individual funds and trained specialists to handle the transaction by doing an Internet search.

- A DonorsChoose.org gift certificate allows recipients to pick from a variety of classroom projects that are seeking funding around the United States. Teachers write a proposal addressing a classroom need such as "Green Technology Fuel Cell Solar Hydrogen Technology Kit so the students can have hands on experience with the energy sources of the future." You may fund all or part of a project.

- Facebook aficionados may welcome a heads up and a little cash to start or boost fundraising for a favorite cause. The "Causes" application allows users of this social-networking site to publicize their favorite cause, recruit friends, and donate to almost any non-profit. Check to see if the graduate is already using this application and if not, encourage her with a donation.

- Sustainable, eco and green travel entered our vocabulary recently and have no definitive definitions. In general though, they all stress the importance of travelers respecting and conserving the destination's economic, environmental, and socio-cultural balance, as well as taking responsibility for the impact of their own actions and impact in respect to traveling. The demand for this type of travel has exploded, so options abound close to home and around the globe for students ready for a graduation trip.

  o Remember that when it comes to the Earth, the most cost-effective trips are those that involve the least actual travel, thus requiring the least expenditure of fuel in getting to the destination and using it once there. Gifting a grad with an eco-trip? Choose a place where, for instance, participants hike or bike instead of require a car to get around.

  o Check out our Valentine's Day chapter for ideas on finding eco-friendly hotels and resorts.

  o In general, eco tourism in the Americas focuses more on outdoor adventures, while in Europe farm stays or work programs tend to be the norm. Asia offers lots of adventure travel as well as eco-cultural tours.

  o Know the difference between eco-holidays that focus on creating a light footprint in every aspect of the operation and those that allow vacationers to experience nature close up. Both may be considered "green," depending on your definition. If the graduate is interested in choosing an up close and personal look at nature, be sure to clarify in advance how responsibly the entire operation is managed.

o Find socially responsible eco-travel organizations by checking with Green Globe (www.EC3Global.com). Utilize their search to plan a trip with organizations that are taking positive steps toward environmental sustainability and have earned Earth Check or Green Globe certification.

o For a fascinating learning experience, the graduate might like to try "wwoofing" (from the phrase "working weekends on organic farms"), the recently-coined term for an organic farm stay. Hosts exchange food, accommodations, and opportunities to learn about organic lifestyles in return for volunteer help. Wwoof. org offers hundreds of prospects around the world. Go to the website, click on the United States, and type in any state to find organic farms close to home which have the added benefit of alleviating the global implications of long-distance travel. As a gift, you can pay the small fee charged to cover the costs of planning or shell out for carbon offsets to address the cost of travel (TerraPass.com, CarbonNeutral.com, RenewableChoice.com or CarbonFund.org.).

o Voluntourism.org offers a unique way of choosing and planning a volunteer travel experience by asking tourists to assess their values, then matching them to potential trips. Next they start you thinking of questions to ask about potential destinations and activities so you can make a decision. Once the trip is selected, the site can walk the traveler through trip preparation, processing the experience, post trip, and preparation for future adventures.

o A great gift for the traveling graduate is a bag containing "green" personal care products like organic toothpaste and shampoo with unnecessary packaging removed and recycled. Make the bag itself one that can be expanded for use in carrying groceries, laundry, or souvenirs.

o For a grad who is into backpacking, a small stove to cook meals from locally grown ingredients, a solar powered radio, or a water purifier would be welcome gifts.

o A digital camera with a reminder to take pictures and leave behind flowers, rocks, shells, and other items in the natural landscape, and one or two extra memory cards.

o A tree-free paper travel journal and recycled pens.

CARBON CONTROVERSY

Purchasing carbon offsets to "neutralize" the emissions from events or air travel seems like a great idea. So what's the problem? Critics claim that offsets allow people to make un-earth friendly choices, then buy their way out, neatly staving off a guilty conscience. Some point out that the ability to buy offsets may reduce the likelihood that purchasers will strive to make needed changes toward sustainability. Others believe that at the very least, the carbon offset industry's term "carbon neutral," is a misleading gimmick. Additional concerns include the difficulty of regulating the offset market, doubts about the effectiveness of offset projects, and the potential for scams.

We'd like to suggest a happy medium. Strive to make the best possible eco-choices. But when your wedding, vacation or event requires travel or high energy use, buy offsets or offer them to your guests. True, trees may be planted in some faraway place, but trees will be planted. For more and updated information on the pros and cons of carbon offsets, and attempts to ensure the money donated toward them is well-spent, do an Internet search.

Green Weddings

 When my husband and I married in 1999, the word "green," for the most part, was associated with St. Patrick's Day, golf, and lawns. In retrospect, many of our wedding choices were "green," although to be honest, at the time we were driven more by budget awareness than eco-awareness.

Yet our wedding is proof that a magical, memorable and earth-friendly wedding can also be affordable. We saved on décor, for example, by holding our ceremony in a sunlit park and the reception at a nearby beach front art gallery. (Who needs expensive décor when you can treat your guests to vibrant flowers, light dancing off ocean waves, and fascinating paintings?)

We saved on food by choosing a vegetarian buffet (much of which was locally grown) that also served as décor. We selected fresh, colorful foods with an emphasis on green (one of our wedding colors). At the hands of our caterer, the buffet table was transformed into a sculpture of elegantly arranged baskets, herbs, and greenery surrounding aromatic dishes that won over even committed meat eaters.

I had hoped to wear my mom's wedding dress, but it was too small. So she took it apart and made, among other things, the precious pillow that carried our rings. And from the pillbox hat she'd worn when she and my dad had married 30 years before, Mom fashioned a draw-string purse. I was thrilled to wear her original multi-layered veil onto which Mom had hand-sewn hundreds of tiny pearls to make it extra special for me.

 We rented tableware and linens, and the centerpieces were edible and/or reusable. Flowers (including my bouquet and those for the bridal party) were locally grown. Instead of hiring a band or a DJ, we asked musician friends and family to play (which also brought a bit of "us" into the event, although I'll never forget the look on Ryan's Jewish grandmother's face when my brother's Tex-Mex band, outfitted in outlandish sombreros, took to the stage). After the reception (at sunset), in place of hiring a limo, my new hubby

and I walked hand-in-hand, in full bridal garb (a previously owned dress for me and a rented suit for Ryan), down the beach to our nearby hotel.

If we were getting married today, in addition to all we did then, we would use tree-free or recycled invitations, eliminate the programs, purchase ethically sourced rings, and register for donation-for-a-cause gifts.

In our defense, green weddings were still uncommon in 1999. Eco-friendly information and resources were as difficult to find as a Prius in Antarctica. But today's brides and grooms seeking to make their weddings an extension of their love for each other and the Earth have unlimited green options available, no matter their budget or wedding fantasy.

To help make your wedding choices easier, we've compiled a green wedding checklist that, like our other checklists and advice we offer, should be taken as a suggestion. If something we say doesn't work for your soon-to-be-spouse or your soon-to-be-mother-in-law, your great-aunt-Sue, or you, leave it off the list and find other ways to reduce your wedding-day footprints. Planning your big day is stressful enough. Turning it green shouldn't be. Have fun, make it your own, and above all else, remember to focus on what matters most to you as a couple.

Green Wedding Checklist

Paper goods: save-the-date announcements/invitations/programs/thank you notes

- ☐ Save-the-dates can be done through e-mail, and so can RSVP's.

- ☐ Are printed programs and menus really necessary?

- ☐ Invitations, place cards, and thank you notes are made from tree-free, 100% post-consumer waste recycled fibers or plantable seed papers and mailed in eco-friendly envelopes. Hand deliver when you can if you don't have to drive to do it.

Attire
- ☐ Use your mother's, grandmother's, or friend's gown, veil, and accessories, or have them remade to suit you.

THIS SUPER GREEN GIFT WILL BRING LASTING MEMORIES

If the bridal bouquet includes roses, turn one into a bush as a lasting reminder of the wedding day. Simply cut four to six inches from the stem and place in water. Change the water every day. In four to six weeks, small buds should appear at the base. When roots reach four inches, plant in a pot. Keep indoors and continue to water daily. Move the pot outdoors in warm weather. Surprise the bride on her first anniversary with her own heritage rose bush.

- [ ] Rent or borrow the dress. If you enjoy vintage gowns, check out your local shops for recycled dresses. Also try Craigslist and eBay for bargains.

- [ ] Rent or borrow the suit/tuxedo.

- [ ] Rent or borrow the bridal party's attire.

- [ ] Give your bridal party color swatches and ask them to select dresses/suits that will coordinate but that they'll surely wear after the wedding. Better yet, choose a color (or two) that most will already have in their wardrobe and invite your friends to wear something they own and like. You should approve the choices, of course, but especially for those who are continually asked to be bridesmaids, this thoughtful action can mean a lot.

- [ ] Children's clothing can be as expensive as grown ups, yet many, especially girls, already have perfectly acceptable party clothes. The ring bearer can look as adorable in a shirt, tie and pants he already owns as in a tuxedo. Take a look at current wardrobes before buying new.

- [ ] Make or purchase bridal attire from earth-friendly fabrics such as organic cotton, silk (Peace Silk preferred), and hemp. Many designers now make eco-conscious and eco-luxurious attire and accessories. For starters, try Annatarian.com, GetConscious.com, Rawganique.com, and ThreadheadCreations.com. (You can even buy a sustainably sourced, custom-made bridal corset from MyCorset.com.)

- [ ] After the wedding, contribute attire and accessories to GlassSlipperProject.org, MakingMemories.org, or similar organizations that help create fairy-tale experiences for others.

Rings

- [ ] Use heirloom, antique, reclaimed/recycled, found, or ethically and ecologically sourced metals, stones, or other materials. (See the jewelry section in Mother's Day for more information on jewelry.)

☐ Take a look at the exquisite reclaimed wood wedding bands from TouchWoodRings.com.

Ceremony locale

☐ Have your wedding and reception within walking distance of each other so that the wedding party and your guests don't have to travel during the event.

☐ Choose a cozy location (one that's not too large) and let your guest provide the heat during the winter.

☐ Have your wedding during the daytime hours in months that are not too cool or warm to avoid the need for lighting, heat, or air conditioning.

Flowers

☐ Use organic, locally grown, or wild flowers.

☐ Make a big impression carrying single flowers instead of a massive bouquet. Think simple and elegant rather than over-the-top.

☐ For centerpieces, choose live potted plants, then gift them to the wedding party participants or guests.

Food & Beverages

☐ Offer a fresh, local buffet artfully arranged to double as décor.

☐ Serve cold food and eliminate the financial and ecological cost of keeping it warm.

☐ Plan only for the amount you'll need.

☐ Send leftovers home with the guests (don't forget to have some saved for you!) or take what you can to a food bank or shelter. One couple we know took their leftover cake to the local fire station to be shared among a group of guys who could have cared less that it wasn't wrapped.

☐ Ask your local bakery to create your cake from all natural, organic, and locally sourced ingredients. Vegan cakes are also gaining in popularity.

- ☐ Buy (or ask your caterer to buy) drinks in the largest containers possible, with a preference given to glass above aluminum and aluminum over plastic. Serve drinks in reusable glasses.

- ☐ Serve organic (and if possible, local) alcoholic and non-alcoholic beverages.

- ☐ Serve organic, Fair Trade, shade grown coffee and organic, Fair Trade teas.

Décor

- ☐ Rent, borrow, or buy used linens, tableware, glassware, serving pieces, and other decorative items.

- ☐ If using paper napkins, be sure they're 100% recycled or compostable.

- ☐ Use live greenery or natural décor that can later be planted, composted, or consumed.

- ☐ Use recycled, repurposed, or reclaimed materials (for your centerpieces, place-card holders, and other décor items) that can also be recycled, repurposed, reclaimed, or otherwise enjoyed after the ceremony.

- ☐ Ice sculptures are virtually zero waste.

- ☐ Use LED, solar lights, or 100% beeswax or soy candles.

Favors

- ☐ Use consumables, beeswax, or soy candles, live seedlings, seed favors, or make donations to a worthy cause in your guests' names.

- ☐ Make sachets with fabric swatches and organic herbs found locally or in the bulk section of your natural foods store.

Gifts

- ☐ Register at iDoFoundation.com, JustGive.org, AfricanDowry.org, or similar sites where you can create a donation registry or register for gifts that give back to causes that matter most to you.

- ☐ If you register for specific items, check to see if they are available from stores that are as eco-friendly as possible.

- ☐ Register for gifts of experiences that are close to home—rock climbing, canoeing, rollerblading, biking, theater tickets, or aquarium visits. Choose fun activities that you might enjoy trying together.

Traditions

- ☐ Provide organic lavender or bird-safe, biodegradable rice for tossing.

- ☐ Use a garter belonging to a relative or best friend

- ☐ Purchase a Fair Trade, tree-free wedding album from GXOnlineStore.org for your guests to sign or for you to store your photos. Or create a digital album to view online or put on a DVD to be viewed on a television.

- ☐ Regarding your tears of happiness, know that some facial tissues are embedded with pesticides meant to fight off colds and flu. Choose a good old fashioned hankie instead, or go with tissues made from recycled fibers without the use of pesticides or chlorine bleach.

Transportation

- ☐ Walk, ride a bike, or even skateboard away from the wedding. If you'll be too tired and want someone else to do the work, in some locations you can hire a bike-drawn chariot. If it's raining or freezing out or you're craving a little more luxury, use a hybrid, electric, or bio-diesel chauffeur service.

- ☐ Purchase carbon offsets (from sites such as TerraPass.com) for guests who have come from near and far to attend your big day.

Honeymoon

- ☐ Choose a travel company, airline, or destination that already has offsets built in. Go to ClimateCare.org for a list of some of these businesses.

- ☐ Choose destinations that are closer to home.

- ☐ Visit green and eco-considerate hotels, resorts, or bed and breakfasts. (See Valentine's Day Chapter.)

Lynn crafted a pillow from her wedding dress fabric and converted the pillbox hat she wore at her own wedding 30 years before, into a drawstring purse for Corey.

- ☐ Turn your honeymoon into a vacation that helps other people, endangered animals, or the planet. Go to CharityGuide.org for more information.

Miscellaneous

- ☐ Choose a wedding planner who understands your vision for an eco-savvy wedding and who has experience, or at least and interest in, green special event planning.

- ☐ Request that your photographer use a digital (not film) camera. Limit the number of prints you order. Instead, choose digital wedding albums that can be placed on a CD or DVD and simply viewed on a computer or TV. Ask wedding participants to avoid printing photos as well. Given access to the digital photos, they can easily create slideshows of whichever ones they choose using one of many online services like Shutterfly.com.

- ☐ After your wedding post leftovers from bags to bells on RecycleYourWedding.com.

- ☐ Have a zero waste wedding: Elope (walk) to the nearest courthouse in a borrowed dress and suit having purchased nothing but the wedding license and needing nothing more than the love between you.

Wedding Anniversaries

Most Americans are familiar with the idea that certain gifts are associated with particular anniversaries, the most well-known probably being the 25th (silver), 50th (gold), and 75th (diamond). The history of the traditional list dates back to medieval times when a garland of silver was bestowed by a spouse on his wife of 25 years. Other anniversaries were noted in Europe throughout history by the giving of gifts of wood or metals.

In 1937 the American National Retail Jewelers Association produced a comprehensive list, associating a type of gift with every anniversary up to the 15th, then each fifth year after that to the 60th.

That list has been modernized (no doubt by people hoping to sell more high end products including real estate—yes, it's true that one "modern" listing matches the gift of land and improved real estate with the 41st and 42nd anniversaries, respectively), with the basic concept remaining the same. Generally speaking, each year's gift is progressively more valuable, honoring the continually growing commitment of a couple over time (although this does not explain the unlikely modern gift for the 44th anniversary—groceries).

Since we agree with the sentiment (in fact, we believe couples should consider putting a little less money and thought into getting hitched—which just about anyone can do—and a little more into commemorating anniversaries—which represent proven commitment), we'd like to propose an ultra-modern anniversary gift list with—surprise, surprise—an emphasis on sustainability.

But unlike modernists whose gift ideas tend toward the financially extravagant and attempt to underscore that stuff=love (I love you so here's a bunch of stuff to prove just how much), our Green Anniversary Gift List above all else honors the couple through generosity of spirit. Few of the listed gifts require or include mass consumerism. For instance, a first anniversary gift might be a poem written on handmade paper, while a fourth anniversary present could be an evergreen seedling or fruit tree that will continue to grow along with the marriage. For years 25, 50, and above, instead of buying new jewelry gifts, consider family heirlooms or recreated pieces from precious metals you already own. No matter which year you're celebrating (and congratulations, by the way!), let your creativity, time, and energy be your primary gifts to your love (or others in your life whom you are celebrating). Everything else will be just icing on the cake. And by considering the Earth in your gift choices, you'll be honoring not only your marriage but the future of marriages on the planet.

And if you don't see a gift that seems fitting for the happy couple or the year that you'd like to celebrate on our list? Start a new tradition by making up your own; just be sure each gift comes from the heart. And who knows? Maybe your ideas will catch on and 100 years from now, happy couples will have you to thank for a meaningful and sustainable contribution to wedding anniversaries.

Corey and Lynn's Green Anniversary Gift Guide

Anniversary	Traditional	Modern	Green
1st	Paper	Clocks	Recycled or tree-free paper
2nd	Cotton	China	Organic cotton
3rd	Leather	Crystal/Glass	Recycled glass
4th	Flowers, fruit	Appliance	Organic flowers/fruit or energy star appliance
5th	Wood	Silverware	Reclaimed wood or tree planting
10th	Tin/aluminum	Diamond	Recycled aluminum
20th	China	Platinum	Estate or heirloom china
25th	Silver	Silver	Recycled Silver
40th	Ruby	Ruby	Eco-travel
50th	Gold	Gold	Recycled gold
60th	Diamond	Diamond	Cultured diamond
75th	Diamond	Platinum	Fund a green project

Birthdays that Give Back

No child old enough to understand her birthday is too young to understand the importance of giving back. Celebrating a birthday by acknowledging the needs in the world gives deeper meaning to the event than cake, candles, ice cream, and even loads of tangible gifts can.

Giving can be the main event of the party. For instance, a summer birthday might be celebrated at a park where there is a need for removal of invasive weeds. The party might include identification games about weeds, prizes for whoever picks the most, etc. Beach clean ups, writing letters in support of organizations trying to stop the importation of toxic toys, helping plant a community garden, sorting clothing and toys at a local food bank— the list is endless.

If you're not sure where to start, go to VolunteerMatch.org and type in your zip code. In the drop down menu, indicate your area of interest and up will pop dozens of opportunities. Seek out organizations that offer bite-size projects where a group could contribute a few hours. You can also call local organizations, let them know you'd like to volunteer your crowd of children or adults, and ask what they have to offer. Many will be thrilled to have you.

If you're not ready to make giving the central theme of your birthday celebrations, you can still do good while having fun. Ask guests to bring the same number of canned or packaged foods as the age of the birthday child. So if she's seven, request that each guest bring seven cans. During the party, the children can decorate bags and include the words, "This donation is made in honor of Lizzy's 7th birthday." Afterwards, take your daughter to the food bank to distribute the bounty.

 And if you're not a kid anymore? I've done this for my birthday, asking guests, instead of gifts, to bring contributions to the food bank. I can't tell you how great it is to deliver the bags. It's a wonderful feeling to know that others are benefiting from my turning a year older. (And by the way, I haven't asked people to bring my age in food, but maybe this year I will. Hmmm, I'm 63. I'd need a bigger van to carry everything!)

As part of every birthday celebration, we suggest you consider enjoying time together in a "giving" environment. Depending on your interests and those of your children, you will find choices that meet your own needs and values. But whatever you do, putting your energy and enthusiasm toward bettering others' lives and/or the life of the planet cannot help but bring meaning to each year we enjoy the privilege of being alive.

It's important, especially when you're dealing with children, to talk with the birthday child first about what you are thinking of doing. Involve him in all decisions about the activity and organization. Also be sure to find ways to make the child feel happy as well as important as this is, after all, a celebration in his honor. And doing for others doesn't necessarily mean no gifts. This is a decision only you can make, with your child, of course. If you do decide to forgo gifts though, you might want to consider rewarding your child's altruism by giving him one present he badly wants.

Birthdays planned around giving instead of receiving help children to take the focus off materialism. (By the way, for help thinking about this idea and discussing it with your child, take a look at BirthdaysWithoutPressure.org, ECHOAge.com, or read *Raising Charitable Children* by Carol Weisman.) If you need ammunition to convince yourself that this is the way to go, just do an online search for charitable birthday party and you'll read about everyone from five-year-olds asking guests to donate to a no-kill animal shelter to Prince Harry, younger son of Prince Charles and Princess Diana, who marked his 18th birthday by foregoing a lavish celebration and instead set up a schedule of charity work to remind the public of his mother's commitment to causes.

If you believe your children's ideas about "how birthdays should be" are too entrenched, why not serve as a role model, and before asking him to consider the idea, do it for your own birthday. Be sure it is a fun experience for everyone, then ask your child if he would like to do the same.

Below are some suggestions for activities that could be adapted to giving and celebrating. Be sure to let your guests know in advance where you'll be going so they can dress appropriately. Of course, you'll consider the age and abilities of guests and reassure them that along with a bit of work will come fun too. Ask your contact at the organization about games or activities that can be a part of the volunteer effort.

You could make this a tradition in your family by sticking with one organization every year or choosing a new one annually. Once you start down this path, we bet you'll come up with loads of ideas. Share them and your experiences with us on our website, CelebrateGreen.NET.

Age	Where to go	What the group might do
1-4	Organic farm/orchard	See the animals. Pick fruit or vegetables if allowed.
	Dog rescue organization	Pet dogs and talk with them.
	Ronald McDonald House	Take books, old toys and games.
	Home	Make cards for ill children that you can take to a local hospital after the party.
	Fire department	Instead of presents, ask parents to bring a donation. Call ahead and arrange to visit the fire house and bring the donation.
5-7	Park	Plant a tree in honor of the birthday child. Help with planting or painting pots for plants, beautifying the park.
	Animal food bank	Take food and help sort.
	Big Brothers/Big Sisters	Have mom and dad organize an outing for "bigs" and "littles," doing something together with them like starting a garden or painting recycling bins.
	Farmer's Market	Hand out fabric shopping bags.
	Environmental organization	Plant acorns.
	Owl organization	Help with creating owl habitat.
	Family service organization	Help prepare healthy brown bag lunches for children.
	School or camp	Build a solar oven.
	Home	Assemble baby supply kits to give to new moms in need.
8-12	Beach	Help clean up, storm-drain stenciling, applying marine debris awareness labels to recycling bins.
	Pet Rescue event	Help animals find a good home by talking with the public.
	Parks Department	Pot seedlings.
	Foster Care support group	Put on a green party for children in foster care.
	Local library	Read books about the environment to younger children.
	Backyard gleaning program	Help harvest fruits or veggies from local homes that have gardens to support the local food bank.
	Non-profit thrift shop	Sort clothes.
	National forests	Reseed after fires.
	Home	Make teddy bears for sick children.
Teens	Therapeutic riding program	Help disabled children ride, or help with barn maintenance.
	River Restoration program	Help clear debris and mulch.

Age	Where to go	What the group might do
	Special events	Fundraising events need staff to interact with the public and people to fill bags and hand out T-shirts.
	Native plant organizations	Save native species from destruction by digging up or replanting in protected areas.
	Trail building groups	Help build or maintain trails.
	Wildlife Rehabilitation	Feed animals. Help release rehabilitated animals.
	Seal organization	Help protect seals from humans observing them on beaches.
	Tree giveaway programs	Help wrap, prune, and organize trees.
	Organic farm	Help with a birthday party held at the farm.
	City	Paint over graffiti.
	Greyhound rescue	Walk dogs and socialize with them.
	Bicycle organization	Lead a mountain bike tour for underprivileged kids.
Adults	Thrift store	Sort contributions
	Nursing home	Put on a green celebration for anyone having a birthday that month.
	Nursing home	Help beautify grounds.
	Animal rescue	Take photos of animals for use in online adoption sites.
	Senior center	Prepare a fun, healthy locally sourced lunch.
	Agencies that collect blankets, etc.	Make your birthday a sewing bee. Everyone can be given a square to decorate, then you can sew a blanket to donate. Or, if all your guests happen to knit, they can each contribute a hand knitted square.
	Green Festival	If the birthday happens around the time of one of the Green Festivals in Seattle, Chicago, San Francisco, or Washington DC, there are a number of opportunities to help out in areas such as registration and set up. And if you volunteer, you get free admission to the festival as well (GreenFestivals.org).
	Childcare facility	Hold and rock babies.
	Public rose gardens	Help with pruning.
	CSA (Community Supported Agriculture) organic farm	Weed, plant, harvest.

Family Reunions

Scale is the main difference between a family reunion and many other celebrations. Reunions have been known to bring together hundreds of family members from newborn to 100 from countries around the world.

Happily, many Internet sites offer great advice on how to plan these fun get-togethers, (try Family-Reunion.com for free, or FamilyReunion.com, a paid site), but few help you do it in an eco-friendly way.

So if you're in charge of the masses and you're also interested in keepin' it green, you'll want to spend some planning time figuring out how to have great fun and be eco-friendly.

- **Theme**: Many families choose a theme. Why not make yours "green"? If everyone agrees, ask them to think about ways the reunion could be as eco-friendly as possible. You could vote on the suggestions and award a prize to the winner.
- **Invitations**: Use Evite.com or a similar online invitation system not only for the invitation, but to keep in touch during the process and for thank you's afterwards. Skobee.com allows everyone to contribute ideas and includes maps and other extras.
- **The place**: Consider the impact of your decision on where to gather. The best place from an eco-standpoint is the closest to home for the majority of people. But if you are going to travel far, at least consider an eco-resort. Do a search for eco-travel or eco-hotels and see if you can't find a great place that meets more than simply your need for space. (Find some suggestions in this book's Valentine's section.)
- **Budget**: In your budget, consider including the purchase of carbon offsets or a donation to an eco-organization at your destination.
- **Getting there**: Encourage carpooling or taking the bus or train.
- **Getting around once you're there**: If people are driving, encourage them to bring bicycles. Or rent them once you get to where you're staying.
  - o Encourage riding during the reunion by creating a scavenger hunt where people ride bicycles from clue to clue. A mini one can be set up for kids as young as three who can ride tricycles.

PAPER NAPKINS, WHAT A WASTE!

Before you pick up that cheap bag of napkins, consider the math:

100 people at your family reunion

3 meals a day x 4 days = 1,200 paper napkins to the landfill.

And that's not counting paper towels!

o You also could set up a contest to see who rides or walks the most while you're at the reunion. Give each participant a pedometer, and if the bikes don't have an odometer, estimate. At the end of the day, everyone marks on a large board how far they biked or walked. (Or you can do this by family group.) At the end of the reunion, give out prizes to those who walked/biked the farthest.

● **Games and Activities**

o Have everyone bring items to trade with each other. Kids can gather toys they're tired of. Adults can contribute items they never use. (Lynn's rule is...if we haven't used it in five years, it goes to a thrift store.) You can play the "White Elephant" game, lay items on a table and allow everyone to take what they want, or use the items for prizes.

o Encourage physical games. A family "Olympics" can involve everyone. Break up into teams that include a mix of kids and adults. The teams can make flags, then stage a parade. Next set up active competitions like running races, long jump, hula hooping, basketball throw—whatever works for your family.

UNIQUE!

SUMMER QUINOA SALAD
● ● ● ● ● ● ● ● ● ● ● ●
Choose local and organic ingredients whenever possible

Make for a crowd by assuming approximately 4 oz. per person.

INGREDIENTS
2-3 cups cooked quinoa
1/2 c minced red onion
1 c minced parsley or fresh basil
1 c small diced cucumber
1 c sliced cherry tomatoes
1/4 c lemon juice
1/2 c extra virgin olive oil
kosher salt and fresh ground pepper to taste

DIRECTIONS
Toss all ingredients together. Add seasonings to taste. Platter on layers of fresh sliced cucumbers, tomatoes, fresh basil or greens.

Contributed by Pam Samper, chef, Ravishing Radish Catering, Seattle, WA.

THREE BEAN SUMMER SALAD

● ● ● ● ● ● ● ● ● ● ● ● ●

Choose local and organic ingredients whenever possible

Make for a crowd by assuming approximately 4 oz. per person.

INGREDIENTS
1# cannellini beans
1# black eyed peas
1# edamame beans
1# minced red onion
1# sm diced red pepper
1# sweet corn kernels, blanched
2 c fresh basil chiffonade
1 pt. Italian vinaigrette
kosher salt and fresh ground pepper to taste

DIRECTIONS
Toss all ingredients together. Add seasonings to taste.

Contributed by Pam Samper, chef, Ravishing Radish Catering, Seattle, WA.

o **For the women in the family:** Bring some organic cosmetics and let everyone try them out. Many women have never used (or even seen) chemical free make up.

o **Craft table:** Invite everyone to bring contributions of recycled materials. Use this as an opportunity to introduce your family to chemical free crayons, paints, and glue.

o **Make a family tree:** You can use a live tree (get permission first) or a branch if you can find one that is not attached. From recycled paper, have each person cut out a leaf shape and write their name and any other information they'd like on it. Then punch a hole in the "leaves" and hang them from the tree branches using string.

o **Volunt**eer: Visit VolunteerMatch.org and type in the zip code of the place you'll be meeting. Then see if you can find an opportunity for the group to lend a hand for a day.

o **Digital photos and videos:** Use a computer to download everyone's pictures onto a free site like PhotoBucket.com. No need to print out photos when you can share them digitally in slide shows that can viewed online or transferred to a

DAD MOM
SON DAUGHTER DAUGHTER
GRANDSON GRANDSON

- o **Hold a green conversation:** Volunteer to lead a discussion around living green. Be sure to get the kids involved in this one. Ask questions rather than lecture. Avoid showing up with a list of scary statistics. The idea is to find out what family members' perceptions are about living an eco-aware lifestyle, what that means, and what changes they might want to make. Your role would be to answer questions, make suggestions, and keep it light.
- o **Arrange a talk:** Ask a local park ranger to host your group on a walk on their home turf while speaking to the group about trees, wild flowers, preserving the forest, or whatever topic might be interesting and timely.

- ⦿ **Food:** Assuming you're away from home and in a place where your group will be doing the cooking, put together meals with locally grown ingredients. If the season is right, a fun outing for the group might be going to an organic farm and picking produce, then making a tasty dinner. Before you leave home, research what's in season and look up some easy, healthful recipes so you have them ready to go.

- ⦿ **Recycling:** Be sure that clearly marked recycling containers are available in everyone's rooms and for all outdoor activities. (Assign children 8-12 responsibility for ensuring containers are in place. They'll most likely enjoy contributing in this way.) Check first with the place you're staying and if they don't provide the containers, bring biodegradable bags (BioBags from DirtWorks.com, for example).

- ⦿ **Souvenirs:**
  - o Encourage everyone to "take only pictures, leave only footprints." If you gather in a natural setting, ensure that members of your family do not pick up materials from nature unless there are no rules against it.
  - o Encourage everyone to "buy local." Almost every town in the United States has at least one store where you can purchase items made by local artisans.

- ⦿ **Giveaways:**
  - o Organic T-shirts with your family's name
  - o Check out RecycledProducts.com for everything from recycled wood award frames to EcoSpun tote bags to take home your treasures to buttons, magnets, and stickers.
  - o How about a copy of this book for everyone at the reunion?

Office Parties and Other Business Celebrations

Office celebrations are a part of the American business culture. Some companies put on one or more companywide events annually. Others periodically host a series of informal bashes. At larger companies, when a milestone such as a 20th anniversary hits, celebrations can last an entire year.

And while many companies today are starting to "think green," few carry over their values when it comes time to party. At small companies, party planning may fall to a group of "volunteers," while larger ones may employ someone as a special events planner. Either way, whoever is planning often knows little about how to make a celebration eco-friendly, or if she does, assumes that doing so will mean breaking a very tight budget. In addition, green can feel like a noose when what people really want to do is break loose.

You don't have to go to extremes like the New York party decorator who directed the museum for which he was planning an annual shindig, to shred its office paper for six months, to which he added years of tax returns and personal papers, turning the resulting 6000 pounds of shreds into topiaries and chandeliers on a grand scale.

But if you share your office with some creative types, there's no reason not to come up with décor from the recycled detritus of your everyday cube life. How about staging a companywide contest involving tablescapes with prizes like coupons for organic coffee?

If you've read the rest of this book, you know that being eco-friendly can be both cost-effective and fun. Your job, therefore, if you choose to accept it, is to help incorporate the 3Rs and the 3Gs into office parties in a cost-effective way.

How to do that?

Here's a matrix that will help you (and those who need a bit of convincing). Think about areas you can cost-effectively green up. Remember, it's unlikely that you'll get an enthusiastic reception if you insist on every one of these options. Instead, why not suggest them as alternatives. Once you've tried out one or two and they've met with success, the next time, people in the organization will likely to be more open to additional changes. Take it slowly. Celebrate successes no matter how small.

BYOW
Bring your own water to today's big office shindig!

Note that on the chart below the X in the center column, "Save money," indicates that by going green in these categories, you'll save dollars that could then be put toward a few items that might cost more.

Eco-oblivious office parties	Save money	Eco-aware office party alternatives
Paper invitations hand delivered or sent by mail	X	Electronic invitations
Throw away plates, cups, utensils	X	Reusable or recycled plates, cups, utensils
One-time use décor including cut flowers, generating large amount of waste	X	Reusable centerpieces including plants that can be given as gifts or placed in the office to improve air quality. Fabric table cloths and napkins. Rent or borrow décor or make from commonly available items that can be reused or recycled.
Throw greenery in dumpster		Compost or chip greenery to use as mulch
Menu cards, programs	X	Do without menu cards and programs if possible. If not, print on 100% recycled paper with soy inks and be sure to have everything collected for recycling.
Live band requiring electrical input for equipment, lighting, etc.	X	Digitally recorded music played through the company's existing system
Party favors and decorations made from plastic or other non-renewable resources		Party favors and decorations made by local artisans, Fair Trade companies, and/or from recycled materials
Ignore thermostat settings	X	Plan party for the coolest time of day in summer and warmest in winter. Assuming it's a winter party, put thermostat very low or turn it off and see if the guests provide enough heat to keep a comfortable temperature in the room. In summer, plan the party outside if possible to avoid having to use air conditioning.
Center party around food and drink	X	Center party around fun, healthy activities like ice skating, bowling, games, walking, or doing good for the community
No thought given to location in terms of driving distance for attendees.	X	Party located where employees can get to it without driving long distances. Encourage carpooling.
Drinks provided in individual cans and water in individual bottles	X	Drinks provided in large pitchers, punch bowls, or glass bottles. Non-disposable cups and glasses.
No recycling containers		Clearly marked recycling containers for food, bottles, cans, wrappings, etc. as needed.
Food provided by caterer with no thought to health, locale, or sustainability		Food provided by caterer with emphasis on sustainable, organic, preferably local sources.

Eco-oblivious office parties	Save money	Eco-aware office party alternatives
Giving non-sustainable gifts to employees		Give eco-friendly items from sources like RecycledProducts.com or GreenWithEnvyGifts.com. A few examples: ◉ Organic dark chocolate bars ◉ Recycled or sustainable wood pen ◉ Recycled glass awards ◉ Fair trade picture frame
Or offer employees a sum to donate to a local charity of their choice.		
Giving gifts wrapped in non-recyclable paper and tape		Imaginative gift wrappings like reusable shopping bags, oven mitts, handmade boxes that will be kept, string that will biodegrade, bandanas
Leave all the lights on, bring in decorative lighting, and/or use candles.	X	Have party earlier in the day and keep lights off, and if using decorative lighting, ensure that it is LED or CFL. Keep air cleaner by avoiding candle use, unless they are 100% beeswax or soy.
Regular coffee or tea		Fair Trade, organic coffee (shade grown) and teas
Poor planning resulting in leftover food that goes into the trash.	X	Careful planning. Less food purchased and leftovers are recycled or sent home with guests. Unopened bags, boxes, and cans can be taken to a local food bank. Check with your local waste disposal company to see if you can recycle the food scraps.
Party benefits only those attending		Party results in an effort for the community. Invite party-goers to bring any of the following, which can then be donated: ◉ Books to local book drives ◉ Coats to local coat drives ◉ Used athletic shoes to Nike's recycling program that turns shoes into athletic surfaces ◉ Eye glasses recycled by local Lions Clubs
After party clean up using polluting cleaners	X	Clean up using eco-friendly products

Everyday Celebrations

Naming a day, week, or month to recognize a cause is as easy as doing it, no congressional approval necessary. As a result, someone somewhere has selected one or more days to promote just about every concept, no matter how bizarre.

But the days of note we've listed below were created to raise awareness about issues critical to those of us who are interested in eco, green, animal, vegetable, people and/or earth-friendly ideas. (By the way, please don't write incensed notes to inform us that we've left out Be Kind to Crustaceans Week. We selected the days we thought might be of most interest to readers. We'd need another book to list every one in existence!)

Whether you choose to do anything special to recognize a particular day or not, is up to you. But if you have children, using this calendar might be a convenient way to bring conversation about these topics to your breakfast or dinner table.

To find out more about any event listed below, including the date on which it occurs (which in many cases changes each year, which is why we only state the month), perform an online search for the name or seek out even more special days at BetterWorldCalendar.com.

January
Global Family Day
Poverty in America Awareness Month
Whale Awareness Month

February
Perseverance Day
World Wetlands Day

March
End Racism Day
Energy Day
International Women's Day
National Agriculture Day
National Nutrition Month
World Forestry Day
World Pillow Fight Day (See
   PillowFightDay.com to read about its
   important purpose.)
World Water Day

April

Arbor Day
Earth Day
Global Education Action Week
Hope Day
National Park Week
Reconciliation Day
World Health Day

May

Bike Month
Clean Air Month
Dialogue Day
Endangered Species Day
Families Day
International Compost Awareness Week
International Day for Biological Diversity
World Fair Trade Day
World Naked Gardening Day
World Turtle Day

June

End Torture Day
Interfaith Day
National Trails Day
World Day to Combat Desertification and
    Drought
World Environment Day
World Ocean Day
World Refugee Day

July

International Day of Cooperatives
National Simplicity Day
World Week of Action for Captive Dolphins
Parents Day

August

Civil Rights Day
Forgiveness Day
International Day of the World's
    Indigenous People
National Compassion Day
World Breastfeeding Week

September

Green Consumer Day
Interdependence Day
International Day for the Preservation of
    the Ozone Layer
World Carefree Day

October

Child Health Month
Fair Trade Month
International Day for the Eradication of
    Poverty
International Day for Natural Disaster
    Reduction
International Walk to School Month
World Egg Day
World Food Day
World Habitat Day
World Mental Health Day
World Rural Women's Day
World Smile Day
World Vegetarian Day

November

America Recycles Day
Buy Nothing Day
International Day for Preventing the
    Exploitation of the Environment in War
    and Armed Conflict
Kindness Day
Tolerance Day

December

End Slavery Day
Human Rights Day
Imagine Day
International Animal Rights Day
International Mountain Day
National Day of Artisans
Volunteer Day

P.S.

ALL THE GREAT THINGS WE WANTED YOU TO KNOW THAT WOULDN'T FIT ANYWHERE ELSE

1 We're fairly confident that after reading *Celebrate Green!*, you'll want to order copies for all your friends and family so they don't miss out. Just go to CelebrateGreen.NET for freebies, special offers, and discounts.

2 Get exclusive extras, download more fabulous recipes, sign up for our blog and updates, find out where we're appearing, "meet us" via our videos, all at CelebrateGreen.NET.

3 You know our ideas on celebrating green. Now send us yours. Let us in on the challenges you've faced while greening up your own celebrations. Amusing or moving, as long as they're not boring, we'd love to see them. E-mail us via CelebrateGreen.NET.

4 We are available for consulting and speaking at seminars, retreats, and workshops. If you think we're fun in the book, you should meet us in person! You know how to contact us.

5 When it comes to this book: **Reduce**: We know everyone wants his or her own copy, but feel free to loan it to others. While we'd love to sell more books, we're really all about spreading the message. **Reuse**: When the book reaches the end of its lifespan due to endless thumbing, turn it into something useful. (And send us a picture.) **Recycle**: This book should decompose nicely when its time comes. Please dispose of it properly. By doing so, you're giving its pages a chance at a second life as a countertop, a chair, wedding invitations, or who knows, maybe even our next book. Stay tuned!

Furoshiki, a traditional type of Japanese wrapping, is eco-friendly because the cloth can be used over and over again and takes the place of paper and ribbon. Once you learn some of the simple techniques, you'll be hooked. The illustrations below come from Furoshiki.com where you can find genuine Japanese furoshiki to purchase and all the instruction you need to become an expert.

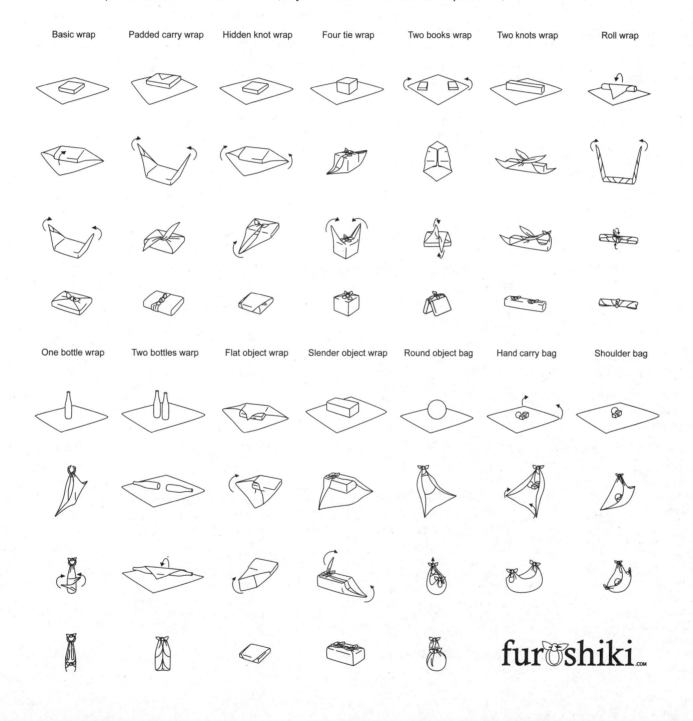

Basic wrap   Padded carry wrap   Hidden knot wrap   Four tie wrap   Two books wrap   Two knots wrap   Roll wrap

One bottle wrap   Two bottles warp   Flat object wrap   Slender object wrap   Round object bag   Hand carry bag   Shoulder bag

furoshiki.com

Websites

The websites below are mentioned in this book. We thought it would be helpful to categorize the sites to make it easier for you to find those you might want to contact, regardless of the holiday or celebration.

Note: At the time *Celebrate Green!* went to press, all websites were functioning. However, by the time you read this, some may no longer exist. Also, sometimes companies change site addresses, so if you can't find one listed as written here, try a search for the company name. (And remember our website, CelebrateGreen.NET. Being the smart readers you are, we'll bet you know why we decided to capitalize the NET throughout the book. Did it work? Is CelebrateGreen.NET seared in your brain? Although we don't mind you visiting our friends at CelebrateGreen.com, you'll save a click when seeking us out by remembering we're at the NET.)

CANDY, CHOCOLATE
Chocleteer.com
CocoaCamino.com
EcoExpress.com
LakeChamplainChocolates.com
NaturalCandyStore.com
RainforestFriendly.com
Sjaaks.com
Skobee.com

CARBON FOOTPRINT, REDUCE
Footprint-es.com
GetCarbonCreditCO2.com
TerraPass.com

CHARCOAL
CowboyCharcoal.com
Kamado.com
WickedGoodCharcoal.com

CHILDREN: CLOTHING, TOYS, EQUIPMENT ETC.
AmericanApparel.com
Animalz.com
AToyGarden.com
CottonMonster.com
DreamALittle7.com
EcoToyTown.com
FamilyFun.com
Fleurville.com
GreatGreenBaby.com
GreenBabyCo.com
GreenDimes.com
GreenGamma.com
HerbKits.com
JamTown.com
KateQuinnOrganics.com
KidBean.com
Kee-Ka.com
LaLaNatural.com

MagicCabin.com
NovaNatural.com
PlanetHappyToys.com
PlanetPals.com
SarahsSilks.com
SoothingTheWomb.com
TheEarthFriends.com
TreeInABox.com
WeeGeneration.com
ZiaAndTia.com

CHILDREN SAFETY AND HEALTH
AskDrSears.com
ChildrensEnvironment.org
HealthyChild.org
HealthyToys.org
iParenting.com
KidsInDanger.org
LaLecheLeague.org
RootsAndShoots.org
SafeKids.org
TinyFoodprints.org
Treeswing.org
WAToxics.org

COSMETICS
BlissWorld.com
CosmeticDatabase.com
FairlightCosmetics.com

CRAFTS/CRAFTING
CraftersForCritters.com
DIYNetwork.com
EcoArtWorks.com
EcoGlue.com
Etsy.com
ReadyMade.com
ThreadHeadCreations.com

DRINKS INCLUDING ALCOHOL
Beau-Coup.com

BeerTown.org
Biodynamics.com
BrewOrganic.com
ButteCreek.com
FreyWine.com
LoftLiqueurs.com
MaisonJomere.com
ModMix.com
OrganicVintners.com
OrganicWineJournal.com
PeakBrewing.com
SantaCruzMountainBrewing.com
SCOJuice.com
SkySaddle.com
SouthernWine.com
StoneMillPaleAle.com
WildHopLager.com
Wolavers.com

ENVIRONMENTAL NON-PROFITS
ABCHomeAndPlanet.org
Audubon.org
CarbonCounter.org
CarbonFund.org
CarbonNeutral.com
ClimateCare.org
Earth911.org
EcoLifeFoundation.typepad.com
EcologyFund.com
EnvironmentalDefense.org
GreenVolunteers.com
JCarrot.org
MadisonDialogue.org
NDCF.org
OrganicConsumers.org
Panda.org
PulmoAmigos.org
Quartos.org
RenewableChoice.com
Ripple.org

SalmonSafe.org
SierraClub.com
SierraClub.org
TheRainforestSite.com
WorldWildlife.org

FARMING, FARMS, PRODUCE, FOOD, EATING

100MileDiet.org
AdoptATurkey.com
Annies.com
AnsonMills.com
AzureStandard.com
BellasCookies.com
Budget101.com
CalliesOrganics.com
CarolinaPlantationRice.com
Consorzio.com
DiamondOrganics.com
EatWellGuide.org
FoodNews.org
GoodFlowHoney.com
GoVeg.com
GreatOlives.com
HeritageFoodsUSA.com
HawaiiSeaSalt.com
KokoGm.com
LocalHarvest.org
MBayAq.org
MilkRanch.com
MoPecans.com
NourishingBalance.com
OrganicConsumers.org
PickYourOwn.org
RaysHickoryNuts.com
SeasonedSkewers.com
SeedSavers.org
SeedsOfChange.com
SproutPeople.com
SunBDCorp.com
VellaCheese.com

FLOWERS

AboutFlowers.com
CaliforniaOrganicFlowers.com
Demeter-USA.org
ExpoFlores.com
FairFlowersFairPlants.com
Floverde.com
My-mps.com
OrganicBouquet.com
TransfairUSA.org
Veriflora.org

GENERAL NON-PROFITS

AfricanDowry.org
AmnestyUSA.org
BirthdaysWithoutPressure.org
BuyAMeter.org
BuyHandmade.org
Candle-Safety.org
CatalogChoice.org
ChangingThePresent.org
CharityGuide.org
DonorsChoose.org
EcoCenter.org
EcoPsychology.org
FairTradeFederation.org
GlassSlipperProject.org
GlobalExchange.org
GlobalFundForWomen.org
GolfAndEnvironment.org
GrandmotherProject.org
Green-E.org
GreenFestivals.org
GXOnlineStore.org
Heifer.org
IFFilmFest.org
JewishWorldWatch.org
JustGive.org
Kiva.org
LaborRights.org
MakingMemories.org
MarchOfDimes.com
MyGreenElectronics.org
NWFilm.org
OxfamAmericaUnwrapped.com
Ripple.org
ShopTheGreastCancerSite.com
StopGlobalWarming.org
SurfRiderSD.org
TheHungerSite.com
ThinkOutsideTheBottle.org
TownHallCoalition.org
Tree-People.org
UNICEF.com
UthandoProject.org
VolunteerMatch.org
Voluntourism.org
WomenForWomen.org
WomensBeanProject.org
WorldCentric.org

GIFTS

3RLiving.com
AbundantEarth.com
Amazon.com

BambuHome.com
BetterWorld.com
BiggDipperWaxWorks.com
BorealisPress.net
BottleCapLure.com
ChopStickArt.com
CountryMeadowSoaps.com
EcoExpress.com
EcoLibris.net
Eco-me.com
EcoPatio.com
FindGift.com
Gifts.com
GiftsWithHumanity.org
GreenAndMore.com
GreenEarthOfficeSupply.com
GreenFeet.com
GreenGiftLinks.com
GreenHome.com
GreenLinkCentral.com
GreenMaven.com
GreenWithEnvyGifts.com
HempBasics.com
HempMania.com
LiveGreenOrDie.com
MagellanTraders.com
OrganicAvenue.com
PlayReThink.com
PriceGrabber.com
PristinePlanet.com
Rawganique.com
RecycledProducts.com
Re-Modern.com
Shopatron.com
SimplyBiodegradable.com
SoGoGreen.com
Solio.com
TerraKeramik.com
Terrapax.com
TheFindGreen.com
TheGreenGardenStore.com
Tree-Free.com
TreeLeafCards.com
VitaminDesignShop.com
VoltaicSystems.com
WorldOfGood.com
X-TremeGeek.com

GIFTS: FAIR TRADE, BENEFIT A CAUSE

BridgeForAfrica.org
CrossroadsTrade.com
EcoArtworks.com
Econscious.com

Equalexchange.com
eShopAfrica.com
EthicalShopping.com
EticaFairTrade.com
Feed1Bags.com
FreeRice.com
Gaiam.com
GiftsWithHumanity.org
GiveMeaning.com
GoodSearch.com
GreatGreenGoods.com
IAmAPeaceKeeper.com
Ilala.co.za
Lucuma.com
MadeBySurvivors.com
MrElliePooh.com
NonProfitShoppingMall.com
OaxacanStuff.com
OneWorldProjects.com
Orenoque.com
SaveYourWorld.com
Swahili-Imports.com
TaraLuna.com
TeesForChange.com
TenThousandVillages.com
Uthando.com

GOVERNMENT
CPSC.gov
EPA.gov

GREEN/ECO INFORMATION
AFreshSqueeze.com
BetterWorldCalendar.com
BigGreenPurse.com
Care2.com
EcoEarth.info
EcoSearch.org
EnvironmentallyFriendlyHotels.com
GreenWashingIndex.com
Grist.org
IdealBite.com
ProjectHouse.vpweb.com
TheDailyGreen.com
TheGreenGuide.com
TreeHugger.com
TreeHuggingFamily.com

HOLIDAYS, CELEBRATIONS, SPECIAL OCCASIONS
ArborDay.org
CelebrateGreen.net
EarthDay.net
ECHOage.com

FamilyReunion.com
Family-Reunion.com
GreenHalloween.org
iDoFoundation.com
InspiredBirthdays.com
LivingChristmasTrees.org
PillowFightDay.com
RealChristmasTree.org
RecycleYourWedding.com

JEWELRY, GOLD, SILVER, DIAMONDS
ApolloDiamond.com
Chatham.com
CommunityMining.org
ConflictFreeDiamonds.org
CredJewelry.com
EthicalMetalSmiths.org
GemEcology.org
Gemesis.com
GreenGold-OroVerde.org
GreenKarat.com
KirsetnMuenster.com
LauraBeamer.com
MadisonDialogue.org
MiningWatch.ca
NoDirtyGold.com
TobyPomeroy.com
TouchWoodRings.com
VerdeRocks.com

LOW COST, NO COST OR RE-USED DÉCOR, GIFT ITEMS RESOURCES
Craigslist.org
eBay.com
Freecycle.com

MEN'S: CLOTHING
Ecolution.com
JaanJ.com
TerraPlana.com

MISCELLANEOUS
EC3Global.com
EcoBusinessLinks.com
SaveASnowman.com
ShalomCtr.org
TerraChoice.com
Walking.About.com
WasteFreeHolidays.com
WordSmithAndCompany

PHOTOGRAPHY, VIDEO, ONLINE INVITATIONS
EarthCinemaCircle.com
Evite.com

GreenSender.com
HolliDunn.com
IronWeedFilms.com
PhotoBucket.com
Shutterfly.com
SmileBox.com
StoryOfStuff.com

SHOPPING BAGS, HANDBAGS, BACK PACKS, WRAPPING
Act2GReenSmart.com
ArtisanGear.com
CelebrateGreen.com
ChicoBags.com
DirtWorks.com
Ecoist.com
Furoshiki.com
WrapSacks.com

TEA, COFFEE (ORGANIC)
CaffeIbis.com
ShopStashTea.com

WOMEN: CLOTHING, SHOES, ACCESSORIES
AlpacaUnlimited.com
Annatarian.com
AuroraSilk.com
ClothingMatters.net
DeborahLindquist.com
EarthErotics.com
EcoLogicDesigns.com
Ecolution.com
Eco-Me.com
GetConscious.com
GreenElectronics.com
Guild.com
HelenKaminski.com
HolleyKnives.com
LadiesWhoLaunch.com
LaraMiller.net
LoyaleClothing.com
Mohop.com
MoonDropClothiers.com
MooShoes.com
MoralFever.com
MyCorset.com
Sternlein.com
TansuStyle.com
TheGreenLoop.com
TheRomantic.com
UnderTheCanopy.com

The GreenSmart Glossary

Newly coined eco-terms can be confusing. We've defined some in this book's content, but called on Tom Larsen's excellent GreenSmart Glossary to fill in the rest.

This is no ordinary glossary. Not only does Tom provide the definitions, but he's added information that will help you make more informed choices.

For additional definitions, check out the full GreenSmart Glossary at Act2GreenSmart.com. And if you are stumped by a term you think should be included, send it to Info@Act2GreenSmart.com.

Note: *Opinions expressed in this chart are Tom's.*

Term	Definition	Upside (Optimist)	Balancing Act (Cynic)
Biodegradable	Used to describe the properties of items that will naturally decompose if left in exposed outdoor environments.	If something disintegrates to become useful to the environment, that's usually good. Disintegration and decomposition are not the same though.	Anything can be made poorly enough to "degrade" or even be toxic after biodegrade-ability. Even organic cotton, dyed with toxic dyes, could be biodegradable and toxic.
Carbon footprint	The process of calculating the amount of carbon created in any given process or enterprise	Companies (and some people) have a deep seeded need to quantify everything. This metric is the one currently in vogue.	Carbon is good for the soil, bad for the air. Deconstructing human existence into the amount of carbon we convert is like monetizing the value of a life; it's just a common denominator.
Carbon offset	A new method by which carbon emissions produced by one process or practice can be offset by reducing carbon emissions produced by another process or practice.	A method constructed to make people invest a little money to allow them to feel good about something being done somewhere to mitigate the carbon producing practice in which they are engaged.	This is another murky area. If a tree is planted today, how much carbon does that "offset" over its lifetime relative to a vehicle driving around over its lifetime. It's not very perfect as a common denominator.
Conservation	The practice of resource management that seeks to balance the resource's consumption or utilization between natural and human needs.	In its truest sense, conservation strikes the closest possible balance between human interaction with resources and no interaction with resources	In its worst definition, considered to be the "leave it entirely alone forever" concept.
Earth friendly	Generally practices or products that have a small impact on the earth's resources.	See Eco-friendly or Environment-friendly.	See Eco-friendly or Environment-friendly.

Term	Definition	Upside (Optimist)	Balancing Act (Cynic)
Earth friendly	Being an informed purchaser. Knowing or having an understanding of what effect what you are doing, buying or using has on the environment.	If you have kids, you're likely more eco-conscious now than you were 10 years ago.	If you're still throwing things out the car window, you're eco-UNconscious.
Eco-friendly	A term used to describe products that are not harmful to the environment in either their production or post usage life	In it's best form, a term that can help consumers and others distinguish environment improving products.	Can be used to describe a broad range of products that are not of themselves eco-friendly, but, may be a better choice than "less eco-friendly" alternatives.
Environmentally friendly	A general (non-technical) term that identifies a product or practice that does not harm the environment.	Not unlike eco-friendly, just a longer word.	If it's not environmentally friendly somehow, it's not even IN the Green universe. This represents the minimum charge for admission.
Fair-trade	Defines a payment practice and overall business relationship based on delivering to generally artisanal or agricultural producers a fair wage based on costs of production.	A great concept with relatively short supply chains where producers are only a step or two away from consumers, or for products that require a relatively uncomplicated production process – e.g. wine.	Doesn't really translate to manufactured goods very well. A major component of some extreme green's sustainability perspective.
Natural	Used to describe the contents of a food or material. The term is general only describing non-synthetic or non-synthetically treated substances	Natural materials are most often closer to sustainability than synthetic materials.	Natural has no boundaries. It is possible to consider coal or oil natural. Asbestos is natural. This term is always open to scrutiny.
Off-gassing	The evaporation of volatile chemicals in non-metallic materials at normal atmospheric pressure, like paint, nail polish remover, petroleum, rubber, etc.	In a landfill for example, the off-gassing of mostly methane gas from decomposition can be harnessed to create electricity.	If it smells like chemicals, it's going in your lungs and some ventilation and limiting your exposure is a pretty good idea.
Organic	A food and agricultural term describing the practice of growing/raising the food in the absence of pesticides, hormones, synthetic fertilizers and other toxic materials in cultivation. In some cases a legal description of the process of growing/raising food products.	Almost always a term defining produce, or ag materials. Almost always a positive attribute. May be the only term with a legal definition (FDA) and standard.	Is organic produce, packaged in cellophane, or flown in from far off lands a better choice than locally grown non-organics? A buyer's and shopper's dilemma to be sure.

Term	Definition	Upside (Optimist)	Balancing Act (Cynic)
Post consumer waste	Defines a specific type of recycled material. These materials in a previous existence, were a consumer product that has been returned and processed to become a "new" item.	The ultimate definition of the "global village" where we willingly sort waste to be reconstituted into useful new stuff.	Less waste would be good, but, since waste is a pretty much a given, this term doesn't carry much trade-off.
Recyclable	An identification of any of a number of materials that are universally accepted by waste recovery companies (aluminum, glass, paper, plastic) that CAN be recycled.	A great way to distinguish credible companies from others. Products are only recyclable if the consumer can put them in a bin – mono-materials only.	An all too often greenwash term to redescribe a virgin material product as green by virtue of its ultimate recycleability. Without scrutiny, this term is almost meaningless, now. Grocery bags being banned worldwide are recyclable.
Reuse/repurpose	The practice of using an item in a second way, not having to have re-manufactured it.	When you take your old shop tools and convert them to lawn art or take old CDs and make bird deflectors	If it goes in the recycle bin to be transformed, like aluminum which is melted to become a new can, it's recycling.
Sustainable	The ability of something to replenish itself without damaging the ecosystem in which it exists for an unspecified long period of time	Being sustainable is the optimum goal, in creation of goods as well as social structures for humanity.	Almost nothing that humans make can be fully sustainable. Some type of resource is unreplenishably consumed or byproduct created that compromises a some percentage of full sustainability. Humans are not hunter gatherers anymore.
Toxicity	The point at which the introduction of a toxin to a system will begin to damage the system.	Toxicity is dose-dependent. Any substance becomes toxic beyond a certain threshold for a given system or organism. Vaccines are derived from staying below the toxicity threshold, insecticides are derived by going past the toxicity threshold.	Even water introduced at high enough levels can be toxic. The FDA, CDC or any other organization can not determine the toxicity point for every given toxin or potential toxin. Toxic to one is not toxic to all, either.

Index

Spring

Notes & Ideas

Spring

Notes & Ideas

Summer

Notes & Ideas

Summer

Notes & Ideas

Fall

Notes & Ideas

Fall
Notes & Ideas

Winter

Notes & Ideas

Winter

Notes & Ideas

About the Authors

Corey Hope Colwell-Lipson is a wife and mother of two. She is also a licensed marital and family therapist and board certified clinical art therapist specializing in the transition to parenthood. Corey grew up in a family that prioritized "love over stuff," nutrition, and fitness. So it's no surprise that her early interests in health, ethics, human and animal welfare, and environmental issues evolved into a passion for helping people walk lightly on the Earth while creating meaning in their lives and for the lives of future generations. In 2007, Corey started the Green Halloween® movement and later co-founded The Green Year®, LLC, with her mother and friend, Lynn.

Lynn Colwell is a Renaissance soul, admitted laughaholic and probably one of the few women on Earth who doesn't crave chocolate. An accomplished life coach with clients around the U.S. and Canada, Lynn also has been a writer for more decades than she likes to admit. She wrote the only authorized biography of humorist, Erma Bombeck, in addition to hundreds of articles for well-known magazines including *Reader's Digest* and *Mothering*, and enthralling trades like *Plumbing Equipment News*. Addicted to crafting, Lynn is also the family tech guru. Her curiosity about everything from aardvarks to zymurgy (yes, it's true, she liked to peruse the dictionary as a kid), not surprisingly, led her down a meandering career path. She owned a children's clothing business with her sister-in-law, Debbie. (the same Aunt Debbie whose apple pie—or lack thereof—broke Lynn's heart on page 110). She was a Lamaze childbirth instructor, darkroom hired hand (if anyone reading this remembers life before digital), and spent years in public relations and corporate communications. She once turned down a position as vice-president of community relations because she didn't think it would be much fun. Assuming you're already read this book and aren't starting at the back, you'll know that in many areas, Lynn has been an avid recycler her whole life, but before the eco-movement picked up steam, people just referred to her as cheap.

Lynn's proudest accomplishments are her marriage of 40 years, her three children (all far more productive members of society than she), and this book.